THE ⠀⠀⠀⠀⠀⠀⠀⠀⠀ IN SPORT

THE EVOLUTION OF ENGLISH SPORT

NEIL WIGGLESWORTH

FRANK CASS
LONDON • PORTLAND, OR.

First published in 1996 in Great Britain by
FRANK CASS PUBLISHERS
Crown House, 47 Chase Side
London N14 5BP

and in the United States by
FRANK CASS
c/o ISBS, 5824 N.E. Hassalo Street
Portland, Oregon 97213-3644

Copyright © 1996 Neil Wigglesworth

Reprinted 2002

British Library Cataloguing in Publication Data

Wigglesworth, Neil
Evolution of English Sport
I. Title
796.0942

Library of Congress Cataloging-in-Publication Data

Wigglesworth, Neil.
   The evolution of English sport / Neil Wigglesworth.
      p. cm.
   Includes index.
      ISBN 0-7146-4785-7. – ISBN 0-7146-4219-3 (pbk.)
      1. Sports–England–History. 2. Sports–Social aspects–
–England–History. I. Title.
   GV605.W54 1995
   796'.0942–dc20   95-37821
                                                 CIP

ISBN 0-7146-4219-3 (paperback)
ISBN 0-7146-4785-7 (hardback)

Typeset by Vitaset, Paddock Wood
Printed in Great Britain by
Bookcraft (Bath) Ltd, Midsomer Norton, Avon

For Dora

Contents

List of Illustrations

Preface

Sport may be a single word but it is not a single thing.
(Richard Holt, *Sport and the British – A Modern
History*, 1989)

Although it has been said many times it is worth repeating that until
recently sporting history has been written by middle-class amateurs,
many of whom were Oxbridge graduates. Taken with the fact that
many original records also come from similar sources it is not surprising
that much of the history produced suffers from a narrowness both of
cultural and geographical perspective. The growth of the many varied
sporting clubs and the development of sport throughout the country
are vast topics which have largely escaped the attention of these
historians who have tended to concentrate upon the activities of a
metropolitan elite.

In order to help redress the balance of reporting in favour of the
provincial 'quasi-amateur' it has been necessary to use original material
from many clubs and organisations nationwide. This takes the form of
minutes from over one hundred sports clubs together with accounts,
annual reports, correspondence and press reports which have been
used to illuminate the evolution of sporting activity through reference
to themes identified in the first chapter. It is hoped that such an
approach will present a wider perspective on sport, firstly by representing the views of the ordinary participant and secondly by setting the
sporting activities in the context of relevant geographical, economic
and social environments.

1

Introduction

No sport can be insulated from the
wide society in which it is played.

(E. Dunning and K. Sheard, *Barbarians,
Gentlemen and Players*, 1979)

The ways people enjoy themselves and the ways that these enjoyments
are exploited are of considerable importance for social history and yet
it is only recently that they have become subjects of legitimate inquiry.
There were many instructional treatises on field sports published in the
sixteenth century which in their turn followed in a long tradition of
material concerning courtly etiquette. Although these addressed themselves exclusively to the class of 'gentleman', they can be seen as the
precursors of present-day inquiries into the social science of sport,
recreation and leisure. 'What's a Gentleman but his pleasure?' rings
true for an Elizabethan age when servants and artisans of any occupation
were prohibited from a whole range of designated unlawful sports,[1]
and yet we can see in Stow's Survey of London in 1599 that there were
almost countless ways in which the ordinary citizen found immense
recreational pleasure. So successful and communally disruptive was
this pursuit of pleasure that a royal Declaration of 1618 sought to define
which sports were and were not socially and legally acceptable, whilst
Peacham's English Recreations of 1641 provided a cultural commentary
for gentlemen, concluding that a 'gentleman should have some knowledge in all the arts but not seek excellence in any': an attitude that has
informed English perceptions on sport ever since. Despite a massive
commercialisation of leisure pursuits during the eighteenth century, it
is not until 1801 that we find a work given over to a social survey of
sport which sought to form a just estimate of the English by looking at
their sports and pastimes.[2] The traditional emphasis on gentlemen's
recreations continued with the appearance of material on the playing
of sport in the newly popular public schools, with Sydney Smith's
contribution[3] placing it firmly in the realm of an academic discussion
which did not extend to the state system for a further century.

The nineteenth century witnessed a growth in the spread of organised sport and physical recreation brought about by a wide variety of social, political and economic factors and yet little evidence was produced to place it in a cultural context. A notable exception was the volume on sports and pastimes edited by Anthony Trollope, a fanatical fox hunter, in 1868[4] which made some attempt at social commentary, an approach he continued with considerable venom in *The New Zealander*, a posthumously published work criticising upper-class hypocrisy. Such criticism lay in a long English tradition of argument and reasoned dissent which stemmed from humanitarian rather than political motivation, but the widening franchise led to a new class of politically aware writers whose aims included further extentions of franchise, education and leisure time endorsing Marx's dictum in *Capital* that 'man deprived of leisure is dulled in mind and broken in body'. Despite centuries of punitive laws banning the lower order from hunting, playing football and gambling, society had entered an era in which the struggle for leisure became an overtly political act with the role of women assuming greater importance with the first steps in their educational enfranchisement being taken. Females of the lower orders had to wait another half century to enjoy the freedom that the upper-class Victorian and Edwardian lady experienced as of right and not until relatively recent times have they begun to take part in sport to the same extent. Lady Greville in her *Gentlewomen's Book of Sports* of 1880 made the point that it was only then for the first time that females could indulge in formerly 'unladylike' sporting activities like rowing, and from this period onwards they played no little part in sporting cultural history.[5]

The pervading atmosphere of this period, despite many outward manifestations to the contrary, was one of radical change: behind the magnificence of royal and state occasions, the general pomposity of artistic culture and the flamboyance of dress and manners lay an enormous underclass of people whose expectations of life were changing for the better. Much of the radicalism stemmed from Christian groupings whose religious teaching often resulted in the growth of social aspirations producing social movements which affected every aspect of life from politics to popular culture. This in turn prompted virulent reactions from the middle and upper classes who felt threatened by the mass incursions into previously privileged areas of society. In the realm of sport the process had been put in motion by the gradual commercialisation of competition during the eighteenth century which produced during the following century a class of professional sportsmen whose very existence threatened the nature of sport and the position of its regulative bodies. Professionalism became the subject of interminable reports in metropolitan and provincial journals in which writers extolled the nobility and cleanliness of sport untainted by the 'greed for gold'.

The Edwardian era saw the entrenchment of amateurism in London and the home counties and professional progress in the north of England, with the result that many sports were badly disrupted producing policies of separate development as means of survival. The First World War, whilst advancing the cause of women, had the effect of depressing the sporting scene generally. Texts of the post-war period reflect nostalgic views of pre-war playing fields dappled in sunshine conjuring up images of peaceful serenity which were to be rudely shattered in a variety of sports up and down the country. Initially, however, the country appeared to slip back into the social divisions of a century before, a phenomena criticised bitterly during preparations for the second conflict by those who questioned the wisdom of employing the elements of boarding, classics and team games in the education of leaders for an increasingly cosmopolitan and technological society. The contempt in which this and many other anachronisms were held explains in large part the overwhelming victory enjoyed by the Labour Party in 1945.[6] For those in public schools, the Second World War, like the First, only confirmed the belief that their methods had been instrumental in securing victory, and thus despite reforms elsewhere their traditions, including a Corinthian emphasis on team games, were if anything actually strengthened.[7]

Although much social history has been written during the post-war period, there was at first little effort made to use sporting themes as social commentary, but during the 1960s there were several works which highlighted particular aspects of sport in society that led in turn to a systemisation of approach.[8] The basis of this approach was a concentration on examining sports 'from the inside to inquire into the relation between the sport and the participant':[9] an approach employed in the present work. In pursuing such an approach we can identify elements of sport's social pathology determined from within by the pressure exerted by class culture. Some sports remained impervious to all but the most crushing outside influences, such as wrestling and bowling, whilst others allowed themselves to be socialised by the dominant culture as a means of gaining social status, for instance rowing and cricket. Many commentators have remarked that group leisure activities provided the middle class with opportunities to confirm and consolidate social standing through emulation of those above them in the social scale, whilst their patronage of those below them gave the lower orders similar chances of emulation. The complexity of this two-way process acting throughout class culture can be simplified to some extent by recourse to three objective models for sport: that of consumer with commercial ramifications exemplified by horse-racing and football; that of participant with recreational ramifications exemplified by the field sports; and that of recent origin lying mid-way between the two and brought about by the commercial influence of television exemplified by golf and tennis. Whatever it might be, the predominant culture is faithfully reflected in the characteristics and value structures of sport since there is overwhelming evidence to suggest that sport plays a vital role in socialising participants into the dominant ideology of society. Over the centuries the dominant ideology has resulted increasingly from economic rather than cultural determinants so that the complexity of class culture has been gradually replaced by the relative simplicity of cash culture. During the period of industrialisation when cash first began to threaten class, there could be found a mutual accommodation between the two which in recreational terms effected a maintenance of amateur structures and values and strengthened symbolic rivalries such as those between the north and south (as in cricket and rugby), London and the provinces (as in rowing and athletics) and adjacent towns and sections of towns (as in football). Each of these rivalries finds expression in the development of sports, as does the cultural rivalry between the sexes following upon increasing female independence which manifested itself particularly in sport both causing and reflecting a modification in the definition of gender roles.

It is obvious therefore that the socio-economic implications of sporting activity are extensive and diverse and that each sport has its own story to tell. Cricket is particularly well served with hundreds of histories culled from mountains of written and pictorial material which indicate its growth from bucolic roots and development through patronage by gentlemen who used it for the purpose of gambling which led to teams full of servants hired for their playing abilities. This was commonplace in the eighteenth century when footmen and chairmen were hired as runners in pedestrian matches, grooms as jockeys and watermen as scullers, all for the purpose of wagering. Practically every known sporting activity was utilised by the nobility for betting: cock-fighting was promoted by the Earl of Derby, pugilism and pedestrianism by the Duke of Cumberland, coursing by Lord Orford, cricket by the Duke of Dorset and horse-racing by George III, whilst rowing was patronised by the Dukes of Richmond and Northumberland. Pigeon shooting and fishing were mere excuses for gambling, whilst yacht racing using hired sailors as skippers had been common from the time of Charles II. Activities which began in honest trade or mere playfulness became objects of attraction for thousands with the result that specific venues were established and permanent facilities installed. The era of the spectator had begun and the huge popularity of race meetings, cricket matches and prize fights indicated society's need for excitement and group identification. As the audience and market expanded attempts were made to make leisure activities exclusive and grandstand owners made huge fortunes by segregating customers and selling off select enclosures and boxes at enormous premiums. In the nineteenth century the new factory systems operating mostly in the north of England strengthened the workers' desire for diversionary excitements and reinforced their need for a group identity whilst only allowing them the time and energy to spectate. So it was that any diversion attracted large, enthusiastic crowds and that the new northern rugby and football clubs attracted fanatical support which derived from a determination not to bow the knee to London or the south of England and resulted in a new identity and independence for many provincial towns. By the last quarter of the century the combination of supply and demand for sporting entertainment had produced an industry orchestrated by large commercial interests.

This commercialisation of sport had the effect of producing two classes of participant: those who had the ability to play for money and those who continued to play for amusement only, a simple dichotomy considerably complicated by the gradual evolution of a variety of intermediate sub-classes. Long before the noble patronage of sport, most recreational activities enjoyed considerable popularity as rural sports usually centred on the local public house whose landlord would make facilities available in return for extra custom: the first commercial exploitation. Hunts and point to point races would meet at a host of country inns, boxing was carried on at the Adam and Eve tavern at Chelsea, badger-baiting, dog and cock-fighting were well known at the White Lion in Brighton, cricket at the White Head in Leicester and a whole variety of sports including rowing took place at the Red Barn in Battersea. Such venues and hundreds more throughout the country became traditional as many active and retired sportsmen became landlords. The later commercialisation and professionalisation of sport took activities away from their origins leaving the majority of participants continuing to play at an amateur and purely recreational level.

Whilst the patronage of the aristocracy had produced many individual sportsmen who were professional in all but name, the industrialised areas of the country saw the emergence of a whole new professional class of players which began to threaten traditional sporting organisations based in London and the south of England. The first 'open' golf championship was held in 1860 with great professionals like Tom Morris and Sandy Herd taking part, whose counterparts on the river were scullers like Mark Addy of Salford and Harry Clasper of Gateshead, and soccer personalities soon emerged when the larger clubs began paying 'expenses', a trend later followed in rugby union. The Football Association succumbed to pressure and sanctioned professionalism in 1885 whilst the Rugby Football Union declined to do so forcing the Northern Union to become the Rugby League in 1922. Cricket, meanwhile, compromised and retained its respectable image by denominating cricketers as 'players' or 'gentlemen' and providing separate facilities for them, an arrangement only allowed to lapse as recently as 1962. The leaders of northern and midland athletic clubs concluded that 'they could very well do without the South and hope that the northern members will treat the southerners with silent contempt'.[10] This attitude softened as 'payment in lieu' became generally accepted and the major championships were moved occasionally away from London and into the provinces. Professional boxing became entrenched in the regions, particularly in Manchester and Birmingham, during the 1890s and continued to flourish, especially in the period following the end of the First World War when unprecedented numbers of men, many of them Jews, blacks and Irish, were desperate to box for money. By the end of the nineteenth century a contemporary commentator concluded that 'cycling is contaminated with professionalism, athletics is considerably below the standard of purity, cross country amateur status is reprehensible and in football professionalism infests the game from end to end'[11] and could have added for good measure that the infestation affected all but a very select number of those sports that he failed to mention.

The difference between playing for wages and playing for fun was considerably obscured by the cross-over in culture during the nineteenth century when the traditional class culture based on heredity gave way to a cash culture based upon the ability to pay producing the much maligned 'pseudo-amateur'. Those who could do so bought themselves into the aristocracy and those unable to do so emulated their privilege by establishing exclusive societies which was the very ploy used by the old nobility to ensure segregation from the masses. Just as eighteenth-century aristocracy established governing bodies for sport, so too did the new middle classes of the ninteenth century and for similar reasons: the Jockey Club was established in 1750 for

the particular purpose of securing a place at Newmarket where aristocratic owners could meet immune from the rufffians, whilst the
Marylebone Cricket Club (MCC) grew from the necessity of regulating
the game to reduce cheating and thus facilitate fair wagering, a
motivation which also gave rise to the Broughton Rules in boxing
sanctioned by several gentlemen at Broughton's amphitheatre in 1743
and designed for genteel performances in West End theatres. Initially
the game of golf saw the indiscriminate mingling of the classes as 'all
distinctions of rank were levelled by the joyous spirit of the game'.
However, as Browning goes on to say, 'the club system made an end to
this arcadian simplicity',[12] a process exemplified in golf by the Royal
and Ancient Club of 1754 and in rowing by the Leander Club of 1818.

The eighteenth-century desire to isolate and control the encroaching
sporting masses became the nineteenth-century desire to isolate and
control professionalism and foster amateur ethic, the one being a
matter of convenience whilst the other was promoted as a matter
of principle. This element of righteousness had been assiduously
acquired at the muscular and Christian public schools attended by all
the putative rulers of the sporting scene, but whilst they might agree
with many contemporary critics that it was to the nobility that they
were indebted for the excellent tone which pervaded the English
character, they also suspected that the same nobility lacked the moral
fibre to fight sporting professionalism since it was they who had first
promoted the trend a century earlier.[13] The new middle-class righteousness also stemmed from the classical tradition so strongly followed at
the schools which encouraged the belief that nobility of action lay in
purity of motive, which in sporting terms meant playing the game for
the players' enjoyment only, a view even extending to a denigration of
passive 'spectatorism'.[14]

From such a background grew the amateur ethic incorporating
attitudes which were 'unintellectual, combative, manly, Christian and
patriotic',[15] thus excluding the professional on every count: his scientific
training disqualified him under the first heading, the unfair advantage
he derived from it under the second, his propensity to cheat under the
third, his profiteering under the fourth and the baleful example he
therefore inevitably set his compatriots under the fifth. It was consequently considered a Christian and patriotic duty to marginalise him
as far as possible and to this end the new men set about re-regulating
each sport in order to exclude them: the old Jockey Club strictures of
1750 were gradually strengthened until by 1837 every aspect of the
sport came under central control; similarly the relatively loose almost
advisory guidelines of the MCC were tightened in 1835; and even in

yachting, where no specific reason to do so existed, rules and regulations were introduced with the establishment of the Royal Yacht Club in 1820. The unruly and hugely popular game of football was regulated on a strictly amateur basis with the formation of the Football Association in 1863, as was rugby with the Rugby Football Union in 1871, athletics with the Amateur Athletic Association in 1880, boxing with the Amateur Boxing Association of 1880, followed by the Amateur Rowing Association in 1882, finishing with the official ratification of the Royal and Ancient Golf Club as the ultimate authority in golf during 1919. It is instructive to note that in every case the promoters of the new rules and the governing bodies were public school and Oxbridge men and all the original member clubs were to be found in or near London.

The enforcement of a strictly amateur code had enormous social, cultural and geographical effects on individual sports with the intransigence of southern-based governing bodies leading to the establishment of the Northern Rugby Union, the Northern Counties Athletic Association, the Northern Cross Country Association, the National Amateur Rowing Association, and the northern cricket leagues. It also fuelled the northern traditions of professional boxing and steeple chasing, the latter being dismissed as 'dominated by sportsmen rather than racing men and infested with crooks'.[16] In each case the sentiments expressed by Owen on the split in rugby union can be applied when he remarked that 'thanks to a few hard headed and far seeing members of the governing body the first class game was saved for the amateur and not permitted to develop into a public entertainment'.[17] Cultural differences caused the game of association football to be lost to the amateur and the middle classes eventually retreated from the game altogether as it was taken over by professionalism, mass spectatorship and commercialisation and became identified as a 'passion not a recreation'.[18]

The predominantly southern middle classes seemed unable to come to terms with a nothern sporting fervour which resulted from scarcities of money and leisure time since they themselves had plenty of both. Their lack of understanding translated into a condescension often mentioned by Matthew Arnold who noted in *Culture and Anarchy* in 1869 that a true ruling culture would refrain from teaching down to the level of inferior classes and seek instead to do away with the concept of class altogether. Rather than do this, however, the new rulers began to concentrate on purely recreational involvements, withdrawing themselves from open competition as rowers did for example in their espousal of boating. In football the Corinthian Club was established in 1883 to promote the true amateur spirit of playing the game for its own

8

sake and the Rugby Union became more determinedly amateur as time went by. In sports like hunting, which had always linked classes together from 'peer to peasant', the social distinctions and etiquette began to assume a prime importance with some hunts requiring references and establishing long waiting lists. The sheer cost of many recreations excluded many who might otherwise have taken part: Major Wingfield introduced the game of lawn tennis in 1873 as a purely commercial venture, selling kits at 5 guineas to those with gardens large enough to accommodate the court; and at the same time croquet began to enjoy great popularity again with people who had moved out into the new rambling suburbs and could afford the space to play it. The seclusion and security of a large garden also explains the growing fashion for target archery particularly amongst women. Whilst middle-class women took up these recreations, the men continued to play at the old school games such as rackets, fives and the newly emerging squash, and even fencing experienced a resurgence of interest towards the turn of the century to such an extent that it was regarded as too much of a recreation to be looked upon as a true sport. Other middle-class recreations included skating on the artificial ice of the new refrigerated rinks and cycling with the newly improved safety cycles, both of which soon ceased to be exclusive following further technical developments: the rinks became commonplace with entrance charged in pennies and the mass production of cycles produced a social revolution by providing cheap transport, thereby radically altering the most ordinary processes and methods of social life. The new class of cyclists became known as 'cads on castors' and questions concerning their irresponsible actions were asked in the House of Commons and it must have appeared that there was no hiding place from the rowdier elements of society.[19] Other factors were also working against exclusivity in recreation since for the first time in many years the working classes began to enjoy longer periods of leisure time, which together with slightly higher wages provided the basis for the leisure revolution of the present century. The range of activities available to them was greater than ever before in music and commercial entertainment as well as organised and recreational sport, all of which gained the status of respectability with little reference to middle-class ideology; leisure was gradually becoming more than merely an antidote for work. The larger industrial and commercial enterprises had already begun to provide recreational facilities for their employees and enabling legislation was passed for the first time to encourage local authorities to provide land for recreational use.

So it was that political, economic and technical developments gradually conspired to extend the recreational franchise to the working classes and in so doing encouraged the leisured classes to seek even further exclusivity in their sport and recreation. The era extending to the First World War witnessed perhaps the most blatant displays of social exclusivity at such occasions as the Varsity and Eton–Harrow cricket matches at Lords and, encouraged by regular royal attendances, the race meetings at Goodwood and Ascot, Cowes Regatta and Henley Royal Regatta, whilst participation was restricted to those clubs which operated the black ball system of membership election. It is not surprising that this period also witnessed the growing fashion for foreign holidays as 'society' shunned the increasingly down-market English resorts and the hey-days of the Grand Hotels. In recreational terms this fashion was mirrored by the advent of skiing as the exclusive sport par excellence which distanced the participant both metaphorically and geographically from much of contemporary society.

Although the First World War seemed to depress sporting activities, most of them had revived by the late 1920s with professional games being played before record crowds and amateur club memberships at record levels. The tension between the two extremes of sport continued as political, social, commercial and technical factors produced new patterns of leisure, bringing about a gradual decline in local forms of sport and consolidating national games, the organisation of which began to cause problems as in football where the authorities looked anxiously towards the future of the game and racing where the public began to demand better facilities and fewer restrictions. The Jockey Club remained an elite body but did alter a little after the war as a contemporary journalist noted 'the old Tory spirit trimmed its sails to the passing breeze whilst maintaining its old authority',[20] a movement also discernible in rowing as the amateur definition was gradually relaxed during the 1930s. The spread of suburbia and a desire for exclusivity, together with greater technical capacity, produced a host of new, private golf courses, particularly around the larger cities like Manchester and Leeds, which mirrored similar expansion in the home counties brought about by the spread of the rail network fifty years earlier. In cricket where amateur and professional played together, there remained the cultural north–south divide, with southern visitors to northern games being overheard to remark what they were witnessing 'wasn't cricket at all'.[21]

The major trend in recreation since the Second World War has been the democratisation of leisure activities brought about chiefly through the increased use of cars, the spread of television and the establishment of the Sports Development Council in 1965 following upon the National Playing Fields Association of 1925 and the Central Council of Recreative Physical Training of 1935, later to become the Central Council of Physical Recreation in 1944. Media coverage of sport has had the effect of commercialising and professionalising those sports not hitherto involved, such as lawn tennis which went 'open' in 1968 and athletics which at the elite level has become professional in all but name. Growing affluence in society would seem to be the main cause of both a dramatic decrease in the number of registered professional boxers since the war from 1,000 to 350 and also an enormous increase in gambling, particularly at the races where betting levies now represent 90 per cent of the sport's income, a supreme example of eighteenth-century private philanthropy giving way to twentieth-century public sponsorship. According to some, the Jockey Club should have prevented the bookmakers from gaining the upper hand but were unable to do so since it had 'lost its identity being unsure of whom it represented if indeed it represented anyone apart from its own members'.[22] This point of view was shared by grass root participants in many sports with regard to their governing bodies. In football the Football Association has suffered the recurrence of hooliganism whose transfer from the field of play to the terraces mirrors a societal trend away from participation towards spectating which has been fostered by the media in all its forms. The game which came of age as a 'passion' one hundred years ago is now accounted a 'madness' with many drawing a parallel between its decline and that of the country.[23] That such a comparison can be made and generally accepted indicates the recognition given to sport as a barometer of social change, the reading of which can give us, as Strutt advised all those years ago, 'a just estimation of any particular people'.

In reviewing the sporting scene in England from the sixteenth to the twentieth century we can discern several major themes emerging which will be used in subsequent chapters to widen the perspective on the evolution of sporting culture. Taken chronologically these themes concern the occupational or bucolic origins of many sports, often involving elements of commercialism which in turn presented opportunities for gambling and business exploitation. Such opportunities were taken up by the aristocracy in the eighteenth century and evolved during the nineteenth century into a systematic professionalisation of the sporting scene. As a reaction to this trend the new righteous middle class preferred a more recreational involvement in sport nurtured by various social determinants resulting in a strictly codified amateur ethic and the rise of the sporting club. Two distinct cultures then existed for many years within the sporting tradition, cultures

11

whose fortunes were determined by a whole range of factors throughout a century of enormous social upheaval and which continued to affect and reflect contemporary society.

NOTES

1. J. Dando and H. Runt, *Banks Bay Horse in Trance* (London, 1595).
2. J. Strutt, *Sports and Pastimes of the People of England* (White, 1801).
3. S. Smith, 'Remarks on the system of education in public schools', *Edinburgh Review*, 16 (Aug. 1801).
4. A. Trollope, *British Sports and Pastimes* (Virtue & Spalding, 1868).
5. For a full treatment of this emancipation see J.A. Mangan and R.B. Park, *From Fair Sex to Feminism: Sport and the Socialisation of Women in the Industrial and Post-Industrial Eras* (Frank Cass, 1987).
6. T.C. Worsley, encouraged by George Orwell, produced two works on this theme: *The End of the Old School Tie* (Secker & Warburg, 1941) and *Barbarians and Philistines* (Hale, 1940).
7. An illuminating comment by a leading headmaster serves to illustrate this point: 'In a sense games provide for a schoolboy the opportunity of exercising those acknowledged moral qualities which war provides for the grown up'. D.R.N. Silk, Warden of Radley College, 'Physical education and the future in boarding schools', Conference report, Marlborough College, 17 April 1970.
8. For these, prior and subsequent similar works, see bibliography under 'social commentary'.
9. R. Cashman and L. McKernan, *Sport in History* (Queensland University Press, 1979).
10. Editorial, *Athletic News*, Dec. 1895.
11. C. Whitney, *Sporting Pilgrimage* (Osgood McIlvaine, 1894), p. 20.
12. R. Browning, *A History of Golf* (Allen Lane, 1965), p. 35.
13. R. Fulford, *The Greville Memoirs* (Batsford, 1963); cf. Lord Greville's comment on the turf quoted on p. 135: 'I feel that my involvement in the turf degrades and stupifies my understanding, that it renders me less agreeable in society, less useful, less respectable in the world and that this consciousness together with the want of cultivation which I would otherwise possess vex and harass me'.
14. H.A. Harris, *Greek Athletes and Athletics* (Methuen, 1964); see the comment on p. 189: 'So long as sport is true to itself its only purpose is the enjoyment of the players, if the interests of the spectators predominate then corruption has set in and the essence of the game is lost'.
15. H. Cunningham, *Leisure in the Industrial Revolution* (Croom Helm, 1980).
16. M. Seth-Smith *The History of Steeple Chasing* (Joseph, 1966).
17. O.L. Owen, *The History of Rugby Football Union* (Playfair, 1955). This comment may be set against the view expressed later in the book that 'the economic balance has swung against the impecunious young businessman and those in the early stages of a profession but happily a liberalised policy of paying legitimate expenses has eased matters for all concerned' (p. 85).
18. E. Ensor, 'The football madness', *Contemporary Review*, 74 (1898).
19. Sir George Jenkinson, *Hansard*, 241, c. 3124.
20. S.G. Galtry, *Memoirs of a Racing Journalist* (Longman, 1934).
21. N. Cardus, *Cardus on Cricket* (Souvenir Press, 1977).
22. N. Robinson representing the Race Horse Owners Association, commenting in the *Observer*, 21 Oct. 1984.
23. J. Walvin, *Football and the Decline of Britain* (Macmillan, 1986).

2

Origins

It has always been common for gentlemen to use their recreations as badges of social and physical superiority over the lower orders.

(Marcia Vale, *Gentlemen's Recreations 1580–1630*, 1977)

Unlawful games such as boleng is comynly used at all divers tymes so that the mayntenance of Archery is cleane lefte unexiecyssid.

(*Southampton Court Leet Records 1569*, M41)

Many of the sports and pastimes mentioned by Strutt in 1801 were ancient even then. William FitzStephen in his Life of St Thomas written towards the end of the twelfth century tells of traditional Shrove Tuesday recreations when boys brought their cocks and men their boars to stage fights for the holiday crowds, whilst bulls and bears were baited by specially bred mastiff dogs. It was not all violence, however, as the boys went off to the fields after the cock-fighting to play at foot, hand or club ball as a further entertainment for the general public. In the Easter holidays water quintain was played in boats on the rivers and during summer holidays there was leaping, dancing, shooting with arrows, wrestling, casting the stone and 'practising with shields'. Winter encouraged ice sports such as sliding, sledging, curling and even a basic form of ice hockey, and all of these activities took place throughout the country in the more prosperous towns such as Oxford, York, Lincoln and Norwich and in smaller towns where weekly markets were held. In the villages rough games of football were already played, one side or even one village against the other, with the most important matches likely to be held on Shrove Tuesday; Sundays and holy days gave opportunities for football, wrestling, boxing and primitive forms of bowls. Nothing that is known in more detail about play in the fourteenth and fifteenth centuries was wholly missing from life in the twelfth and thirteenth centuries.

In subsequent centuries a greater element of spectatorism became obvious in the popularity of jousts, pageants and processions, augmented on holy days by seasonal mummeries and fertility rites which would often be followed by feats of strength and wrestling. Judging by the number of enactments which sought to reduce the time wasted on alternatives, archery grew less and less popular during the fifteenth century, understandable perhaps when the activity was so much associated with duty and compulsion. Evidence of recreational archery is hard to come by since the longbow was never a gentleman's weapon and so there is little information about its use except in war or preparation for war. Acts to promote the practice of archery whilst proscribing other activities had been passed in the reigns of Edward II, Edward III, Richard II, Henry IV, VII and VIII particularly and specifically at times of perceived national weakness to outside threat or internal disorder, and in 1477 the Commons petitioned Edward IV to execute these laws effectively for the first time. The games which were popular enough to be proscribed as injurious to the development of archery, were named as handball, tennis, football, hockey, dice, quoits, bowls, skittles and cock-fighting. The Acts supporting archery were henceforth prosecuted with greater vigour, at least for a time, as we can see in court records around the country which itemise the fines levied for playing bowls, as at Amtphill in 1502 where 11 men were fined 20d each or at Leighton Buzzard in the same year when several boys were fined 12d each for playing tennis. On both occasions the miscreants were encouraged to develop their shooting skills at the butts and large practice fields adjacent to the banks of the River Ouse in Bedford.

The most popular sports were merely extensions of childish games played with the most easily acquired implements, namely sticks and stones: hence football, hockey, bowls, skittles and quoits are all variations on hitting and aiming, whilst handball and tennis were the same but using another commonplace article, a ball of wool later compressed and stitched. It was the nature of such activities that rules were lacking: play continued until boredom set it, skill broke down, the strongest prevailed or sufficient disruption occurred to encourage what authority existed to bring activities to a close. Some systemisation was introduced when bowls and skittles gravitated to the public houses where wooden alleys were erected inside the premises and greens laid conveniently close. Towards the end of the fifteenth century it seemed likely that some games were approaching regulation: already jousts and sword play had acquired the elaborate observances required by noble participants, and largely due to the demands made by the leisured class the balls for tennis and bowls were being standardised, as were rackets, introducing a consistency of performance which paved the way for rules of play. The shape and size of the playing areas continued to be determined by local considerations and games played by the poorer classes were pursued on an ad hoc basis for centuries to come.

If the inn attracted the village bowlers it also served as a meeting point for the local hunts, even though hunting itself was restricted to the gentry – a restriction which also applied to fishing and fowling activities reserved for the benefit of those living in big houses. Although fishing for the poor was often a matter of poaching to aid survival, it was also recognised as a sport, at least by the author of *The Treatise of Fyssynge with an Angle* (1496) who wrote that it should be undertaken principally for 'solace and to cause the helthe of your body and specially for your soule'. Such therapeutic value ascribed to sport was claimed for football by Richard Mulcaster in *The Schoolmaster* (1561) since it 'strengthened and brawneth the whole body by provoking superfluities downwards'. However, these attitudes so early expressed failed to gain general acceptance until the nineteenth century when other humanitarian views were expressed concerning activities of previous eras. The cruelty of baiting animals, one of the few recreational activities which appealed to both master and man, was roundly condemned by, amongst others, Jeremy Bentham when he supposed its pursuit implied 'the absence of reflection or a fund of inhumanity.[1] Notwithstanding this, cock-fighting, bull and bear-baiting were extremely popular displays for a social cross-section of spectators, nowhere better exemplified than in Cambridge where at the animal fairs there would be gathered graduates, undergraduates, college servants and townsfolk. In 1581 a complaint was made to the local constable concerning a bear-baiting which was the occasion for a great congregation of town and gown and a warrant was granted from the justices 'to cease from that disordered pastime'. The university beadle attempted to disperse the crowd but was deliberately pressed against the bears and beat a hasty retreat, only to learn later that the bearward had in fact been lawfully licensed by the constable.[2] Such diversions were widely popular but often the gentry would arrange to watch them at a distance or separately, and whilst their particular recreations were no less bloody they entailed greater skill in execution as in hunting, hawking and fowling. Their athletic pursuits were numbered amongst archery, fencing, dancing, tennis, bowling, golf and swimming[3] in none of which would master and man ever play together – a situation for which we must wait until the more liberal and cosmopolitan eighteenth century.

The two sports habitually but separately played by both sections of society were bowling and tennis, but very different circumstances attended their pursuit. For the common man bowling began with rounded stones flung against a single stake embedded in the ground or at a collection of sticks to be toppled, and progressed to wooden bowls and skittles as technology allowed and custom encouraged. The problems that authority had with the game stemmed from the damage often done with the 'sticks and stones' when crowds of players fell out, and the frequency of play which kept the players from gainful employment, points made in a Declaration of Edward II to the sheriffs of London in 1349. While bowling was actively discouraged among the meaner sort of people throughout the medieval period, the gentry had developed a more sophisticated game on grass areas specially adapted for the purpose, the first example of which were the lawns of God's House Hospital in Southampton in 1187. These lawns, originally laid out for the warden of the hospital, were first used for bowling in 1299 when we find documentary evidence of a Master of the Green being elected.[4] An old plan of the southern section of Southampton in 1611 shows figures playing bowls on God's House Green which is described as a ground where 'many gentlemen and gentile merchants of this town take their recreation'. Meanwhile, elsewhere in Southampton the common men playing at bowls were frequently hauled before the magistrates and heavily fined, as were 19 such in May 1577.[5] Bowling was a popular target for the authorities in its clamp down on people's recreations, presumably because of its popularity and destructive potential and it was exempted from a general relaxation against such activities in the seventeenth century. In 1617 King James sought to mollify many who complained that they were 'barred from all lawful recreation upon the Sundaies after Devine service', concluding that this had the effect of building up religious discontent at the least possible desirable time. Another vital consideration was that any such bar discouraged 'the common and meane sorte of people from usinge such exercises as may make their bodies more able for warrs' and so a general amnesty for previously unlawful sports was allowed at least on Sundays with the sole exception of 'bowlinge'.[6] Bowling by the gentry became increasingly popular during the century and we find specially constructed greens appearing throughout the country at places where 'gentelemen and gentile merchants' congregated[7] whilst at the same time common land continued to be used for its bucolic equivalent.[8]

A similar story of separate development can be told about tennis which in its genteel form evolved from ball games played in the cloisters of monasteries and in the common form derived from handing any available likely object over any available obstruction or hazard such as wall, hedge or ditch. Like bowling it became disruptively

1. The illustration shows the type of court adapted from the French monastic original which was incorporated into the design of gentlemen's houses during the sixteenth century. The game itself has also been modified from the original format so that several players can participate at any one time. Note the presence of the sixteenth-century equivalent of 'ball boys' who would have been members of the domestic staff.

popular and was always cited in Warrants, Declarations or Proclamations as forbidden to the common and mean people, but at the same time the spread of specially constructed tennis courts for the nobility and gentry continued so that by 1500 there were at least ten within a five mile radius of King's Cross.

Although different forms of bowling and tennis were enjoyed by all sections of society and recognised as recreational activities, archery could not be so described since for the common man it had become an irksome obligation whilst remaining a pleasure for his master. The defence of the realm was largely dependent upon the availability of large numbers of skilled archers together with a smaller but still substantial number of horsemen drawn from the landed classes. The longbow was regarded as the military tool of the lowly foot soldier while the better off aspired to all the accoutrements of the cavalryman to be used and enjoyed as evidence of social and cultural superiority. As the era of the military mercenary began, the necessity for a national pool of reservists declined and with it the enthusiasm for

17

practice, aided and abetted by strictures of work on the land and of course, as we have seen, alternative forms of entertainment. The first laws to compel archery practice because of its military importance were introduced in the thirteenth century and all enactments concerning unlawful sports cited its continuing importance until the end of the sixteenth century when it must have been obvious to all that it was no longer necessary. There is much evidence of archery practice grounds falling into disrepair, nowhere more so than in Manchester where the main site lay in Alport Lane which is now part of Deansgate. In 1576 it was necessary for the authorities to order the repair of the butts, apparently with very little permanent effect since two years later the local court observed that 'artillerie in this towne is wonderfullie decayed'.[9] The longbow as a hunting rather than military tool had always been used by the gentry, whose skill at shooting can be traced as a gentlemanly or noble pursuit through written records beginning with the Norse sagas, and they continued to shoot in the country as an integral part of their 'field' sports. By the middle of the sixteenth century when relatively reliable muskets were coming onto the market, those interested in archery as a pure entertainment took to target archery, and although the first mention of organised competition is dated 14 May 1673 at Scorton in Yorkshire, its description as 'ancient' probably places the inaugural event a century earlier. It is somewhat ironic that at the same time as the bucolic form of the activity was becoming moribund the genteel variation was successfully established.

As with other advances in technology the gentry were quick to take advantage of the new muskets for recreational purposes, and shooting with a gun soon became uniquely their sport, representing as it did their social, financial and physical superiority. During the eighteenth century the mass production of muskets, designed to supply the new militia established to counter civil unrest, brought prices down and 'rough' shooting became more popular, resulting in the killing of huge quantities of wildlife.[10] So great was the slaughter that conservation of game was begun, a closed season introduced and a range of licenses levied, all of which restricted access to the sport in a way which continues today due to private ownership of shooting land, ecological pressure on wildlife and the high costs of fees and equipment. Hunting is another recreational activity which has largely retained its privileged nature over the centuries. As a sport inevitably restricted to horse owners it was initially pursued by the nobility alone but gradually spread with increasing levels of horse ownership to the point in the mid seventeenth century when middling landowners and prosperous yeoman farmers were able to participate. Hunting of all kinds was severely restricted in the immediate post-Norman Conquest era when the penalty for illegal possession of game was loss of limb or even life. The Charter of the Forests (1217) softened these harsh Norman penalties and placed limits on the extent of royal hunting grounds, but following the Peasants' Revolt of 1389 Richard II decreed that pursuit of game was lawful only for those qualified by ownership of land. Following seventeenth-century incursions by the rising middle class into the hunting field, Charles II introduced a gentleman's 'game privilege' based on high land qualifications, and despite the cosmopolitan nature of the many subscriptions hunts of the eighteenth and nineteenth centuries hunting remained a sport for the prosperous elite,[11] which to a large extent it remains today.

From hunting naturally grew horse-racing as each hunt member strove to be first to the kill, but this was only one origination for the sport. At least two others in the form of chariot racing and cavalry activity can also be identified. The first recorded horse race in England took place between two Arabian steeds at Netherby in Yorkshire nearly 1,800 years ago. Racing has always had strong royal connections and became a fashionable pastime for the nobility in the twelfth century, but it was not until 1540 that the first racecourse was officially established at Chester. Queen Elizabeth I went to the races at Croydon and in 1616 James I bought the Markham Arabian, a small bay stallion, to use with his royal mares, thus founding thoroughbred racehorse dynasties that have survived to this day. James established race meetings at Newmarket, Doncaster, York and London where the races were anything up to six miles with gold and silver bells, later cups, for first and second prizes. Charles II made Newmarket the sport's headquarters and rode his own horse to victory there in 1671. By the eighteenth century the sport had spread so rapidly and indiscriminately that the artistocrats of Newmarket felt threatened enough to form a loose organisation of control, not founded with any high notion of governing or reforming the sport but initially designed to protect their own interests on Newmarket Heath. The Jockey Club of 1750 grew out of informal social gatherings of racing nobility at various London clubs which were moved to Newmarket with the establishment of the Stewards coffee house in 1752. Such protective regulation was not unique: comprehensive Rules of Racing were laid down as early as 1680 by Richard Legh, who as Lord of the Manor inaugurated a course on Newton Heath in Lancashire in 1678 long before any rules emanated from Newmarket,[12] and similar local regulations can be found at all the original racing venues. Despite such legislation and the Jockey Club's increasing national significance during the eighteenth century, racing like other sports suffered from the nefarious dealings of many of its adherents in rigging competitions for pecuniary advantage and for quite some time became downright unfashionable. *The Times* notes this fact, whilst on the advice of the Duke of Dorset advocating the choice of cricket as a suitable alternative since it made 'far better use of the turf'.[13]

The origins of cricket were rustic and cast in the same mould as other stick and ball games with the addition of a target to be aimed at and defended, which would probably have been a wicket gate or fence protected from a woollen ball by a shepherd's crook. Although initially a rural peasant game it soon became one of the apprentices' rowdy diversions in urban areas and for some time after the accession of George I became the object of unwelcome attention from the authorities nervous about large crowds in those Jacobite times.[14] By this time players had reached a certain level of sophistication born of equipment adaptation and frequency of practice, to which was soon added a refinement of rules and playing conditions introduced by the gentry. Even at village level the game was taken extremely seriously, as memories of play on Halfpenny Down illustrate with leading players like David Harris and 'Lumpy' Stevens walking the ground in the early hours to pitch carefully the stumps so as to embrace such hillocks as favoured their peculiar bowling methods.[15] Such play and players were soon superseded by a metropolitan elite of gentlemen playing at specially constructed venues on White Conduit Fields and New Road, Mary le Bone under their own self-regarding rules which allowed for paid bowlers and did nothing to discourage heavy betting.[16] The support given to the sport by the gentry and its subsequent development through the public schools ensured cricket's status as a national game to be set alongside the ancient sport of football.

Despite the fact that football had been regarded as a public menace for many centuries, with 23 edicts issued against it between the fourteenth and seventeenth centuries, it continued to be the national pastime. Pursued in a totally unregulated fashion by the lower orders wherever space allowed and often where it did not, nevertheless it somehow managed at one level to be accepted by the gentry who made attempts to adapt it for their own purposes.[17] There is evidence that they placed artificial limits on the field of play and began to introduce basic rules,[18] and we have seen how their children were encouraged to play the game by Richard Mulcaster, headmaster of St Paul's School, a lead no doubt followed elsewhere. At the same time public disturbances caused by indiscriminate play at football continued, not

2. Players at Ball – taken from a 12th-century manuscript. Such activities were mentioned by William Fitzstephen in his Life of St Thomas written in the same century. This form of play was the forerunner of all stick and ball games which gained popularity in subsequent centuries including of course cricket.

least in those areas formerly used for archery practice and left in disrepair, as in Alport Lane, Manchester where desperate complaints were made against 'companies of lewd and disordered persons playing football' spilling into the street and breaking windows.[19]

We know that such disturbances were caused by many rowdy land sports over many centuries but water sports were not immune from the general level of performance. The bouts of water quintain mentioned by FitzStephen in 1175 were often followed by a general aquatic 'free for all' and much licentious behaviour was produced by the watermen plying for hire on the River Thames which transferred itself to the wager racing between individual scullers that was such a feature of seventeenth-century London life.[20] The contestants in Doggett's Coat and Badge Race inaugurated in 1715 were regularly pelted and accosted by spectators while running an aquatic gauntlet between London Bridge and Chelsea Bridge and also endeavouring to avoid fouling manoeuvres from fellow contestants. As sanctions were taken against disruptive behaviour in football, bowls, tennis and the like, so too were regulations applied with increasing severity to the watermen, but disturbances reached such a level during the eighteenth century that the Lord Mayor of London was finally constrained to prohibit boat hirers form letting out craft on Sundays 'to prevent the many apprentices that make common practice of going up and down river and frequently been detected in robbing their masters to support their expenses'.[21] A similar injunction against rowing had been issued by the headmaster of Westminster School following several fatalities among pupils out on the river at Chelsea. The fashion for boating amongst the wealthier class waned and was replaced by an enthusiasm for sailing[22] in which the tradition of employing watermen as helmsmen continued.

The winner of Doggett's Coat and Badge in 1730, Jack Broughton, like many before him had used boxing as a training regime for his rowing, and following his retirement as a licensed waterman he set up in business as a boxing coach and trainer. Many gentlemen paid him to train them for physical fitness and their protégés for combat. In order to meet these demands and minimise the risks of serious injury he introduced a scientific element into a previously mindless pugilism, regulating it with the new Broughton Rules for which he became known as the Father of British Boxing. Boxing, pugilism or simply fist-fighting was common in early rural sports on high days and holy days, along with wrestling which was particularly localised in the north-west and south-west of the country with the unique Cumberland style evident in the earliest reports.[23] Further evidence of violent whole body sports is provided by reports of stick-fighting or cudgelling where the object was to render your opponent unconscious, and in Cornwall particularly it was regarded as almost a rite of passage for adolescents as fathers 'encouraged their children to thrash one another'.[24] The genteel equivalent of such barbaric behaviour was fencing and there were even some points of similarity in 'toeing' a line and holding one's ground, but gentlemen engaged fencing masters who often also taught them dancing and whose substantial accounts were settled quarterly.[25] It is instructive to note that while the gentry paid for dancing the common people were frequently fined for the activity as it was associated in the official mind with 'filthie Typlinge and Drunkeness',[26] yet another example of the imposition of double standards applied by the wealthy in pursuit of cultural propriety and domestic security.

A similar duality existed between golf and hockey stemming as they both did from essentially the same activity – striking small objects with bent sticks – with hockey taking the form of an adversarial contest as in football and golf being target-orientated having been refined in Scotland and introduced to England by James I. In Scotland the game was played quite indiscriminately by all classes on land that was generally regarded as free or common land, and even in northern England we can see elements of this practice in operation.[27] In the same fashion both gentry and peasants used dogs for hunting, so much so that one of the first forest laws introduced by the Normans after the conquest forbade their use by commoners who employed them as a vital means of obtaining food. The gentry, however, used dogs in pursuit of game purely as a means of racing them and so great was the variation in their application that the Duke of Norfolk was charged with drawing up a set of rules which he produced in 1580 under the title Laws of the Leash.

Two activities which had strict cultural demarcations were swimming and running. Not only was swimming considered to have proven cultural bona fides in its classical military origins in Greece, but towards the end of the seventeenth century much scientific and pseudo-scientific research suggested that there was much therapeutic value in immersion and exercise in salt water, whereas the common man would take to the water only to wash, play or poach. Running was out of the question for the gentleman whose principal badge of social superiority was his horse, but his man would run as part of the purely athletic activities available at rural sports along with 'leapynge and vaultynge'. Running races were common at feasts and fairs marking holy days and we find mention of them for both men and women at the May Fairs on Kersal Moor, Manchester throughout the sixteenth century where prizes were food, drink or clothing.

In seeking the origins of our national sports and pastimes we can see that they sprang from common roots but developed diversely due to concerns about social superiority and civil security which were not only produced by but contributed towards a cultural apartheid in English society. This radical diversity is evident in all our ancient sports and is also obvious in the more modern activities with which we shall be dealing in subsequent chapters; indeed the ways in which they were either exploited or modified constitute the evolution of English sport. The master and his man occupied separate social and cultural worlds during the medieval period but in the eighteenth century increasing mercantilism and the emergence of a 'middling' class of people inaugurated a coming together in society which is well represented in the sporting scene and it is to this that we turn in the next chapter.

NOTES

1. J. Bentham, *The Principles of Penal Law* (collected works, Bowring, William Tait, 1948).
2. Report in the Cambridge Record Office ms. PB, Vol. 31.
3. M. Vale, *Gentleman's Recreations 1580–1630* (Brewer, 1977).

4. *Records of Southampton Old Bowling Green* (Southampton Records Office BG14/1).

5. *Court Leet Records of Southampton*, Southampton Records Office M109.

6. King James I, *Book of Sports* (version dated 27 Aug. 1617 at Gerards Bromley).

7. See maps of Southwell in Nottinghamshire 1683 (SOIOS) and Marylebone, London, 1703 (DD4P 18/s) both at Nottinghamshire Records Office.

8. For example, clods taken from common land at Chesterfield for the construction of bowling alleys, 1660 (Nottingham Records DD4P 79/10).

9. *Manchester Court Leet Records*, 1578 M30/4.

10. *Shooting Diary of Charles Shaw M.P.* 12 Oct. 1784: 796 pheasant, 514 partridge, 184 hares.

11. Ibid., 16 Sept. 1785: 'I have the strongest passion for hunting but not being able to afford the expenses of horses I content myself with shooting'.

12. *Newton Court Leet Records*, 1678, and *Newton Course Records* held at Haydock Race Course.

13. *The Times* (31 Oct. 1787), 5c.

14. Hostility to cricket can be found in the historical novels of Scott: *Waverley* and *Red Gauntlet*.

15. *The Times*, 'Memories of Halfpenny Down' (4 Sept. 1908), 7d.

16. It is interesting to note that when the pavilion at Lords burned down the greatest distress was caused by the loss of the valuable wine cellar, *The Times* (30 July 1825), 5c.

17. M. Vale, *Gentlemen's Recreations 1580–1630* (Brewer, 1977).

18. Mention of the construction of a 'Futebale Croft' at Oxton in Nottinghamshire in 1570 (Nottinghamshire Records DD/SK/16).

19. *Manchester Court Leet Records* for March 1603.

20. *Pepys Diary*, 18 May 1661 (Bell & Hyman, 1973).

21. *The Times* (21 July 1787), 3c.

22. *Memoirs of Willliam Hickey*, Vol. 1, p. 95 (Hurst & Blackett, 1923).

23. *Cumberland and Westmorland Wrestling Society*, notes for 1871 referring to the original Cumberland 'holds' in use pre 1656.

24. *Dudley Ryder's Diary 1715–1716*, 15 June 1715 (Methuen, 1939).

25. Accounts for a Dancing Master, 1661, giving a total account of £996 14s 0d split between 27 pupils (Nottinghamshire Records DD/5P/7).

26. King James I, *Book of Sports* (version dates 27 Aug. 1617, Gerards Bromley).

27. Preamble to *Alnmouth Golf Club Rules for 1907*, referring to the tradition of exempting from membership 'the working classes who reside in the village of Alnmouth' recognising their rights to play golf on the common land.

3

Commercialisation

There was a prodigious conflux of nobility and
gentry into London.

(D. Defoe, *A Tour through the whole island of Great Britain*, 1726)

Purses of £50 entered at the Cross Keys
No horse to stand at any house that does not subscribe 1 guinea
No person to sell liquors unless he subscribe 10/6d
Balls at the County Hall every night
Cocking at the Woolpack as usual

(Notice for Warwick Races, August 1783)

As we have seen, the public house had always been a gathering place
for recreational activities with skittles and bowls taking place there
and with local hunts meeting there. Given the commercial nature of
the business it is not surprising that the publican should often sponsor
and promote sporting activities to boost trade nor that other promoters
should seek his or her support for their ventures. Horse-racing was the
first activity to be positively encouraged through financial sponsorship
and town councils were often instrumental in promoting local racing in
order to attract people to their areas, much as tourist boards and
chambers of commerce do today. Newton racecourse in Lancashire
was one of the first to be properly surveyed and laid out and Richard
Legh, the Lord of the Manor who was largely responsible for its
establishment, made sure that all the local innkeepers made an annual
donation of 12d towards a silver plate 'to be run for with horses'.[1] All
subsequent meetings here and elsewhere were partly funded by commercial subscriptions to plates and cups for winning owners. The inn
would easily recoup any financial outlay as the incoming crowds would
queue to eat and drink at the 'Ordinarys and Assemblys available as
usual'[2] at each and every watering hole. Always available too were the
cock-fights to attract the racing gamblers before and after the main
meeting, until that is the latter part of the eighteenth century when
a combination of puritan revulsion and official reaction to civil

disruption caused it to become far less common and publicans began to realize that 'cocking' was likely to lead to a revocation of their licences. It was banned throughout the country in 1795 but the occasional prosecution provides evidence of its continuing fascination to the present day, usually in areas of the country like Cheshire and Northumberland where it was always most popular.[3]

Later in the Victorian period the public house became a second home to many, providing as it often did 'light and heat, cooking, furniture, newspapers and sociability'.[4] But all these facilities were available in the urban coffee shop and to a lesser extent the rural inn during the eighteenth century and it was often the latter which provided the base for local sports teams, the most celebrated of which was certainly the 'Bat and Ball' on Hambledon Down. This provided the Hambledon village cricket eleven with a headquarters from which they proceeded to beat most opposition, including a full England eleven, returning in their resplendent uniforms of sky blue waistcoats with black velvet collars to drink their ale and sing their songs well into the summer evenings.[5] Publicans soon realised the commercial attractions of sporting contests and those lucky enough to run establishments close to open ground promoted events of all varieties. In the London area cricket was guaranteed to pull large crowds, especially when the games featured the more bizarre contestants: four men aged 74, one-armed and one-legged veterans, one man and a dog versus two gentlemen and so on.[6] Often enough a newly opened inn would present such an attraction to publicise its existence and secure future trade, as did the 'Westend' by organising a match between married women and maidens in 1838 which attracted a staggering 3,000 spectators,[7] or even the new Montpelier Tea Gardens at Walworth in 1796 which was considerably less successful.[8] Cricket grounds were hired by publicans for other promotional events, such as hugely popular pedestrian matches like that between the Manchester Pet and a local East End man on one October holiday in 1843 which many thousands might be expected to attend.[9] So frequently did they attend and so disruptively that the authorities gradually reduced the number of bank holidays during the 1830s and 1840s from 40 annually to 4 in order to minimise the civil disturbance caused by the drunken behaviour at such events.

Publicans, often sportsmen themselves, would encourage any activity that they thought might increase custom and bowling alleys and greens were often added to licensed premises, boxing rooms were not uncommon and there is even evidence of a fives court being built onto a public house in Nottingham.[10] As cock-fighting declined it was necessary to replace it as a source of gambling with other activities. Many of these were simple bar room games of chance but gradually, and particularly in the north of England, bowls and boxing became staple activities attracting bookmakers and punters with many a bloody fist-fight fought out in the paddock behind the local inn until it too, like cocking, was outlawed. Bowls certainly had a more respectable pedigree, at least on the genteel side, which could be said to have begun in Elizabethan times but remained largely unregulated until the eighteenth century when the first fully documented match was held on the oldest known green on 1 August 1776 in Southampton. This competition known as the 'Knighthood Competition' has been held ever since and can be viewed as the precursor of the semi-professional handicap games which grew up in the Victorian era sponsored by publicans and breweries, the most famous being the 'Talbot' and 'Waterloo' handicaps established in Blackpool in 1873 and 1907 respectively. A continuity of sporting tradition was ensured regionally around the country as sportsmen became publicans and so we continue to see boxing publicans in the East End of London, bowling publicans in Lancashire, cricket publicans in the Yorkshire Dales, whilst in the Newcastle on Tyne area there are publicans well known for promoting the 'mining' sports of quoits, coursing, dog-racing and pigeon-flying, all of which have their roots in eighteenth-century industrial development but were semi-professionalised during the nineteenth century.[11]

The public house was the traditional centre for the many rural sports which originated in the holy day diversions of the medieval period. The fairground attractions of Salford's Kersal Moor sports in the seventeenth century were centred on the Kersal Cell and similar parallels can be drawn elsewhere around the country where the publicans saw opportunities to begin or extend their 'season'. These traditions continued and even strengthened during the Victorian era by a process of diversification. Most of the old athletic sports could be found, for example, at the Golden Ball Sports at Overton in Lancashire including 'a sculling match, a wrestling match, a quoiting match and a swarming up the maypole for a new hat'.[12] Similar events were held throughout the nineteenth century at Ironbridge Fetes (The Bridge Inn), Leeds Fair (The Hyde Park), Hereford Games (The Boar), Lancaster Quayside Sports (The Blue Anchor) and so on around the country.[13] The Poulton Sports in Lancashire indicate the extent to which the old traditional elements of such diversions were maintained: advertised as 'Old English Sports' they included jingling matches, climbing poles and leaping for prizes which had been awarded for centuries such as large cheeses, pairs of boots and new hats, but just as important from the publicans' point of view was that most common of all activities at such events, namely the 'Quaffing of Ale'.[14]

The other major source of sport sponsorship was support given by the nobility and gentry who had for centuries participated in sporting activities but had never to any large extent until the eighteenth century sponsored or promoted them for entertainment. The beginning of this phenomenon can be traced to the changing financial climate which attracted, as Defoe mentions, a 'prodigious conflux of nobility and gentry from all parts of England into London'[15] who financed theatres, gardens, clubs and sports indirectly through investments and directly through their own gambling, spectating and participation. The wealth created through 'stock jobbing' and the new mercantilism by this new class of entrepreneur led to a revival in the fortunes of the public schools, as the children and grandchildren of this initial 'conflux' learned the manners and made the contacts necessary to establish themselves as a social and financial elite which determined the nature of English society and stamped its personality on the sporting scene.[16] Much of their initial activity required an element of exploitation in utilising the sporting prowess of others for entertainment, a principle well understood by their forbears whose own sporting activities were serviced by 'servingmen' and labourers identified later by Whig economists as 'beasts of burden produced by nature for the purpose of being useful to the consuming classes'.[17] Horse-racing had long been the sport of kings and courtiers and its organisation since the seventeenth century had depended upon hordes of farriers, blacksmiths, stable staff, grooms and jockeys who laboured long and hard to produce racing results for their masters for whom victory came to mean thousands of pounds in winnings and stud fees. By the eighteenth century most towns of any size had a racecourse, however basic, and several days were set aside each year for a meeting which was promoted by the town elders as a commercial venture whose success was invariably underwritten by local nobility subscribing to the prize funds. Such a situation pertained at Stockport in 1764 when the local meeting was threatened with financial ruin until the Lords FitzHerbert and Egerton came to the rescue, at Warwick in 1754 where 16 of the 48 subscribers were local aristocrats, and in Lancaster in 1772 where the steward was Lord Stanley and the 'Noblemen's Purse' stood at 150.[18] Such support was common wherever there were race meetings. As we have seen, racing became depressed for some time and the aristocracy began to patronise and gentrify cricket during the eighteenth century. A reference work of the day sums up the situation when it defines cricket as a 'sport formerly confined solely to the labouring classes but becoming daily more fashionable among those whose rank and fortune entitle expectations of very different conduct'.[19] This trend continued unabated for many years, aided by the appropriation of the sport by the major schools, and by 1845 *The Times* thought the phenomena sufficiently interesting to publish a substantial list of those noblemen who supported the game and the particular clubs to which they gave allegiance.[20]

Whilst cricket became at least a metropolitan focus for genteel entertainment, hunting and shooting maintained their fascination for the country dweller; and if cricket was confined formerly to the labouring classes and subsequently gentrified then hunting was formerly confined to the landed gentry and gradually democratised. Early feudal hunting, usually for hares, provided free sport for the friends and associates of the large landowners but gave way towards the end of the eighteenth century to fox hunting 'subscription' hunts whose members would contribute considerably towards the master's expenses. This change, like others, can be traced to the emergence of a wealthy commercial 'middling' class whose strove to emulate their social superiors by aping their customs and practices. The new hunts with the new money built magnificent kennels to house expensive hounds which was roundly condemned by humanitarians at a time when the rural poor lived in hovels, and was quite unlike the previous generation of hunt followers who mocked such 'vain expense' and advocated building 'for use not state'.[21] These different attitudes lay in the motivation to hunt since the original landowners hunted at least partially for pest control, particularly after the middle of the eighteenth century when foxes became a real problem, whereas the new class of hunter joined a hunt for entertainment, outward show and possible social advancement. For the former 'fox hunting was a form of warfare where sport is a secondary consideration'[22] whilst for the latter the exhibition predominated with the result that sponsorship of hunting changed dramatically from the functional involvement of hereditary landowners to the financial investment of an urban commercial class. Not surprisingly such a change is also discernible with regard to shooting, which was opened up to any purchaser of a Game Certificate by the Game Reform Bill of 1831. This swept away all the archaic qualifications which pertained until that time. Ironically, reform was initiated by the landed gentry themselves who suffered so greatly from indiscriminate shooting that it became easier to certificate the offenders than to apprehend and prosecute them,[23] and from then onwards the activity became legitimately democratised.[24] This change to an overtly commercial environment encouraged the landed gentry to charge for

ir land, which they began to do on a large scale for the
inevitably led to further problems of enforcement,
allowfield near Newcastle on Tyne where a long-running
en Sir Edward Blackett and John Ridley concluded with
ere would 'never be anything but unpleasantness between
Ridley, the tenants as long as he has the shooting'.[25] The courts
were full of such litigation for decades to come.

From the earliest times the gentry, whether watching or performing,
would gamble on the result of any sporting activity, indeed on the
outcome of any activity at all.[26] Horse-racing and breeding were to a
very large extent the products of the desire to gamble and this proclivity
ran through the generations and into the culture of the public schools
where there was 'much gambling, contracting of debts and drinking'.[27]
Many of the wagers laid were on horse-racing and all meetings had
clerks whose job it was, amongst other responsibilities, to solicit
wagers, collect sweepstakes and subscriptions and generally administer
the financial side of affairs to the satisfaction of the stewards. This
frequently led to unfortunate consequences, not only for the individual
concerned but ultimately to the reputation of racing itself. We find
examples of this at Lichfield races during the second half of the
eighteenth century when the clerk to the course was a Mr Hands who
in 1786 found himself owed £1,021 19s 0d in unpaid sweepstakes, the
result of 'the failure of noble lords to pay their accounts' with the
consequence that the following year the races were in debt and in
danger of failing altogether. The subscriptions for 1787 totalled a mere
59 guineas and Hands was obliged to trawl the surrounding area for
further support from leading inhabitants and business people to secure
the event. Due to economic depression the races at Lichfield as elsewhere continued to find life difficult and by 1797 the situation for
Hands had become perilous as income failed yet again to match
expenditure. He was accused of financial impropriety by the stewards
Lord Spencer and Sir Robert Williams who advised him rather
menacingly to 'make payment of race money into Cobb's bank and do
so before he obliges them much against their inclinations to proceed to
very unpleasant measures'.[28] It was the prevalence of such difficulties
that led the Jockey Club to become increasingly engaged in regulating
financial affairs at race meetings,[29] but the legalisation of off-course
betting by the Gaming Act of 1845 proved disastrous and was subsequently outlawed by an Act of 1853 (and not reinstated until 1960).
Even control of on-course betting was more tightly regulated by the
Tattersall Rules of 1866 which banned gifts to the judges and barred
jockeys from betting. The gambling instincts of race-goers was further

indulged by the provision of cock-fighting at public houses during race meetings with large wagers being laid such as the 50 guineas a main fought every morning during the Lancaster races of 1772 between the gentlemen of Yorkshire and Lancashire, and the 500 sovereigns laid on one main between the gentlemen of Warwickshire and Stafford-shire at the Swan Pit during the Anson races of 1827 – 32 years after the activity was declared illegal. So common was betting on cock-fights in Northumberland that in 1785 a betting guide was produced listing every permutation of odds for any number of contests up to 30 at which point it concluded that 'at thirty battles in a match it is 918624303 to 155117520 not a drawn match'.[30]

This mania for gambling extended nationwide across the social divide but was particularly notable amongst the leisured class who were able to wager huge sums of money, almost on a whim, whether on horses, cocks, cricket, boxing, rowing or pedestrianism. With cricket becoming fashionable amongst the gentry towards the end of the eighteenth century it too grew rapidly into a source of wagering. Even out of London large crowds were attracted to well-promoted matches between county-based teams whose players bet on their own performances and were backed by local gentry. One such early game at Nottingham in 1791 was played for 1,000 guineas before a crowd estimated at 10,000.[31] Rowing had been a focus for genteel entertain-ment since the first Doggett's Coat and Badge race of 1715 and became particularly fashionable following the Ranelagh Regatta of 1775 by which time wagering on watermen's 'wrangles' had become common-place with the 'greatest wager ever rowed' taking place in August 1765.[32] Prize-fighting had long attracted the attention of the gentry with the first recorded fight taking place on 18 January 1681 between the Duke of Albemarle's footman and a local butcher which was by all accounts for entertainment only. In 1719 Figg established himself as a 'master of the noble science of defence in Oxford Road near Adam and Eve court' teaching gentlemen 'the small backsword and quarter-staff'[33] and the art of pugilism which became regulated by the Broughton Rules and institutionalised in the Pugilistic Club inaugurated by gentlemen in 1814. It became common for money bouts to take place in the public schools where upper-class life was faithfully reflected in microcosm and one such match resulted in the death of Lord Shaftesbury's son Ashley at Eton in 1825. An eye-witness writing to Shaftesbury records that the opponents fought for two hours and ten minutes and 'as in all prize fights they allow a man if his opponent falls to tumble on him and if his knee comes down on chest or head so much the better; Wood his opponent fell on Ashley's throat and it was this

3. A cricket match card of 1782 (courtesy of Lords' Memorial Gallery and Library) illustrating the gentrification of the game and its adaptation from bucolic origins for use as a form of gambling. Note that all players were accorded the title 'Mr' despite the fact that some at least would have been hired for their cricketing abilities. For example, Mr Lumpy was John Stevens from the Hambledon Club and David Harris a team mate from the same illustrious Hampshire club. Note also that the bowler is bowling underarm deliveries.

that killed him'[34] – so much for Broughton's Rules and the Noble Art. Such bouts were not confined to the schools or to the upper class and were common around the country, usually at fairs but often promoted by the local publican between a local favourite and a hopeful pretender. This is exemplified by a fight for £5 a side at Whittlesford in Cambridgeshire on 21 January 1863 between the son of a local farmer and a man 'who hawks fish about'. They fought for one hour and ten minutes but 'the farmer being bigger and in better condition gave the fishman a good punching'.[35] Publicans also promoted pedestrian matches on a casual basis wholly for the purposes of gambling on running grounds often owed by them and found in most suburbs or adjacent to the public house itself. Such events were extremely rough and ready and the source of much corrupt practice, with matches being outrageously 'fixed' resulting in crowd violence, added to which handicap events such as walking backwards, wearing weighted clogs or pushing wheelbarrows caused great physical damage to the contestants. Despite the regional popularity of stars like 'Crowcatcher', 'Gateshead Clipper', 'Norwich Millboy', 'Manchester Pet' and the female 'Folkestone Bess', the activity became less common due to the greater regulation demanded by the authorities and the emergence of alternative entertainment, but individual attempts on speed and distance records continued until the turn of the nineteenth century. One such alternative entertainment which became hugely popular in the twentieth century was dog-racing, first mentioned in *The Times* on 11 September 1876 where the correspondent concluded that 'the new sport which we might call simulated coursing is undoubtedly exciting and interesting'. It became a staple gambling activity for the working class, a point to which we shall return later.

The promoter of sporting events be he publican, gentleman or Lord Mayor knew that first and foremost his venture would stand or fall on the number of spectators attending since upon this would depend the level of commercial activity and hence the profit realised. London theatres like Astley's would engage in promotional work, particularly on the river on whose watermen much of their business depended by inaugurating sculling races and then parading the victors with the prizes as part of the evening's entertainment. At the same time and across the cultural divide, the major gentlemen's clubs were responsible for promoting the first regatta on the Thames in 1775, an unprecedented event owing much to Venetian regattas viewed with some envy by those on the Grand Tour, and introduced as a fashionable diversion to the River Thames. Such was its success despite inclement weather that 200,000 people turned up to view the resplendent aquatic display and to spend their money at the many stalls and booths on the riverside, whilst the gentlemen took to the grandstand seats and wagered on the only truly competitive race of the day. This situation was curiously paralleled a century later at the height of the popularity enjoyed by the Oxford and Cambridge boat race when 'Hammersmith Bridge was a black festoon of human beings swarming like flies'.[36]

It was impossible to control and therefore exploit these massive crowds, but since in other sports it was in the sponsor's interests to do so great efforts were made to provide spectators with enclosed facilities. Cricket was amongst the first sports to grasp the commercial implications of enclosure and the first intimation of this was a notice in the *Daily Universal Register* of 22 June 1785 stating that White Conduit Fields in Islington were being enclosed for the 'security and amusement of the Lordling Cricketers'. Such efforts were being replicated throughout the country as the passion for the game spread and large crowds were attracted to temporary enclosures, notably at Nottingham, as we have seen, and Sheffield, where in 1822 there was 'an assemblage at once so numerous and respectable that the city seemed to have poured out its whole population'.[37] As the game became more sophisticated and the crowds larger still, the county sides established themselves at various headquarters around the country. By 1900 most of the 16 first-class sides played to crowds of 10,000 or more. It was not long before the conservative elements in the game began to criticise its commercialisation, arguing that it had become a spectacle demanding for its success a sufficiency of 'stars' which made it necessary that players should spend their whole lives practising thus 'converting the game from an occasional pastime of geniality to a more or less mechanical trade'.[38] Even the small amateur clubs became aware of the commercial imperative.[39] During the Second World War and the return of the one-day game, the Wisden of 1942 (Cricketers' Year Book published by Wisden) records that such games, though hugely popular, attracted the 'kind of spectator not wanted at county cricket', and since this time cricket along with other sports has had to temper social desirability with economic necessity.

A desire for social exclusivity allied to a keen commercial instinct informed the development of horse-racing during the eighteenth century as public demand for access encouraged promoters to provide enclosures for owners and grandstands for the prosperous whilst continuing to cater for the ordinary race-goer with course-side paddocks. The Jockey Club provided its members with separate facilities at Newmarket in the 1760s and around the country a similar trend operated as racing was gradually opened up to a greater cross-section of paying customers. At Fulwood near Preston the original grand-stand had been erected in 1790 but by 1805 it had become necessary to upgrade the facility so as to 'guard against every accident', thus allowing the owners to raise prices and exclude a socially unacceptable element from entry. Naturally this element was made welcome at lower prices elsewhere on the course.[40] For the first time since its inception in 1678 the Newton course in Lancashire was provided with a 'magnificent grandstand' in 1824 due to the influx of visitors from Manchester and Liverpool and the desirability of making superior facilities available for the more prosperous race-goer. Lord George Bentinck, Jockey Club steward 1836–46, became aware of developments elsewhere and was the first steward to recognise the commercial advantages of providing adequate facilities to all classes of spectator. He introduced at Newmarket differently priced enclosures with amenities varying according to the price paid, a policy eventually applied even to the most humble venues.[41]

Traditionally football had been played on any open ground, but also often in the most inappropriate places where it caused damage and disruption. As an essentially rural sport which transferred to an urban setting, along with the people who were sucked into the developing new towns of the industrial areas, it became usual for the game to take place in those areas enclosed by neighbouring yards and factories sometimes adjacent to churches. Local teams from different areas of the same town played each other home and away and resultant town champions would take on those of nearby towns, so that a league system grew naturally from the industrial demography. As support for each team grew their playing areas were developed according to income, with the first investment invariably being a perimeter wall of sufficient height to deter gate-crashers interspersed at regular intervals with turnstiles for raising revenue. The level of support was the prime determining factor of club development as even amateur church teams were able to pay expenses for particularly skilful players whilst those unable to do so continued to fare badly. Although the distinction between amateur and professional teams became increasingly marked, there was never any hesitation in either camp about enclosing the ground and charging for entry; the only difference was the level of revenue thus raised. So in 1899, for example, we find Tottenham Hotspur Football Club 'with a very fine enclosure capable of accommodating twenty-five thousand spectators and annual gate receipts of six thousand three hundred and ninety nine pounds',[42] whilst in Lancaster the local club printed 5,000 tickets for admission to their field for a local cup match.[43] Rugby football progressed more slowly along the same route as the teams representing working areas of the north of England found that paying expenses to players financed from substantial gate receipts jeopardised their amateur status as defined by the Corinthian rugby establishment based in the south of England. As crowds grew bigger in the north, gate money became huge and was spent on ground improvements and regular team tours, and resulted in an inevitable acceptance that the movement of players between teams was accompanied by financial incentives. As in association football, the strictly amateur teams continued to charge admission to their ground; so Bolton Rugby Football Club was not alone when in 1906 it enclosed its ground with canvas sheeting, erected a small stand and charged 3d entrance.[44] However, unlike the Football Association the rugby authorities were not prepared to accept any remotely quasi-amateur activity and the Northern Rugby Union became the Rugby League in 1922. By 1929 attendances of 40,000 at cup finals became too large for any northern ground to accommodate and the game had to move to the country's largest sporting enclosure, Wembley Stadium.

Even the relatively minor sports were unable to avoid the commercial imperative of matching unavoidable expenditure with commensurate income which subscriptions alone never covered. The first cyclists soon found that competitive activity demanded a subsidy only forthcoming from spectators' contributions, with one of the newest clubs at Warwick constrained to levy a resented 6d entrance charge to its annual tussle with Leamington Cycle Club in 1883, only to find that the income raised was quite inadequate as 'the Warwick people do not seem to appreciate such things and next year we must hold it at Leamington'.[45] The rural fairs of bygone times which were self-supporting had been largely replaced during the nineteenth century with sports organised on rented fields by parochial committees which required a level of cash income to balance the books so that commercial prospects became the overriding consideration. Interestingly this was so in both the north and south of England, particularly in times of economic depression. Hence in Darlington during 1920 'the question of holding the usual sports was considered favourably only with regard to gate monies', whilst at the same time at Sutton in Cambridgeshire the prospect of extra income from admission charges for dancing and spectators was the deciding factor in proceeding.[46] There were those who for reasons of commercial advantage supplied the needs of sportsmen by providing facilities well adapted to 'the business of general athletic entertainments', as did the Sherriff of Hull who in 1889 associated with representatives of the local cycling, athletic and harrier clubs to capitalise the Hull Athletic Ground Company Limited. This and other similar companies around the country sought to construct grandstands and racing tracks and provide facilities for athletic sports which it was hoped would attract crowds of 20,000 and provide shareholders with substantial profits.[47] These and similar developments which stress the commercial aspects of sporting activity indicate a general trend towards 'spectatorism' which began in the eighteenth century and became overwhelmingly obvious during the Second World War.[48]

The self-sufficiency of former centuries, based upon the rural tradition of barter and payment in kind, was eroded as the country became more urbanised, work more sophisticated and payment more complicated with larger transactions facilitated for the first time by notes issued by the newly established Bank of England in 1694. These were not confirmed as negotiable until 1704 and in practice this negotiability did not become common in the provinces until the second half of the century. Smaller transactions were completed, however unsatisfactorily, in gold coin of various denominations until difficulties were eased in 1819 by the issue of 'token money' whose metallic content was well below its face value. Given these financial restraints and the possession of 90 per cent of the nation's wealth in the hands of a few hundred landed aristocrats, it is not surprising that sport as spectator entertainment evolved during the eighteenth century in London where both men and masters moved, the former to seek work and the latter to seek greater prosperity and pleasure. Much of the work entailed serving the gentry either in the capacity of household servant or temporarily hired help, and much of the pleasure was gained through gambling on the performances of these 'servingmen' whether it be as pugilists, scullers, jockeys, pedestrians or cricketers. As the century progressed this personal patronage gradually gave way to a more institutionalised form of commercialism based upon event and later club organisation, and personal entertainment gave way to collective business interests. Early examples of this can be seen at Lancaster in 1698 when the races were inaugurated to coincide with the assizes with a view to promoting the town as an important social centre, and at Gravesend in the same year when the corporation established a regatta to support the industry of its watermen.[49] Both councils, as most others at this time, were predominantly constituted of gentry and it was this class of person which continued to mix business with pleasure in promoting sport, particularly horse-racing, as we can see from the race accounts of three such men – William Horton esquire, John Baldwin gent. and Samuel Armitage esquire – who had been made responsible for collecting race subscriptions for Skircoate Moor Races near Halifax on 3 August 1736. They managed to solicit the support of 11 local aristocrats at one guinea each, 30 gentlemen at half a guinea, 70 tradesmen at 5s, 162 minor tradesmen at 2s 6d, and 72 private individuals at 1s, giving a grand total of £66 4s which ensured a good day's racing for all. Many of the individual races at this and other meetings were advertised according to their subscription, and so we find 'A Gentlemen's Sweepstake of 100 gns.' at Lichfield in 1752, 'The best of three 4 mile heats for the Town Purse of £50' at Stockport in 1763, and 'The Noblemen's Purse of £50' at Lancaster in 1772. Towards the end of the century the popularity of racing declined somewhat, especially in less fashionable areas, partly due to the aristocracy withdrawing financial support and this led to local corporations increasing their investments in order to counter this trend. For instance, at Lancaster the council presented the 'Gold Cup' for 100 guineas in July 1817 in order to halt the decline and even helped to lay out a new course on Lancaster Moor, but to no effect as the meeting finally ended in 1858. At Lichfield in the 1770s where a similar situation presented itself the local authorities approached the problem by laying greater emphasis on the meeting's social side by promoting more Race Balls, always hosted with great pomp in the Guild Hall or Town Hall. At the Fulwood course near Preston, the crisis was precipitated by the demise of four of the course shareholders; six more were hurriedly co-opted and after a ten-year hiatus profits rose to nearly £200. However, this was still regarded as insufficient and so the rent of the ladies' stand refreshments area was raised from £7 to £20 and 'all stake and basket people and all tents and booths were to pay £5'.[50]

Despite efforts made by public school administrators of sport the grosser examples of commercialism grew, and even in rowing, that bastion of Corinthianism, regattas became dependent upon commercial profits to survive against the competition from alternative athletic entertainments.[51] Cricket also made the journey from individual patronage to business concern: the gentle involvement of large landowners in sponsoring their local teams, as at Hambledon whose fancy costumes and hats were so provided and where a 'dulce lenimen was provided for the ladies',[52] gave way over the years to private cricket tours of professionals promoted by the likes of Arthur Shaw of Nottingham and James Lillywhite of Sussex which grossed in the region of £25,000.[53] In boxing the era in which a household servant would be trained and backed by his master gave way to out and out entertainment exemplified by James Burke, the all-England champion in the 1840s, who dressed as a clown in the ring and played in panto-mime when out of it. This form of the sport evolved into a business-like exploitation in the late nineteenth century by promoters such as Martin Lane in Manchester who took Billy Marchant from the fair-ground boxing booths and made him into a champion. In Manchester, as in other large towns, boxing became increasingly popular and another local promoter, Jack Smith, attracted large audiences and top London fighters to the Grand Theatre in Peter Street and was so successful that he opened another venue at the Alhambra in Openshaw before finally moving by popular demand to the Free Trade Hall. Again in Manchester we can see athletics developing from the simple rural sports on Kersal Moor to Mr Reilly's promotions of 'Monster ATHLETIC Fetes' at Pomona Palace, usually held to commemorate or advertise some notable occasion like the opening of Manchester town hall in September 1877 when a 'variety of old English sports' was supplemented with a large programme of events for money prizes.[54] Another promoter, Harry Hardwick, established the Northern Cross Country Association in 1882 and used the Manchester racecourse for championships. By 1888 athletics meetings were also held at Belle Vue in front of crowds of 10,000 but their popularity waned as that of boxing grew in the 1920s due to the rival attractions of other activities such as football and hiking. The commercial aspects of athletics promotion were high on the agenda of the fledgling Olympic Games almost from the initial event, and by 1904 in St Louis the business influence in the guise of the World Fair Movement was already under-mining the Olympic Ideal, a point to which we shall return in greater detail later.

Other sports were similarly involved at varying levels in the pursuit of financial viability, with golf leading the way by advertising daily and weekly charges for visiting players with club representatives often co-opted onto municipal attractions committees,[55] whilst the Profes-sional Golfers' Association solicited large sums in sponsorship for its championships.[56] Fishing clubs arranged holiday permits for holiday-makers and together with rowing clubs arranged preferential rates with railway companies; and swimming clubs promoted displays by professional swimmers whilst making deals with programme printers, as did bowling clubs.[57] Such levels of commercialisation across the sporting spectrum were bound to lead eventually to the growth of a sporting industry as entrepreneurs exploited the market for recreational invention and innovation. Horse-racing had long been associated with gambling and during the nineteenth century Tattersalls and others began to organise and develop its business potential. Horse breeding and sales became big business and the Racing Calendar was first published to offer a shop window for the racing industry in all its forms.[58] Coursing, although minor in comparison, nevertheless shadowed horse-racing in its development as a commercial business with meetings attracting a similar gambling fraternity, sponsorship and sales of animals.[59] It evolved, as most rural sports did, into a highly organised urban entertainment in the form of greyhound-racing at tracks like that constructed at Belle Vue in Manchester in 1926 at the cost of £25,000. The national game of football had attained 'industry' status well before the turn of the nineteenth century and a union was established in 1898 to represent the players' interests to club owners, though not with any great success. At this time proprietors legally owned players as assets of the club and simply bought and sold them often just to turn a quick profit,[60] a practice bitterly resented by the union which rightly described the game in its Annual Report for 1945 as 'Big business with sufficient money to provide security for all'. Both football and horse-racing attained enormous popularity between the wars due in part to their promotion through the sporting press and increasingly through the medium of radio, numbers of which rose to 8 million representing 71 per cent of households by 1939. The original form of tennis first played in monasteries and adapted by the aristocracy had its rustic version which became sufficiently refined over the centuries to be called 'field tennis'[61] and was commercially exploited by Major Wingfield in 1874 as a game for the garden lawns of middle-class suburbia. Henry Jones, a founder member of the Wimbledon Croquet Club, saw the potential of the game and prevailed upon the club committee to set aside land for 'lawners' and provide £25 for equipment, whilst he set up changing rooms for which he charged entrance fees. The club championships beginning in 1877 became such a commercial draw that over the years the committee was able to extract payments from suppliers such as Slazenger and merchandise its own products in the form of towels, clothing, china and stationery. Joint income from such items has latterly amounted to £30 million per annum, to which must be added many more millions from television revenue in recent years. Returning to athletics for a moment we can see that its business potential was fully understood if not realised in the Victorian era by recourse to the prospectus for the Hull Athletic Ground Company Limited, the object of which was to attract to one large recreation ground the whole of the athletic population of the town, to carry on any business calculated to financially benefit the company and in order to do so to take advice from 'professional men qualified for their work who have made this class of business their special pursuit'. However, like tennis, the full commercial potential of athletics as a sporting entertainment was to be realised only in the television era, although the development of the running shoe began with Joseph William Foster, an amateur athlete with the Bolton Primrose Harriers, who began a business producing 'Foster's Shoes' in 1900. Through many intervening stages this has evolved into Reebok UK, responsible for retailing tens of millions of pairs throughout Europe. Foster's originals were used not only by the local running clubs but by increasing numbers of cycling enthusiasts encouraged onto roads by new and improved bicycles, the finest of which was James Starley's safety bicycle of 1886 which was the first model to enjoy huge nationwide sales with the result that by the turn of the century there were over 500 cycling clubs in England.[62]

Looking back over the evolution of commercialism in sport we have seen that at some level or other it has always been present, beginning with the donation of prizes in kind by tradesmen at holy day recreations which became more highly organised rural sports often sponsored by local publicans. Such sponsorship was supplemented in the eighteenth century with patronage by the gentry and promotion by municipalities, both of which led to a great increase in the levels of gambling and spectatorism which in turn encouraged event organisers to seek further commercial development. This demand led to a business exploitation of commercial potential which is only reaching its fullest extent today in the age of global communication. One major effect of the commercialisation of sport was the growth of professionalism and it is to this topic that we turn in the following chapter.

NOTES

1. Newton Court Leet records for May 1678.
2. Stockport Races, public notice for 3, 4, 5 July 1764.
3. Cock-fighting banned on licensed premises in Hucknall following a major disturbance with people injured, 1782 (Nottingham Record Office, DD473/1). Latest prosecution for cock-fighting: Kellow, Co Durham, 20 March 1995.
4. B. Harrison, *Drink and the Victorians* (Faber 1971).
5. It is interesting to note that the 'Bat and Ball' has now (1994) become a themed pub concentrating on food and tourists.
6. *The Times* (21 May 1788, 10 Aug. 1788, 20 June 1793).
7. *The Times* (11 Oct. 1838).
8. *The Times* (12 Aug. 1796).
9. *News of the World* (1 Oct. 1843), 8b.
10. Nottinghamshire Records 1834 (DDTB 5/6/1).
11. For example, see *Newcastle Daily Chronicle* (23 Jan. 1885), 6a, where 25 public houses sponsored a range of sporting activities from sculling to quoits.

12. Golden Ball Sports notice for July 1841. It is instructive to note that the licensee today encourages custom by promoting water sports nearby.
13. Reference to any local paper during the summer months indicates the extent: *Southport Examiner* (22 Sept. 1843); *Wellington Journal* (24 Aug. 1872); *Lancaster Guardian* (26 Aug. 1884); *Worthing Intellinger* (18 Aug. 1888); *Morecambe Visitor* (18 July 1841); *Sunbury Comet* (21 Aug. 1877); *Isle of Wight Observer* (21 Aug. 1877) etc. etc.
14. *Bedfordshire Times* (21 Aug. 1859), 6a.
15. D. Defoe, *A Tour through the whole island of Great Britain* (London, Vol. I, p. 33c).
16. Note the comment in *Athletics and Football* (Longman, 1888, p. 7) that sporting activity is an 'opportunity for making lasting friendships and connections which are often of the greatest value in later life'; an example of this is to be found in verse four of the Eton Boating Song: 'And nothing in life shall sever the chain that is round us now'.
17. E. Edwards, *Edinburgh Review*, Vol. xxvii, 1830, p. 56.
18. Race notices for 23 Aug. 1763, 14 Aug. 1754 and 22 July 1772.
19. Dr Willich, *A Domestic Encyclopaedia* (London, 1802).
20. *The Times* (12 May 1845), 5b.
21. William Somerville, *The Chase*, 1735.
22. Peter Beckford, *Thoughts on Hunting*, 1781.
23. Public notice of 1824 on Buckingham Game Duty (Buckinghamshire Records GD/30/1).
24. For example, Northumberland Records 'Sunderland Collection' Game Duty for April 1869: 'Gamekeepers licenses, 64 at £2; Licenses to kill, 520 at £3'.
25. Letters concerning shooting rights at Fallowfield near Newcastle 1874–79 (Northumberland Records Office SF/10/1).
26. See the *Betting Book* at Whites Club of London. For example: 3 Feb. 1743, Lord Montford bets Mr Wardour 20gns. that Mr Shepherd outlives Sir Hans Sloan; 16 July 1746, Mr Heath wagers Mr Fanshawe 5gns. that the eldest son of the Pretender is dead; 14 Jan. 1748, Mr Fanshawe wagers Lord Dalkeith 1gn. that his peruke is better than his Lordship's.
27. J. Chandos, *Boys Together, English Public Schools 1800–1864* (Hutchinson, 1984).
28. *Observations on Lichfield Races*, 1768–97, by the Clerk of the Races (Staffordshire County Records LR/4/1).
29. See one particular case at the Derby of 1841 where the betting transactions of Richard Gurney were placed under scrutiny. The Jockey Club oversaw his financial affairs and organised a creditors' compensation scheme (*Jockey Club* minutes, 5 Feb. 1842).
30. Cock-fighting near Belford in Northumberland (Northumberland Records Z/ALA/19).
31. *The Times* (6 Sept. 1791), 5e.
32. *Aquatic Register* (10 Aug. 1765).
33. Taken from his business card of 1719: note the nomenclature of 'noble science' – 'noble' to imply an elevated social pedigree and 'science' for its appeal to advanced intellect, both setting the activity aside from common brawling.
34. Northumberland Records, letter dated 15 March 1825 (ZMI/576/50).
35. *Diary of N. Maynard* in the Maynard Collection (Cambridgeshire Records R58/5/5).
36. A. Trollope, *British Sports and Pastimes* (Virtue and Spalding, 1868), p. 195.
37. *The Times* (2 Sept. 1822), 5a.
38. *The Times* (4 Sept. 1908), 4d.
39. See the AGM minutes of the *West Kent Wanderers Cricket Club* for 24 Nov. 1913, which stresses 'hopeful prophecy but sanguine expectation' and the financial necessity of providing chairs and a tea tent to encourage attendances and those for *Durham Cricket Club* (10 March 1914) where gate money of £69 12s 6d was vital for the payment of the club professional.
40. *Fulwood Race Course* minutes (9 July 1805) (Lancashire Records, DDX/103/4).
41. Even at the most rural meetings like Bungay Steeple Chase there were price gradations: Admission to Grandstand, 12/6; Paddock, 10/6; Course 7/6; and by 1915 motors were charged 15/– to park (Minutes, 22 April 1915).
42. *Tottenham Hotspur Football and Athletic Company Ltd*, first AGM (30 July 1899).
43. *Lancaster Football Club* minutes (8 Oct. 1899).

44. *Bolton Rugby Football Club* minutes (2 April 1906).
45. *Oken Bicycle Club*, letter in the minutes for 29 Sept. 1883.
46. *Darlington Sports* minutes (18 March 1920).
47. Memorandum of Association of the *Hull Athletic Ground Company Ltd* (Nov. 1889).
48. *Mass Observation Archive* (University of Sussex), 'Sport in Wartime' (29 Oct. 1939): 'There were the amateurs, the professionals, the supporters, the betting organisations and the gamblers' and in April 1942: 'It is a pity that the Englishmen's idea of sport is changing since now it consists mainly of being spectators rather than players'.
49. See Lancaster Assize records at Lancashire Records (ZX/14/3) and the *Gravesend Chronology* based on corporation records and held at Gravesend Reference Library.
50. *Fulwood Race Course* minutes for 9 July 1829 (Lancashire Records DDX/103/4). This element at the big race meetings grew uncontrollably, witness Derby Day, as recorded by W.P. Frith in his *Autobiography and Reminiscences*, 1887: 'Acrobats and every type of performance, nigger minstrels, gypsy fortune tellers, carriages of pretty women together with the sporting element'.
51. For example, the larger regattas on the River Thames at Bedford, Hammersmith and Reading featured side shows, wrestling, minstrels, illuminated boats, dancing and so on and even Henley Regatta was inclined to consider the commercial potential of 'admitting niggers and comic singers' (*Henley Royal Regatta* minutes, 25 May 1882).
52. *Hambledon Cricket Club* minutes for September 1784. Not relevant here but of interest nevertheless is the minute for 29 Aug. 1796 which mentions 'Mr. Thomas Paine the author of *The Rights of Man*' at one of the club's games; at this time he was wanted by the authorities for sedition.
53. Not all such ventures ended in profit. At the London Lord Mayor's court Miss Agnes Rowley of the Lady Cricketers claimed payment of £11 for a failed tour of the provinces managed by a Mr Wood (*The Times*, 16 March 1892).
54. The costs of the proceedings were as follows: prizes for athletic sports £110, trade procession £100, wages £30, balloon £25, illuminations £25, insurance £20. Total £310. Smaller events were not immune from the need to raise money: the *Public Notice for the Linton Sports* of 1879 stipulated in large type that there was to be 'No free admission and No Half Prices'.
55. See the minutes of *Appleby Golf Club* (2 Nov. 1894) and *Lancaster Golf Club*'s Annual Report for 1913.
56. For example, *Professional Golfers' Association* minutes for 8 July 1908.
57. Fishing: *Warrington Anglers' Association* Rules for 1903; rowing: *A Social History of English Rowing* (Cass, 1992), pp. 37–9; swimming: *Warrington Swimming Club* minutes (2 May 1884, 10 May 1894).
58. See edition Number 1 on 4 April 1811: seventy horses for sale at a total of 8,000 guineas, one hundred and twenty advertisements for horses at stud with fees totalling 14,400 guineas, fifteen meetings advertised over a two month period apart from the large established venues, places such as Abingdon, Bodmin, Tremadoc, Northampton, Stamford and Northwich. Apart from the *Sporting Calendar* there were *The Sportsman*, *Sporting Life* and *The Sporting Chronicle* all selling 300,000 copies a day during the 1880s.
59. See the *Notice for the Lytham Open Coursing Meeting* for 8/9 Feb. 1843, promoted at the Clifton Arms Hotel by the Lord of the Manor, Thomas Clifton.
60. See the *Football Players' Union* minutes for 2 Feb. 1921: Mercer of Hull City FC signed for £40 and sold for £4,000 was awarded £500 and Meehan of Manchester United FC sold at a profit of £3,000 and awarded £325, 'both men of excellent character who had no desire to leave their homes or clubs'. Such behaviour on behalf of the club chairmen brought them a bad press and as early as 1908 the Union was advising free bargaining for wages and transfer fees which would, it claimed, 'save gentlemen of high social position from being pilloried in the public press' (minutes, 15 Dec. 1908).
61. See *The Sporting Magazine* for 29 Sept. 1793 where Field Tennis is reported to be 'threatening to bowl out cricket'. It is interesting that Wingfield's exploitation of tennis was mirrored in 1903 by W.G. Grace who with his partner Arthur Weintrand attempted

to market (with remarkable lack of success) 'Table Cricket, suitable for house or garden' (*The Times*, 11 Nov. 1903).

62. The updated version of this model, the 'Special Rover Bicycle' of 1894, was widely endorsed in advertisements by Viscount Bury, President of the National Cyclists' Union.

4

Professionalism

The professional takes a pleasure in his
business and is generally a capital fellow
whose only failing is to spend improvidently
what he earns easily.

(*The Times*, 20 May 1882)

The idea of receiving money for winning sporting contests dates at least from the sixth century when Solon decreed that any Athenian gaining victory at the Olympic Games should be paid 600 drachmae. By the beginning of the nineteenth century the three-fold influence of rural sports, gentlemen's patronage and commercial exploitation had produced a class of competitor who was able and willing to derive financial benefit from any number of sporting activities. If we stay with the Olympic Games for a moment and trace the progress of track athletics from that time, we can see that running has always attracted those prepared to train hard since victory represented not only the winner's laurels but usually privileged status in society and for the Athenians and others some financial reward. Even the Corinthians were advised on good authority 'to run so that ye may obtain the prize'[1] with no emphasis or implication that simply taking part was acceptable, and the notion of deriving some practical benefit from victory was evident in the provision of much needed prizes in the form of food, drink and clothing in medieval sports. Pedestrian matches were made for large sums of money in prizes and wagers, whilst running initially for small sums of money was common at local athletic meetings up and down the country during the nineteenth century. The major games provided substantial prize funds for what were nominally amateur athletes, an activity against which the sporting governing bodies fought long and hard. At the Olympic Games, reconstituted in 1896, the concept of strict amateurism soon disappeared and inducements in kind were offered in the Games of 1906 where, for example, the Greek winner of the marathon 'won' a year's free board at his local restaurant. The manufacturers of equipment, particularly shoes, were

45

not long in entering the market place by covering the expenses of champion athletes who endorsed their products. Winning gradually became the whole purpose of competition as financial inducements and national prestige became paramount with 'professional' attitudes towards preparation and performance being encouraged by national amateur sporting bodies who feared international humiliation. Hence the Great Britain athletics team for the 1928 Games was sent abroad piecemeal with many missing the opening ceremony so that athletes could continue training at home for as long as possible before their event.[2] Whilst the professionalisation of British athletes was heavily criticised from various quarters it continued due to increasing inter-national competitive pressure and paid dividends at the Los Angeles Games in 1932 which was acclaimed 'a triumph atmospheric conditions being perfect, the fastest track ever constructed and the largest number of world records broken', with Britain winning four gold, six silver and four bronze medals.[3]

Meanwhile, on the domestic front the Morpeth Olympic Games in Northumberland had been professional since 1874 when £7 had been given as a prize for the premier 130 yard race, which was to rise to £75 and a gold medal by 1925. So popular did the meeting become that in 1921 a splendid new track was laid to improve race times and total prize money rose to £340, with the result that the meeting was established as 'second to none in the U.K. and whoever won the Morpeth Handicap other places including Powderhall treated him with great respect'.[4] Cash prizes were common in the north of England, not only for athletic events but also at flower shows and brass band contests, and their award was not held to disqualify the winner from what continued to be considered essentially amateur events. An essential component of the 1889 prospectus for the Hull Athletic Ground was the 'offering of sums of money for prizes for the purpose of encouraging sports and athletics generally'. Even in the south of England where the sums of money were admittedly much smaller, the tradition of cash prizes was common: both Sutton and Linton Sports in Cambridgeshire, certainly between the years 1877 and 1921, gave money prizes for all their events. Such sports had grown over centuries from original rural sports events where some material payment for winning was considered normal, and in the less prosperous areas where need rather than greed continued to be a determining fact of every-day life the tradition continued and grew. Two of the very first rural sports maintained their popularity with the labouring class in the forms of wrestling, particularly strong in the remote areas of Cumberland and Cornwall, and boxing, which flourished in urban areas and the booths of travelling fairs. In Cumberland wrestling was regarded as the king of sports, being the chief outlet for the display of physical fitness and training and because only limited opportunities for leisure and pleasure were available until well into the nineteenth century. Huge contests were staged at Carlisle, Keswick, Penrith and Whitehaven drawing the cream of wrestlers from around the region: champions such as Richard Chapman of Patterdale, a policeman during the 1830s, who became landlord of the Ship Inn at Maryport where he continued to promote and umpire the sport. Although Cumberland wrestling had been common in the seventeenth and eighteenth centuries at fairs, it was not until the early nineteenth century that it bacame a mass spectator attraction with thousands attending at the major centres where each bout would be fought for substantial sums.[5] As early as 1816 Ben Todd, a local champion, won a bout for £30 at the Carlisle ring, only to be accused with his opponent of fixing the fight, with the result that the promoter withheld the prize money and the dispute caused the suspension of wrestling at Carlisle until 1821.

Similar behaviour by contestants in other sports elsewhere was responsible for the withdrawal of the patronage of gentlemen who feared that unfair practices would jeopardise their investments and led them to establish governing bodies designed to protect their interests. Promoters of wrestling were well aware of the bad publicity caused by such collusion amongst participants and a poster for a match at Penrith on 18 July 1863 warned, as many others did, that 'any man known to receive or make a bribe or make a "sham wrestle" will be excluded the Penrith ring and his offence communicated to every ring in the country'. By the nineteenth century boxing had become wholly professional, even becoming known as prize-fighting, and despite the London Prize Ring Rules of 1838 which introduced more regulations against fouls it continued to be unsporting and disreputable as fighters disregarded what rules there were in pursuit of lucrative championships. Leading fighters were seen to fix and foul bouts to the disgust of backers who gradually withdrew into their clubs where boxing could be more rigorously invigilated. Such withdrawal was precipitated in 1843 by a bout between William Thompson, recently released from his twenty-sixth spell in prison for breach of the peace, and Ben Caunt for the championship of England during which there was blatant low punching which caused Thompson to withdraw in the seventy-fifth round. Thompson was typical of many prize-fighters in being one of a large family (in his case 21 children) who only escaped the workhouse by fighting, usually in secret for a pittance on canal barges, river

4. Cumberland and Westmorland style wrestling became the established method since the Cornish style allowed too much violence; early wrestling contests were the subject of much gambling and some fixing but during the early Victorian era they were largely incorporated into rural sports such as these at Grasmere which continue today. The bowler hatted gentleman kneeling behind the contestants is the referee whose job it is to identify foul holds and award points for good style.

steamers, backyards and isolated fields, building up a reputation which gradually led to bigger 'prize matches' and ultimately to unofficial championship bouts. Such activities always attracted the disadvantaged as a means to a living and possible wealth and the fortunes of professional boxing can be monitored in direct relation to the level of economic prosperity with successive recessions producing new generations of fighters. Each post-war period saw a resurgence in the game, particularly pronounced in areas of industrial or commercial decline, as in the Manchester of the 1920s and 1930s where mass unemployment produced a flood of new talent like Jock McAvoy, a future champion, who took up boxing at the age of 19 only when he lost his job as a mill worker. Such is the popularity of the sport at this time that the British Boxing Board of Control was established in 1929 to protect the newcomers to professional ranks from too much physical damage or financial exploitation.[6] Alongside the regulated professional and amateur games there continued to exist the raw pugilism from which both originated in medieval fairs, as illustrated by a case in 1994 at the Stow Horse Fair established in 1476 where two 'travellers' were prevented by constables from continuing a bout for a reputed purse of £10,000 only to finish their business in secret the following day.[7]

We have seen how some of the original 'bruisers' were Thames watermen already well muscled from pulling one ton wherries up and down the river all day and who well understood the concept of payment for competitive success, having been sponsored to row races from the end of the seventeenth century. Genteel patronage originating in bonus payments for speedy passages led to heavy wagering on the Doggett's Coat and Badge Race from 1715 onwards and literally thousands of similar wagers were recorded in the pages of the Aquatic Register during the eighteenth century,[8] and so the basis of a professional class of oarsman was well established. Professional oarsmen were used in three ways: to act as trainers and stroke oars to amateur clubs, to row as gentlemen's champions in wager matches, and to join with gentlemen in joint crews such as that of George Lander (gent.) and Williams, a waterman from Wapping, who won a £100 bet in a timed race from London to Oxford.[9] More commonly, full crews of professionals would be selected and backed for large sums of money similar to the £300 wagered between Squire Osbaldston and Captain Ross, two well-known sporting gentlemen, whose crews rowed a circular course from Brighton around the latter's yacht.[10] As with other sports this sponsorship of practitioners by gentlemen led to the growth of a professional class which earned its living primarily through competitive activity and the middle years of the nineteenth century saw the emergence of several national and international champions whose exploits on waters throughout the country and abroad attracted enormous interest.[11]

Squire Osbaldston was interested in many sports outside his own particular preference of hunting and was heavily involved in promoting cricket, notably the Sussex eleven for which he sometimes played and frequently backed financially, losing on one occasion 300 guineas with his partner Lieutenant Cheslyn.[12] In cricket, as in rowing, the involvement of genteel patronage positively encouraged the growth of professionalism and in a retrospective assessment penned in 1909 Lord Harris maintained that cricket had acknowledged and welcomed professionalism for 200 years, so that 'after two centuries of comradeship on the field there is no need to encourage disputations on the definition of amateur'[13] as there was in football and athletics at the time. Unfortunately this comradeship did not continue off the field where a strict social apartheid was observed and it was often necessary for the club to offer some financial aid to its professional players during the off-season to ensure their welfare. In the north of England where amateur and professional were socially more compatible Lord Hawke of the Yorkshire Country Cricket Club had for years organised 'talent money' for success on the field and established a fund into which bonus monies were paid during the season which was then divided up amongst the professionals at the end of the season. This attitude of *noblesse oblige* to club professionals stemmed from the eighteenth century when servants were employed to supplement gentlemen's cricket teams, often as bowlers, who were specifically engaged for their sporting prowess and prepared, as John Nyren counselled, to use any tactic including the blunt and unexpected to turn the tables on the opposition. We can see this in operation in many an early game, such as that at Stanmore in Middlesex between the Marquis of Aberdeen and four of his relatives together with 'six of his Lordship's servants' against ten of the best players amongst the tradespeople of Stanmore, with the two servants bowling out the other side to win the match convincingly.[14] The concept of 'servant' was modified significantly when men were employed by the gentlemen of the Marylebone Cricket Club exclusively for the purpose of bowling at them for practice, and at the annual Gentlemen versus Players match at Lord's in 1842 these full-time professionals were well beaten by their employers in a display of serious and perhaps self-serving underperformance. Less prestigious clubs followed the lead set by the MCC and employed professionals to help them practise and lead the attack, as did the Bullingdon Club in appointing 'servants and bowlers' in

1850[15] and the Worksop Club in 1863 when 'devoting annual sub-scriptions to engage professional bowlers',[16] with the result that by the middle of the nineteenth century most clubs throughout the country had at least one paid professional player.[17] If we look at the accounts of any of these clubs we find that the wages of the professional(s) and the 'talent monies' given for successful performance made up the greatest single expense and required the club to continue the pursuit of commercialism in order to make end meet and this was even the case with the Corinthian county clubs. Gloucestershire County Cricket Club sanctioned payments of £4 10s for each player as out of pocket expenses and £15 for W.G. Grace in recognition of his commercial drawing power. However, this premium payment was challenged at the club's annual general meeting in 1879 and new rules were intro-duced so that only genuine expenses were to be paid 'except where special arrangements are made by the committee',[18] a stipulation which ensured the continuation of payment to the good doctor. In this regard Grace, although a gentleman amateur, fulfilled the role of reviled 'quasi-amateur' so heartily denigrated by the genteel admini-strators of all the major sports, but because of his social standing avoided the obloquy heaped on those of lesser status who dared to seek payment for their activities.

The situation in rugby became particularly fraught with difficulties of definition as the Rugby Football Union set its face completely against any form of payment to players whether defined as compen-sation for wages lost, expenses incurred or simple gifts, and after several years of subterfuge the northern clubs split from the Union to form the Northern Rugby Football Union which pledged to push forward 'the principle of payment for bona fide broken time only'.[19] Unfortunately the system of licensing set in place to police this principle soon proved inadequate and almost every committee meeting of the Union from 1899 to 1907 has notices of fines against clubs or individuals in breach of law number 1, sub-section c: 'non registered players playing without a permit'.[20] The tradition of professionalism had been established in the north well before the inauguration of the Northern Union and by the turn of the century players were being bought and sold by clubs with all the financial inducements, albeit at lower levels, already evident in association football.[21] Indeed the Union had recognised this fact immediately by forming the profes-sional sub-committee in 1895 to deal with the more flagrant breaches of its code, but by 1900 it sanctioned the existence of a professional class by stipulating on 1 May that 'clubs shall only be able to register players as professional who are in receipt of actual payments for playing football'. Even so these payments remained primarily a compensation for wages lost by absence from regular employment, though undoubtedly they acted as inducements to forego work and for the more accomplished players to play full-time during the season. Governing bodies peopled by gentlemen amateurs were unable or unwilling to see that there remained a spirit of amateurism in the principle of 'broken time payments' even though the Rugby Football Union, for example, later sanctioned the payment of expenses to its amateur club players, recognising that regular training and playing caused genuine financial hardships.

This lack of understanding derived partly from an antipathy towards members of a socially inferior class and partly from an unawareness of the financial difficulties experienced by them. The overwhelming majority of 'quasi' or 'pseudo' amateurs were ordinary working folk who enjoyed playing sport, were good at it and sought merely to supplement a meagre income with small sums of sorely needed cash. The situation is well represented by remarks made at a sportsmen's dinner in 1866 at Newcastle where the speaker chided the gentlemen who criticised the improvidence of the working man by citing the typical Newcastle family situation of ten members living on 18s a week: 'as improvident in one week as many gentlemen would spend on one meal'.[22] This was more generally recognised in cricket than in other sports and regular benefit matches were held to raise money for players' retirements. One such of many examples was that for George Parr, a loyal Lord's servant, who received several thousand pounds from a gate of 6,000 people in 1858. Whilst Parr was almost certainly a full-time seasonal professional due to such patronage and subsidy, the situation in the north of England where gate receipts were lower was markedly different and players continued their 'day jobs' in tandem with their sporting careers. The Manchester Cricket Club, the MCC of the north, employed professional players from the 1850s onwards, most of whom continued their original trades between seasons, one typical example being Thomas Hunt, 'by trade a coachmaker and latterly a professional cricketer in the service of the Manchester Club'.[23] The growing popularity of the association football and rugby football League systems in the north of England led to the inauguration of the Lancashire Cricket League in 1892 which encouraged the employment of professional players by all the participating clubs in pursuit of competitive and therefore commercial success. The clubs arranged matches so that local people working in the mills and factories could watch them on Saturday afternoons and the professional, apart from being a commercial draw, would be employed to coach the amateurs and generally develop the club's team performances. Payment in Lancashire and Yorkshire was mostly for the whole season with bonuses for performances and gate receipts, but elsewhere the contract would be for a set number of games, as with the professional at Whitfield Cricket Club in Northumberland who was paid £51 for ten matches.[24] Naturally payment depended largely on the prosperity of the club in question and many small clubs struggled to attract a professional, as did the Huyton Club in Liverpool which deliberated long and hard in choosing Barrett only to conclude that 'the club could not afford to pay him a weekly wage so that one pound a match would have to do and he would have to continue working at the British Insulated Wire Works'.[25] In cricket during the nineteenth century, unlike most other sports, it was possible to receive money for playing without being stigmatised by the governing body. Indeed it was even possible to move between the 'codes', as Richard Daft of Middlesex did who began and finished as an amateur but between 1859 and 1880 played as a full-time professional.[26] The distinction between amateur and professional in cricket became increasingly blurred as more team members were remunerated either directly or indirectly through the payment of expenses, and it is not unusual to find, as with Bolton Cricket Club, everyone receiving some form of income with the total wages bill coming to £265 for the 1937 season. Many clubs took up the Yorkshire County Cricket Club idea of 'merit marks' awarded for good conduct and skill which usually had the money value of five shillings per mark which the club paid out to players at the end of the season.

Whilst the cricket authorities had assimilated the professional and quasi-amateur painlessly into the playing ranks, that other essentially bucolic but gentrified game of association football had struggled to maintain a Corinthian purity due mainly of course to its mass popularity, particularly in the north of England. As in rugby football payments were made and teams professional in all but name flourished competitively and commercially so that the Football Association was finally constrained to allow the payment of wages to players in 1885, a move which far from setting up a free market in football actually had the effect of binding players legally to one club and moreover determining the maximum wage that could be paid them. The death knell of amateurism had been sounded by the establishment of that handmaiden to professionalism the league system of competition which was introduced during the 1880s in the north and midlands. Rule 18 introduced in 1890 forbade players from joining another club without their club's consent. This restriction, together with a low maximum wage, encouraged players to form a union which they eventually did at the instigation of the Wolverhampton Wanderers goalkeeper W.C. Rose in 1898 with the ungainly title of Players' Union of Association Players which became the Football Players Association in 1907, established to 'provide legal advice in connection with professional engagements including claims under the Workmen's Compensation Act of 1906'.[27] Their affiliation to the Federation of Trades Unions in 1909 precipitated a battle with the Football Association over rights of association which the union finally won, but the only way around the restriction of the maximum wage 'was to continue to pay illegal bonuses and there was hardly a player that had not been paid in that way'.[28] As with many other sports, applications to the governing body for player representation were continually denied an undemocratic policy of confrontation which left the players powerless and reduced to periodic pronouncements which were totally ignored by the Football Association and Football League alike, the first of which maintained that 'officials of the Players Association were unanimously in favour of the proposal to abolish all financial restrictions between clubs and players'.[29] The level of intransigence displayed by the governing bodies in this matter may be gauged by the fact that the maximum wage was only abolished in 1961 and the freedom of transfer granted in 1963.

Despite such difficulties the people's game went from strength to strength and by 1911 34 out of the 36 towns with a population of over 100,000 had professional teams, many of which had already attained the status of substantial businesses. Tottenham Hotspur Football and Athletic Company established in 1899 had by 1915 secured gate receipts of £6,399 and was paying wages of £3,940. By 1933 it returned a profit of £8,954 from receipts totalling £52,192 and 'by retaining the best of the old players and engaging some of the finest athletic talent available' the club looked forward to its first season in the First Division.[30] The club had weathered the financial storm brought on by the declining gates of the First World War which had been exacerbated by an establishment view that professional football had behaved unpatriotically, a view expressed in *The Times* of 7 November 1914: 'the action of football clubs in paying professionals is like bribing a needed recruit to refrain from enlistment', to which both clubs and players responded by pleading near bankruptcy.[31] Some clubs like Leeds City continued to pay players throughout the war and naturally derived considerable competitive advantage from so doing, only to be expelled from the League later, paving the way for the establishment of Leeds United at Elland Road in 1920.[32]

Few sports resisted the move towards professionalism, even those which were taken up primarily by the middle classes such as tennis, cycling and golf. The Wimbledon Championships had become so successful even prior to the First World War that special trains took thousands to the final stages and the better foreign players received legitimate expenses as they were deemed to be representing their countries. In America a professional tennis 'circus' was established in the 1920s and the spread of international competition and the consequent growth in importance of national prestige placed the amateur at a severe disadvantage with the result that there grew up a class of club professionals who were paid to improve the standard of play generally. As the game became an increasing attraction to spectators it was no longer possible for many first-class players to regard it merely as a leisure activity. There continued to be wealthy patrons and players with private incomes but the demands of the game were becoming too great and the opportunities too numerous for lawn tennis at the highest level to remain an amateur sport and during the 1930s many of the best players, including Fred Perry, turned fully professional. In 1935 Herman David, a Wimbledon committee member, suggested an 'open' championship only to be substantially voted down, but the same David as Chairman ushered in the first fully professional event in 1967 which led to open championships throughout the world from then onwards.

Technical advances in bicycle manufacture towards the end of the nineteenth century had considerably widened the quality and availability of bicycles and the number of cyclists grew from a relatively few middle-class exponents to a mass participation of what came to be called 'cads on castors'. Much of the early competition had been in time trialling on existing roads but in France professional races on artificial tracks had begun and the idea was taken up in England with the first such event taking place in Fulham in 1871, the success of which encouraged promoters to build further tracks in London, Manchester, Coventry and Bristol. Further sophistication in manufacture, combined with mass production from some 700 factories by 1900, ensured the continued success of the sport at a recreational level. Much of the initial middle-class interest waned as a reaction to the democratisation of the activity, whilst at the same time many former cyclists began to buy motorcycles and increasingly motorcars as they became fashionable. The professional side of the sport never became entrenched in this country, suffering from many alternative attractions, but several clubs in the north of England continued to thrive and their better cyclists took part in semi-professional events around the northern region.[33] The very best turned fully professional in the post Second World War years, mostly competing abroad.

Like cricket, golf began as a classless activity but became gentrified during the nineteenth century when the gulf between gentlemen and players, club members and professionals appeared and was consolidated. The first professionals were those who were hired to teach amateur club members as in cricket, tennis and rowing, often doubling as caddie master and general factotum. But as competition intensified and spectatorism grew these men spent less time teaching and more time playing, especially after 1857 and the first professional competition at Prestwick Golf Club which in 1861 evolved into the first 'open' championship as, in contrast to tennis, the amateur was allowed to compete with the rest. With the establishment of the championships the pattern was set for golf's further development and since the middle of the nineteenth century the history of the game has been one of expansion and adjustment to meet contemporary conditions whilst remaining essentially the same, with the amateur game flourishing as a recreation in clubs and the professional game prospering in the commercial glare of international championships.

One major determinant of contemporary conditions to which all sports very quickly adapted was technological innovation and this was particularly noticeable in golf as balls, clubs and courses evolved considerably over the years to meet the challenge of new materials. The original solid wooden balls were eventually considered to be too heavy for extended play and were replaced with much lighter but more expensive models made of compressed feathers tightly stitched in leather, which in turn gave way to the leathery product of the gutta percha plant when this substance was first imported in the 1840s. Due to the development of rubber products for tyres in the automobile industry, the next advance was a ball whose centre was essentially solid rubber covered with a gutta percha skin which considerably outdistanced and outlasted any previous model. This development and sophistication of rubber and its derivatives also had substantial influence on the other games of fives, squash and tennis as harder, faster balls became available which affected the styles of play necessary for competitive success. As the flight characteristics of golf balls improved, the clubs themselves evolved to maximise the length driven off the tee, first by using lighter woods and then the new metal alloys developed in the light engineering industries of the 1920s to be replaced by the plastics of the 1950s and the carbon fibres of the 1980s. The original shorter courses of few holes gradually expanded as new terrain came into range with newly improved equipment, and although today's courses remain around the conventional 6,500 yards, the degree of artificial difficulty built into them reflects the skill of the professional player using the finest of modern equipment.

We have seen how improvements in cycling technology increased participation in the sport due partly to the promise of comfort and safety and partly to the good value brought about by mass production. The development of tubular metal fabrication for the cycle industry also had its effects on rowing where weight remained a prime consideration for professional racers and it was used in the cross-bracing of hulls and in the manufacture of outriggers. The cold moulding of lighter woods could then be used to produce 'carvel' built craft which replaced the heavy 'clinkers' and the offset rowing positions of the crew were brought into line to produce much longer, narrower and therefore faster boats. Sliding seats were introduced in the 1870s and swivel rowlocks around the turn of the century, both utilising the lighter metals that were becoming available due to technical advances induced by a growing domestic market in consumer durables.[34]

The common theme of all technological advances in sporting equipment was and remains the combination of lightness with strength and whilst this was most obvious in cycling, rowing and golf, it certainly applied to other sports. In the ball games, for example, the playing characteristics of the ball itself was of the greatest importance but was to a large extent determined by the state of the field of play which was transformed by the introduction of grass-cutting machinery in the nineteenth century. Cricket and bowling had for centuries been played on coarsely cut grass with all the difficulties of accuracy and control that this implied, and heavy rolling was employed along with the local sheep to produce tolerable wickets and greens. With the coming of increasingly sophisticated lawn-mowers, the groundsmen began to produce surfaces which more truly reflected the players' intentions so that the balls themselves evolved in ways which allowed the practitioner, particularly the professional, to extract every ounce of movement from them. Balls and bowls became lighter with the stitching of the former and the bias of the latter becoming more pronounced. The style of the cricket bat responded to this in changing gradually from a heavy club designed to bludgeon to a well-balanced, lightweight implement capable of defending the batsman from the vagaries of overarm deliveries (from 1835) and of a delicacy of placement in attack.

Association football and rugby football were not dramatically affected by technology but even there the trend was away from the larger, heavier, softer balls to the more manageable smaller, pressurised variety which went further more accurately when kicked or handled with the effect that both games became faster and more spectator friendly. A further move towards spectatorism came through the influence of the public schools in codifying the rules and stipulating a uniformity of playing area, which in concentrating play facilitated support and encouragement from the side-lines. A similar move in boxing established a roped-off combat area which together with the 'fair sized boxing gloves' and stricter rules of the Queensbury Regulations of 1867 was designed to promote safer fighting, and commercial considerations brought the sport indoors and elevated the ring. This was significant for the fighter since for the first time he was boxing on an artificial floor usually covered in canvas which became treacherous when covered in sweat and blood, and from this time onwards footwear became an important item of equipment for the professional. It was natural that shoes had always been of prime importance for the pedestrian and many weird and wonderful variations of footwear were contrived to improve perambulation, but wooden soled clogs were generally thought to be the best for comfort over long distances having been individually sculpted for the athlete's feet; for rough terrain they were studded for better traction. For sprinting distances over tracks that were often rolled clay a lighter 'slipper' was used, but as road building technology improved and asphalt became a popular medium for track construction these proved inadequate, especially in wet conditions when the surface became hazardous and was not adaptable to studs. The next development was heavily rolled cinders exemplified in the track laid at the White City for the 1908 Olympic Games. The growing importance of international meetings gave impetus to further technological advances which resulted in the use of synthetic rubber initially in America and subsequently worldwide. The specialist running shoe began production as we have seen at the turn of the nineteenth century in Bolton and evolved to maximise comfort and traction on a variety of surfaces with many being individually crafted, a skill which has been largely lost with the coming of mass production but which is still available at a price.

Much, if not all, of the technological innovation in sport was the result of experimentation by professionals in pursuit of winning performances, which was then commercially exploited to provide the best equipment for the recreational amateur. This process and the status of sport in society generally was promoted by a cult of personality which was a peculiarly professional phenomenon massaged by the mass circulation newspapers and reflected in much of the popular entertainment of the day.[35] The earliest sporting personalities were those of the pre-commercial competitions such as Phelps and Broughton of the first few Doggett Coat and Badge races who were fêted and cursed for their sculling prowess, replaced in the early nineteenth century by Noulton and Parish, cunning steersmen employed by the first gentlemen's clubs, who in turn were eclipsed by the true professionals like Robert Chambers, Harry Clasper and James Renforth whose exploits at home and abroad were the stuff of legend.[36] In cricket the first player to gain prominence during the 1760s, albeit in his own backyard, was John Nyren of the Hambledon Club, to be followed in the 1840s by the Lion of Kent Alf Mynn and the 'Nonpareil' himself Fred Lillywhite of Sussex. Both of these were completely overshadowed by W.G. Grace whose fame extended through three decades from the 1870s. Some of his magic seems to have rubbed off on Jack Hobbs of Surrey and Herbert Sutcliffe of Yorkshire who enjoyed almost similar adulation from the public during the 1920s and 1930s. All the earliest football personalities were only locally or regionally famous and known primarily as representatives of their clubs: Sam Hardy of Aston Villa and Bill Meredith of Manchester United in the 1880s and Viv Woodward of Tottenham Hotspur in the early 1900s. Similar elevated status was enjoyed in rugby league by many fine club players such as John Anderton (Leigh), Fred Houghton (Runcorn) and Joe Varley (Oldham).[37] Although athletics remained a minor sport until the coming of the television age, the first professionals attained regional cult status as we have seen with 'Folkestone Bess' and the 'Manchester Pet', and a similar status was enjoyed by Harold Hutchens and John Gent, their successors on the track during the 1880s, who unfortunately tarnished their image and that of the sport by blatantly fixing a race at the Lillie Bridge stadium in Fulham in 1887. The fame of the early pugilist derived largely from such fixing and fouling but the sport's first personalities were protaganists turned promoters James Figg and Jack Broughton who spent much time and effort in self-advertisement and paved the way for future champions like Daniel Mendoza and 'Gentleman John Jackson' in the 1790s. Two decades later John Gully progessed from pugilism to politics and a fortune in the coal industry, but his prominence was not emulated until Tom Sayers came on the scene in the 1860s and then Bob FitzSimmons in the 1890s, and theirs not until the modern era. In the other combat sport of wrestling the only national figure to emerge was Eugen Sandow who fought throughout the country at fairs and country shows during the latter half of the nineteenth century but found his fortune as a well managed and promoted 'strong man' often performing in the music halls.

Professional personalities were often invited by amateurs to attend their clubs for testimonials and exhibitions designed to promote the association and boost membership: two well-known Lancashire professionals Joe Dixon and James Walshaw staged a swimming match on behalf of the Tyldesley Club,[38] the Yorkshire bowling champion James Kaye attended a testimonial match at the Headingley Club,[39] Harry Vardon and Edward Ray, the two most prominent professional golfers of their generation, played an exhibition match for the Lancaster Club,[40] and Clasper, Chambers and Cooper provided examples of professional sculling at York Regatta designed to 'give a stimulus to aquatic sports'.[41] Such appearances were one way of earning money but were certainly not sufficient to provide a living on their own and most professionals were dependent on basic weekly wages when available, supplemented by match purses, gambling income, sponsorship, tuition fees and benefits in cash and kind.[42] Whatever the sources of income the real success stories were few and far between and for every sporting hero there were dozens of destitute failures who had spent improvidently what they had earned with relative ease. But fortunately there were also equal numbers of those like Robert Nickson, the champion Lancashire bowler who took over the Talbot public house in Blackpool in 1873, who set up as publicans and remained comfortably off, well-respected and secure for life, a tradition that continues to this day.

The tradition of professionalism in sport originated in the rural sports of long ago where those who were particularly adept could win prizes in kind and was developed through noble patronage and commercial sponsorship so that those professionally involved in providing services to sport evolved into professional competitors. By this time the tradition had produced folk heroes, national competition networks, international championships and popular interest capable of selling hundreds of thousands of newspapers daily and bringing whole cities to a standstill. That this level of activity could be produced by a profession that boasted only some 2,500 full-time exponents in 1900 may be difficult to credit but its effects were quite sufficient to produce a positive reaction from the gentleman amateur. Gradually at first, but later with greater urgency, this class of sportsman began to distance himself from professionalism by concentrating on purely recreational activity and withdrawing into strictly amateur clubs. The following chapter, therefore, deals with the development of recreationalism as a prelude to a discussion of the amateur clubs.

PROFESSIONALISM

NOTES

1. 1 Corinthians, chapter 10, verse 24.
2. *The Times* (28 July 1928), 5d.
3. *The Times* (15 Aug. 1932), 12b.
4. *Morpeth Sports* and *Olympic Games* programmes for 1874, 1921 and 1925. It is instructive to note that the winning time for 110 yards in 1925 was 10.5 seconds. Similar handicaps were common in Northumberland and other games were held at Felten, Ashington, Bedlington, Choppington and Haydon Bridge.
5. *Carlisle Journal* (15 Aug. 1859), 6c.
6. It is significant that in 1992 it was considered necessary to establish the Professional Boxers' Association to secure further the interests of growing numbers of competitors after another significant influx of participants.
7. *Observer* (15 May 1994).
8. *Aquatic Register*, 1835–51. There were 5,000 such matches recorded, indicating a rate of five a week for 16 years.
9. *Bell's Life* (28 Sept. 1835), 4d.
10. *The Times* (16 June 1830), 5a.
11. A quotation from William Lawson's *Tyneside Celebrities* (Lawson, Newcastle, 1873) indicates the level of interest: 'When a professional sculling race comes off the heart of town is convulsed, the stations teem with unfamiliar forms and faces. The river steamers groan, the cart wheels rattle over the granite roads, the sound of the forge dies away, the blast of the furnaces is unheard, the counting house and desk are deserted and the academic benches are vacant. All hasten to the banks of the coaly Tyne, the radical and the tory, master and servant, the great white washed and the great unwashed every available elevation clad with living forms. Such conveys only a faint idea of the feelings that animate every breast'.

    The more successful professionals like Chambers, Clasper and Renforth won small fortunes but they were the exception. More general was the story of John Hobbs a Bristol boatman who fell on hard times and was last seen 'dressed in a seedy top hat and frock coat peddling Oxo cubes outside the main gates of Woolwich Arsenal' (*Bristol Ariel Rowing Club* minutes, 20 Aug. 1888). For further information on payment see note 42.
12. *The Times* (25 July 1827), 5a.
13. *The Times* (21 Jan. 1909). Be this as it may there grew up serious disaffection with the status quo and as commercial influences grew in importance the professional 'player' gradually supplanted the 'gentleman' as the dominant partner in the game. When cricket eventually became 'open' in 1962 *Wisden* commented that 'by doing away with amateurs cricket is in danger of losing the spirit of freedom and gaiety which the best amateur players brought to the game. The passing of the amateur could have detrimental effects in the vital matters of captaincy at both county and test level' (Norman Preston, editor, *Wisden's Almanack*, 1962).
14. *The Times* (5 Sept. 1828), 4c.
15. *The Bullingdon Cricket and Dining Club Rules*, No. XIII (22 April 1850).
16. *Worksop Cricket Club*, minutes (10 Nov. 1863).
17. It was common for sporting associations to employ servants and we find them engaged by the Stayley Hunt where the 'huntsman and whip were engaged at the usual salary' (minutes, 22 June 1869), by Bowling Clubs as ground staff (*Walthampstow Bowling Club Rules*, 1898), golf clubs as caddies and caddy masters (*Porlock Golf Club Rules*, 1910) and swimming clubs as instructors (*Tyldesley Swimming Club* minutes, 9 Aug. 1876), and many would evolve into professionals through the intermediate stage of 'quasi amateur' as opportunities for competition presented themselves.
18. *Gloucestershire Country Cricket Club*, minutes (11 Jan. 1879).
19. *Northern Rugby Football Union*, minutes (29 Aug. 1895).
20. An example of the impossibility of control comes in many minutes such as those of the Professional Sub-committee of the Northern Union for 15 Nov. 1901, 'permits were

granted to the following players to take part in tomorrow's games' (there follows 150 names). This would happen every week throughout the season.

21. For example, the *Northern Union*, minutes for 6 Nov. 1900, 'That the Holbeck club be fined £20 for inducing W. Carey a professional of Leeds Parish Church Club to sign professional forms for them' (Carey was also suspended).

22. *Newcastle Chronicle* (10 Jan. 1866), 7d.

23. *The Times* (14 Sept. 1858), 5b.

24. *Whitfield Cricket Club*, minutes (16 April 1898).

25. *Huyton Cricket Club*, minutes (7 March 1919).

26. *The Times* (19 July 1900), obituary 5d.

27. *Association Football Players' Association*, inaugural minutes (2 Dec. 1907).

28. *Football League*, AGM minutes (1909). A minute of the Players' Association of 15 Dec. 1908 illustrates the point, 'that matters were proved conclusively that the whole of the League clubs had broken the rules for their advantage and that the maximum pay rule had failed'. It is interesting that at the time of writing Tottenham Hotspur FC have been heavily fined by the Football Association for making illegal payments to players even though there is no longer a maximum wage.

29. *Association Football Players Association*, minutes (14 May 1908).

30. *Tottenham Hotspur Football and Athletic Company*, 35th Annual Report and Accounts (19 June 1935).

31. *Association Football Players' Association*, minutes (12 April 1915), 'the attitude of the clubs has been that they needed to keep players until the end of their contracts, there was no encouragement to join up'. There was a loss for Union funds of £478 and a proposal to wind up.

32. Leeds City Football Club ultimately a commercial failure had taken over Elland Road from Holbeck Rugby Football Club which had failed to make rugby into a paying proposition.

33. *Darlington Cycling Club*, minutes (30 March 1927), for example, 7 guineas for the half mile championship and 5 guineas for the five mile race. Total prizes of £75 19s 0d.

34. The new sliding seat found acceptance everywhere despite the amateur authorities disparaging its effects on style. Even provincial clubs were eager to try it, a good example being the order placed by the Berwick on Tweed RC for a set of four from James Purves and Sons at a cost of £9 14s 0d in 1872, practically as soon as it was possible to buy them on the open market (*Rowing Club*, minutes 11 Oct. 1872).

35. The degree to which the general public were emotionally engaged by sporting endeavour can be gauged by some news reports on the deaths of sporting personalities. Two such come particularly to mind: that of Fred Archer the jockey who died tragically young, whose demise was reported by *The Times* as producing a 'sense of shock and almost personal loss to millions', and of James Renforth, the champion oarsman of the world who also died young, whose death in 1871 was reported by the *Newcastle Chronicle* as producing 'general astonishment which turned to the stupor of genuine sorrow'. Funerals of such personalities brought out hundreds of thousands of people to the streets.

36. See particularly the music hall songs based on these and other personalities in 'The Songs of Tyneside boatracing' in the *North East Labour History Bulletin* N. 16 (1982).

37. In the last two decades of the nineteenth century an entrepreneurial Yorkshireman, John Baines of Manningham, saw an opportunity to profit from the fever for Rugby Football and began to produce packets of personality football cards which sold at six for a halfpenny. They sold by the millions well into the 1920s.

38. *Tyldesley Swimming Club*, minutes (25 July 1877).

39. *Headingley Bowling Club*, minutes (25 July 1890).

40. *Lancaster Golf Club*, minutes for AGM 1913, 'So much was the match appreciated and so much to the benefit and reputation of the club that it is intended to repeat the experiment'.

41. *Yorkshire Gazette* (30 Sept. 1865), 8a.

42. It is not possible precisely to evaluate the earnings of the early professional sportsmen

since written evidence on the subject is rarely available and where it does exist indicates a bewildering diversity. However, if we take reported winnings and where available the stated wage rates, we can form some idea of career earnings, bearing in mind that few in any sport would continue at first class level for more than 20 years.

In pedestrianism and later *athletics* the top matches were habitually for £500 and this remained the same into the early modern era of Hutchens and Gent; at club meeting level the premium price would be £50. In *bowling* the only evidence appears to suggest that the winner of a tournament took the entrance monies which varied but were rarely over £5, this of course would be supplemented as with all other sports by gambling winnings (or otherwise); *boxing* again was often for a purse of 500 guineas but varied according to the level of importance and degree of promotion, for example, the Sayers vs. Heenan fight in 1860 resulted in a purse of £200 for Sayers, but for his pluck and determination he also received £3,000 in a testimonial. *Cricket* was for the professional something of a moveable feast, the crumbs from which were heavily dependent on club committees; payment was often on a match by match basis of anything between £1 and £5; W.G. Grace regularly received £15 and often played several times a week and did so for over 20 years despite his 'amateur' status and private income. A club professional in the provinces could expect 2 guineas for a day's tuition or £25 a month. *Footballers* received anything between £2 10s 0d and £5 a week, which hardly varied until between the two world wars. This was supplemented by more or less generous expenses and some share of transfer fees if appropriate. *Golf* professionals received generally around two shillings an hour for tuition and £25 for an exhibition match. In *rowing* the club professional, who doubled as boat builder, received £2 a week which often included accommodation in the boathouse; the purse for sculling matches averaged out at around £30 and a testimonial at £100 (Robert Cooper's gift in 1866 – the solid silver salver he also received – was probably worth more); financially the most successful English oarsman was James Renforth whose (short) career total was £2,590, but others like Harry Clasper also made boats ('claspers') which sold well and made him a fortune. *Rugby League* players, few of whom were full-time professionals, started on £2 a match, and if successful were retained at £5 for what was a relatively short season; once the leagues were in place they, like Association players, received certain expenses and some transfer fees. The most highly paid of all professionals by far were jockeys in *horse racing* who from early in the nineteenth century had received substantial riding fees which acted as retainers for particular owners; taking an average of the most successful riders and what we know of their winnings from 1870 to 1914 career earnings (over as much as 30 years) might easily be £75,000.

5

Recreationalism

The gentlemen subscribers to the bowling
green met at the Half Moon tavern where an
elegant dinner was provided. Afterwards
every bowler exerted his abilities and the
medal was declared after which they adjourned
to the Half Moon where the evening concluded
in the utmost harmony.

(*Hampshire Chronicle*, 4 August 1777)

Provision should be made for the healthy
innocent recreation of all classes of people
and it is proposed to establish a society for
the practice of cricket, quoits, archery and other
games. All classes are invited to attend.

(Public meeting, Guildhall, Walsall, 2 June 1846)

Throughout the period when commercialism and professionalism
dominated the sporting scene, there was continual activity in recreational sport which sought to minimise the importance of competition
and foster the notion of taking part for pleasure alone. During the
eighteenth century there had been disturbances on a wide front:
wages, elections, religion, enclosures and food, with most sizeable
towns experiencing some sort of riot. In consequence the militia was
garrisoned in some 43 towns around the country, the officers of which
were responsible for inaugurating many sporting events. So it is that
we find particularly cricket, shooting and rowing matches taking place
in towns such as Norwich, Woolwich, Dover and Berwick which often
led to the establishment of local clubs. Elsewhere the commercial
middling class took its leisure in similar if less strenuous ways, with the
women boating and the men playing cricket and bowls games which
had become the staple recreational diet of this group,[1] indulgence in
which could become something of an obsession,[2] no doubt encouraged
by the traditional close proximity of a public house. For other social
groups cock-fighting, although outlawed, continued to be a recreational

release in the backyards of inns, primarily for the purpose of gambling,[3] whilst boxing and wrestling matches also maintained their popularity initially at inn yards but later in more established venues.[4] As the mercantile class of the eighteenth century evolved into the middle class of the nineteenth with a million more families entering that socio-economic group, opportunities for leisure grew with the increasing prosperity and free time, particularly in the south-east of the country where such growth was disproportionately high. Sporting activity provided this new group with opportunities for exercise, excitement, conspicuous consumption and social advancement,[5] and during the century middle-class participation grew in hunting, shooting, fishing and the major ball games, as well as in bowls, croquet, lawn tennis, golf and boating.[6]

At the same time there was a move towards the provision of recreational facilities for the less prosperous at club, municipal and works level as philanthropists of various persuasions sponsored or subsidised different sports. Joseph Garside in Worksop, for example, in 1863 'liberally provided' a cricket ground for the formation of a new club whose members then solicited 'public and private' subscriptions to level and lay 60 square yards of turf for the wicket.[7] On the Isle of Dogs individual initiatives combined with some church provision ensured that 'admirers of muscular christianity practised boatracing, athletic sports and played in brass bands',[8] whilst a much stricter religious conviction was responsible for a wider provision in Bradford. Titus Salt in his model industrial village of Saltaire (motto: 'Abandon drink all ye who enter here') established ten societies including those for boating, cricket and bowls, so that in the words of a contemporary guide 'mill workers from Saltaire and Shipley or shopmen and lasses could have a good day out'. Similar philanthropy informed the new Manchester Ship Canal Company in its purchase of Trafford Park for its recreational development as golf course and boating lake in 1896. Meanwhile town councils began providing facilities as many urban redevelopment schemes incorporated 'pleasure grounds', as at Birkenhead in 1845, Leeds in 1861 and Newark in 1884; whilst the tourist potential of sporting facilities was fully realised at places like Talkin Tarn near Carlisle and Hollingworth Lake near Rochdale where provision for boating, dancing, bowling and archery was made available in the 1870s. Recreational play amongst the masses was, however, not always welcome or desirable and football, although increasingly commercialised and professionalised, continued to be the popular game of the street where its capacity to cause mayhem remained undiminished. Many letters bear witness to this, all very similar in tone to that penned to the clerk of Bicester Town Council on 6 March 1899 which complained of the 'intolerable nuisance of footballing boys making their goals from lamp posts and lumping against the thin walls of the houses'.

Such behaviour was antipathetic to the rational philosophy which developed during the latter half of the nineteenth century from the application of scientific method to most areas of life in an age of cheap bread, cheap literature and myriad inventions. The increasing severity of local bye-laws, new sanitary and health reforms and a democratisation of schooling all led towards a rationalisation of physical education in the state sector which brought it more in line with its provision at the public schools, and this trend was given considerable impetus by the decline in physical standards monitored by army recruitment during the Boer Wars.[9] Further decline became inevitable during the deprivations of the Great War and its aftermath, so that the government, no doubt bearing in mind the war-winning attributes ascribed to Eton's playing fields, esablished the National Playing Fields Association in 1925 with a view to improving the nation's health. The emphasis as elucidated by the Durham branch of the association was placed on the provision of 'more playing fields, playgrounds and open spaces for locals and their children' and representatives of cricket, rowing, football and rugby clubs attended the inaugural meeting which immediately identified the mining village of East Bolden as a prime target for its activities.[10] Not surprisingly the industrialised areas of the country which suffered both greater ill health and dearth of recreational facilities than elsewhere were the first to form branch associations and apply for funds. The Bolton branch 'felt strongly that there is much need for playing fields especially for the purpose of organised games'.[11] The therapeutic effect of exercise in the economic depression of the inter-war years, the increasing prestige attached to performances at international level and the need to create higher levels of fitness for future conflict all contributed towards a recreational philosophy, the aim of which was exemplified in the stated objectives of the Sunderland 'Keep Fit' classes of 1933, namely to 'make a race of splendid men and women with fit and beautiful bodies and lively daring minds'. The government nurtured this new athleticism by appointing a National Fitness Council in 1937 and a National Advisory Council for Physical Training which funded several full-time organisers for sport, the first of which was for amateur boxing, perhaps anticipating the blood-letting to come.

Much of the post-war recreational activity was greatly facilitated by the mobility afforded by motorised transport using much improved metal roads which represented in the twentieth century as much of a transport revolution as the extension of rail travel had in the nineteenth. The railways had been instrumental in promoting sporting activity since the 1830s when the first lines were built in the urban areas of London, Birmingham, Manchester and Newcastle,[12] and have continued to be so ever since, transporting players and supporters the length and breadth of the country. In the early days certain activities would not have taken place without rail travel which introduced a speed and convenience not experienced before, rendering, as Lord Greville put it on his way to Liverpool races in 1837, 'all other travelling irksome and tedious by comparison'[13] and enabling, for example, city men to visit their rowing clubs every night for training if required.[14] It also had the effect of democratising travel, so that all social classes although naturally occupying separate compartments were able to indulge their particular sporting fancies in ways simply not possible before. The upper classes could for the first time in any numbers follow in person their racing fortunes outside Ascot and Newmarket and also extend their hunting in the shires from weekends to weekdays if so desired. The middle classes used the train to attend their rowing, cricket and rugby clubs as they retreated further into the suburban sprawl and to participate in a greater number of away fixtures as the railway linked both adjacent and outlying areas. In archery it allowed mass shoots at unusual locations[15] and enabled city-based sons of the sea to indulge their passion at weekends and on long summer evenings.[16] For the working classes cheap excursion trains allowed them to follow their local football and rugby teams throughout the north of England, whose league structure and fixture lists had grown as a direct result of rail extensions. Individual participants in the hugely popular activity of fishing were catered for with concessionary fares negotiated for them by their angling associations.[17] All of this was supplemented by 'specials' which took thousands, sometimes hundreds of thousands, to see professional rowing at Newcastle, cricket at Nottingham, rugby at Odsal (Bradford), bowling at Blackpool, racing at Chester and even skating near Cambridge,[18] and many hundreds of other major and minor venues served by a rail network which stretched to 22,000 miles by 1900.

Although the element of competition was vital to the professional and was an integral part of most games even for the amateur, winning was of paramount importance for one whilst being a matter of relative indifference to the other. Amateur sport could be classified under Johnston's original dictionary definition of 'that which unbends the mind by turning it from care'. Notably unathletic, Johnson was once prevailed upon to take to the hunting field with the predictable result that he pronounced it anything but a diversion, and yet for many hunting was the purest recreation of all with the prospect of killing the fox being the least important consideration. The most famous run in the then history of fox-hunting was generally regarded as the Billesdon Coplow hunt of 24 February 1800 which lasted for two and a quarter hours, travelled over 28 miles and failed to register a kill. Any reading of hunting records show many barren days which are nevertheless accounted successes due to the speed of the runs across open country.[19]

An important element in hunting and other recreational activities was that of socialising and much of the language of early clubs admirably reflects this with many styling themselves 'societies'. The Society of Gentlemen Archers, for example, was established in Darlington in 1758 for the purpose of regulating the shooting at targets for a silver medal and for 'the encouragement of the ancient, noble and manly exercise of archery'; and the Mersey Archery Society was established in 1821 and supported equally by gentlemen and ladies whose shooting partners were drawn by lot and there was a stipulation that no one was allowed to win more than twice in any season. Although, as we have seen, archery was considerably gentrified during the eighteenth century with most shooting societies made up only of the leisured class, other similar institutions were less exclusive and at the other end of the social scale we find fishing societies enjoying huge popularity. Walthamstow residents inaugurated their Fishery and Shooting Society in 1838 whose members were required to pay 1s for a day's fishing on water which extended rather unpromisingly from 'France Ware to beyond the coal wharf', whilst Derwentwater Anglers Association was established to 'secure the means of recreation to the true sportsmen particularly the working man' and whose subscription could be paid by a 'day's labour driving stakes into the stream'.[20] In Warrington the venue for much early sporting activity, the Jolly Anglers Society, was formed in 1848 to award prizes for the best fish caught and any breach of the rather informal rules was penalised by fines levied in drink, a situation that obviously failed to impress a less easy-going late Victorian membership since the jolliness was dropped in favour of a more prosaic Angling Association in 1891. During the latter half of the nineteenth century progress was made towards the mass participation in fishing which today makes it the most popular of all recreational activities, with the increase in membership of urban associations particularly noticeable, like that in Sheffield from 7,000 in 1860 to 20,000 in 1900 in large part the result of cheap rail access to local fisheries.

Many early societies were formed by small groups of friends seeking diversions, an excellent example being the Dresden Boat Club of 1839, rule ten of whose rather emotionally worded constitution states that 'any members having once belonged to the club remain as long as the timbers of the boat hold together' and there was a host of sports clubs whose purpose was essentially social. This was often made apparent by their titles as in the Bullingdon Cricket and Dining Club which was established to play cricket once a week but to dine twice weekly, the Billiard Club and News Room of Darlington whose members had the use of a rather battered billiard table but the choice of five daily papers and five weekly illustrated journals, and the Mutual Improvement Society of Preston formed by nine friends in 1883 for the purpose of purchasing a billard table.[21] Often the titles of the clubs belied their true nature so that the Guildford Rowing Club, like many clubs established during the 1880s, provided its members with opportunities for family outings of swimming, canoeing and picnic trips; whilst Warwick Boat Club was so successful as a general club for other sports such as tennis, bowls and croquet that rowing ceased altogether and the name alone remained to represent its origins. Early bicycle clubs provided urban dwellers with access to the countryside and concentrated on social and recreational activities such as the 'moonlight runs and paper chases' of the Oken Bicycle Club of Warwick (1883), the afternoon tea runs to Wilmslow of the Levenshulme Velocipede Club (1869), the 'very grand ornamental riding around pubyards' of the Colchester Club in 1875, or the ambitious five-day tour of Normandy organised by the Finsbury Park Club in 1912. For all such clubs the notion of serious competition was simply inappropriate. This was also the case with lawn tennis in its first years as a frivolous game for suburban back gardens, but the All England Lawn Tennis and Croquet Club initiated a serious championship at a meeting on 9 June 1877 at which it is recorded that 'having chosen the best seats for themselves and friends the committee adjourned', a cavalier attitude which pervaded the championships for at least the first few years of operation. The committee's priorities can be gauged not only by its approach to ticket allocation but by its action in setting aside two rest days on the first Friday and Saturday to avoid a clash with that highlight of the social season the Eton and Harrow cricket match.

As it happened this particular match was always fiercely contested, as indeed during the same period and later was the annual varsity cricket match which had certainly not been the intention of its instigator Charles Wordsworth, who had also been responsible for the university boat race in 1829, since both events had been the result of informal arrangements amongst old school friends.[22] Towards the end of his life Wordsworth criticised the 'professionalism' of the participants which was far removed from his original concept of 'pure recreation', but by then the desire for sporting excellence brought about by the growth of professionalism had replaced the simple pleasures of participation with the overwhelming desire for victory. Fortunately this was not always the case elsewhere and recreationalism continued to flourish around the country during the late Victorian and Edwardian periods and indeed throughout the 1920s and 1930s when, as one contemporary commentator put it, recreation changed from 'pleasure pure to pleasure as a restless and rapid escape from work in shops and offices'.[23] There had been an abundant evidence of this restless desire for escape for many years amongst the urban working classes who had travelled in their tens of thousands on rail excursions to the new seaside resorts, taken up rural pursuits like fishing and joined cycling and rambling clubs in an effort to break the monotony of their daily lives. Rambling became increasingly popular during the 1880s and demand for greater access to the predominantly privately owned countryside grew accordingly, culminating in the Access to Mountains Bill of 1889 which was overwhelmingly rejected after representations from the owners of grouse moors. This conflict of interests rumbled on until the mass trespass of Kinder Scout in 1932 brought matters to a head, following which greater access to open land was negotiated partly through the good offices of the Youth Hostel Association and the Ramblers Association at a time when government was campaigning to promote 'fitness for service'.

For some members of sports clubs the concept of physical fitness attained an importance often greater than involvement in their sport and training for fitness became an end in itself with many patented exercise machines introduced to the market around the turn of the century. Perhaps the most bizarre of these was the 'Rowing Tricycle' advertised as a 'Road Sculler', whose handles resembling sculls were worked backwards and forwards to propel and steer the contraption via a chain linked to the wheels. Such machines represented a move towards a non-competitive essentially solitary recreation already available in fishing, rambling and cycling in which the element of combativeness had been replaced by one of reflection.[24] Although this individualism evolved gradually over the years into the 'outward bound' adventurism of the second half of the twentieth century, the sporting recreationalists of earlier generations were satisfied with the leisurely social gatherings with which they had become so familiar.

5. The Edwardian period saw the production of many bizarre and flamboyant exercise machines. The Water Cycle illustrated here was merely one such – the aquatic equivalent of the land-borne Road Sculler. Alas, neither lasted beyond their initial fashionable popularity.

There is much evidence of this extending well into the present century, for instance in Bolton where the plight of the rugby club in having no fixtures was not considered an oversight; in Bristol where the cycling club was quite happy to accommodate motor cyclists; in Trowbridge where a club was formed 'entirely for the purpose of recreation'; in Warrington where a bowling league was established for the sole purpose of 'cementing good fellowship'; and in Sunningdale where the Ladies Golf Club was content to change club days 'to accommodate members who hunt'. During the Second World War, whilst organised sport suffered very badly due to hostilities, the truly leisure-orientated recreational pursuits like bowling and angling carried on 'much as usual'.[25]

The overriding characteristic of recreationalism had always been its leisurely pace, which had betokened an activity indulged in by gentlemen only in which excellence of performance was regarded as undignified, and many activities developed through the influence of gentlemen and aristocrats. Like much else in polite society sport was subject to the vagaries of fashion and yachting enjoyed a popularity with the aristocracy during the restoration period which continued into the eighteenth century when George II became patron of the Cork Yacht Club in 1720 and the Cumberland Fleet evolved into the Royal Yacht Club. This connection with the sea was always commended as 'patriotic' as it was thought to encourage marine skills useful to the nation, and similar notions were also expressed about rowing which enjoyed a vogue among the gentry during the second half of the eighteenth century. They were later responsible for establishing many 'one boat' clubs like the Dresden Boat Club in Nottingham formed in 1839 by Sir William Anstruther and Lord Inverary for the recreation of an initial membership of seven, being six rowers and one steerer.[26] A similar social environment was envisaged in the establishment of various archery societies which emerged in the eighteenth century when the ancient art of 'shooting with bows' was gentrified. One of the oldest was the Toxophilite Society formed by Sir Ashton Lever of Alkrington near Manchester in 1780. This and other similar societies introduced the sport to the leisured classes and it soon became one of the most fashionable pastimes, particularly amongst ladies, and led eventually to the formation of competitive clubs like the Broughton Archers which practised near Kersal Moor in Salford and whose members were exclusively well-to-do gentlemen. Another such society was the Staffordshire Bowmen established in 1791 and patronised by the Earls of Shrewsbury, who were instrumental in promoting an association 'which was the means of so much social intercourse' and provided shooting grounds at Alton Towers where as late as 1870 200 archers arrived by special train to shoot and have dinner.[27] The development of cricket, another gentrified sport, was largely dependent on similar aristocratic patronage, usually in the form of the provision of a suitable venue. At Alcester in 1861, for instance, some inhabitants had formed themselves into a cricket club for the purpose of spending evenings in the pastime of cricket but soon found great difficultly in obtaining a field to play in so that at last they petitioned the Marquis of Hertford to 'make available a portion of Ragley Park to enable us to indulge in the healthy pastime of cricket'.[28] Such private philanthropy was mirrored in the public sector, especially in the larger conurbations where open space was becoming scarce. Lord Morpeth, as the appropriate minister of the crown, encouraged cricket by reserving areas of London for recreation as he did in 1846 in setting aside Victoria Park in Whitechapel specifically for the purpose of cricket since 'the present rage for building was reducing the small number of available grounds'.[29]

The country sports of hunting, shooting and horse-racing remained a source of recreation for their leisured supporters, although there were those like Lord Greville who questioned the desirability of spending so much time on such frivolous pursuits as he thought his involvement in the turf had tended to degrade his understanding so that he had become less respectable in the world. Evidence of such degradation of morality and understanding as can be found in Greville's diary can also be found in the shooting diary of Charles Shaw MP.[30] Such problems were an inevitable result of a recreational involvement in sport that was essentially social in nature since one of the functions of leisure in all societies is to provide opportunities for sexual encounters, but there were many other lighter social diversions to be enjoyed. An evening of cards followed a day's shooting as invariably as dinner, dancing or theatre followed a day at the races, and the hunt ball was always the social event of the country year which was not surprising considering the social composition of many hunts. Since the days of Nicholas Cox and his 'Gentlemen's Recreation' of 1674 it was common for the local squire and nobility to comprise the local hunt, but by 1800 it had become capable of attracting several hundred followers and by 1860 Trollope could refer to hunting as the national sport since it was visibly supported by a cross-section of those who could afford it from prosperous tradesmen to landed nobility. Leaving aside the big subscription hunts made more available to mass support by railway extensions and the ancient and socially select hunts like the Quorn, the average country hunt more closely resembled the Gatewood Fox Hounds of Berwick on Tweed with its 37 members of whom 11 were minor nobility or the Norfolk Fox Hounds with 27 subscribers paying £500 per annum for two days hunting a week.[31]

If much recreational development was sponsored directly or indirectly by the gentry, then much too was initiated by the church, and when we remember that the playfulness from which much organised activity later developed took place on Sundays after the church services this is perhaps not so surprising. The local country priest was often involved directly in hunting, shooting and fishing along with his colleagues the squire, doctor and justice of the peace. Archbishop Lang in his 'Sermons' of 1913 extolled the virtues of hunting for the clergy, saying that it encouraged some of the finest qualities of human nature, courage, endurance, readiness to face risk, comradeship and honourable courtesies. At a time of muscular Christianity in the second half of the nineteenth century, the church encouraged vicars to embody the principle of a healthy moral mind in a physically fit body, and in the north of England, for example, the Brampton seminary produced some of the country's best wrestlers: men like the reverends Abraham Brown and Osborne Littleton who passed on their skills to parishioners in church wrestling clubs.[32] Much of the social reform of the Victorian era was imbued with the altruism of Christian philosophy and was informed and targeted by priests who lived among the working poor, often in squalid surroundings, and hence much of the recreational provision for workers originated in plans drawn up and promoted by local Christian groups. In 1845 the Manchester diocese encouraged the major cotton manufacturers to provide a recreation ground which was used for cricket, quoits, and football and where ginger beer and coffee could be bought cheaply.[33] A similar initiative in Walsall the following year was responsible for the provision of 'healthy innocent recreation for all classes in the practice of cricket, quoits, archery and other games'.[34] The role of the Mechanics Institutes and the Working Men's Associations, most of which were supported by the clergy, were also extremely important in providing recreational facilities to the impecunious working man and woman, as for instance did the Working Men's College in Great Ormond Street which organised rambling, rowing and cricket for both sexes on a regular weekly basis. An associate of this college was John 'Rob Roy' MacGregor, an ex-Cambridge oarsman and Christian missionary responsible both for establishing many 'ragged schools' for London street children and popularising canoeing through his adventurous river trips in Europe and beyond. Such philanthropy on behalf of the church and its representatives was at least in part a pragmatic if principled approach to the social evils of delinquency and drunkenness, and practically any diversion was utilised to provide what was literally and metaphorically a recreation.[35] The Vale of Derwentwater Angling Association (president, the aptly named Reverend Goodfellow) was established to discourage poaching and encourage honest fishing amongst working men and seven years after inauguration the annual report of 1858 claimed that 'instead of a few idle men making dishonest gain we now see numbers of decent working men fishing while poaching has entirely disappeared'. On the Isle of Wight the establishment of the Ryde Rowing Club in 1877 (president, the Reverend Mackereth) was deemed to be 'of great benefit for the young men of the town both physically and morally'[36] and in Mansfield in 1874 the local church organised the shop apprentices into the Wanderers Cricket Club. In the same year Bolton Wanderers Football Club was established as the Catholic Christ Church Football Club and elsewhere in football ecumenicims reigned as the two church wardens of St Mark's Church of England established what was to become Manchester City Football Club, the local Congregationalist church spawned Everton Football Club and the Wesleyans established Aston Villa Football Club. This constructive approach to social problems was endorsed by Barnett's classic text *Towards Social Reform*, published in 1909, in which a close personal knowledge of individuals amongst the poor was recognised as the starting point for any useful provision for those where 'the line of leisure was drawn just above sleeping hours and where the education ended at thirteen years of age'. Policies in the twentieth century followed much the same pattern with, for example, Sale Harriers being established in 1910 by a group of local churches which staged road races and cross-country runs, and the development of nationwide recreational facilities by the Young Men's and Women's Christian Associations. One particular difficulty encountered in church encouragement of recreation was the disapproval in some quarters of play on Sundays which dated back to the condemnation of unlawful sports in the sixteen century and before. Much of this disapproval became apparent during the first half of the nineteenth century when more working people began to use Sundays for recreational purposes as the only day available to them after a six-day working week in the factories and workshops of the newly established conurbations. For the relatively leisured and church-going middle class this smacked of unchristian behaviour and several organisations were established which sought to mitigate the harmful effects such as licentiousness: the Temperance Movement in 1829, the Lord's Day Observance Society in 1831 and in the same year the Society for the Suppression of Vice which lambasted the 'shameful practice of races on Sunday'.[37] We have already seen how the Lord Mayor of London prohibited boat hirers in the eighteenth century from letting out boats to apprentices on a Sunday and the gentrified sport of rowing continued to discriminate against rowing on Sunday, so much so that in Nottingham the working members of the local club were prevented from using the boats by its middle-class committee with the result that they formed the Nottingham Boat Club in 1894 which positively encouraged Sunday outings.[38] The 'cads on castors' also presented a problem for Sabbatarians and the Lord's Day Observance Society regularly recorded the incidence of Sunday cycling. Indeed on 20 June 1904 1,797 men and 125 women were seen to pass the Red Deer Inn at Croydon on their way to Box Hill, but such runs were rarely official club outings; some clubs strictly prohibited the wearing of uniform or insignia on Sundays in an effort to mollify establishment disfavour.[39] Perhaps it is no surprise to find that the gentrified and socially exclusive game of golf upheld the 'no play on Sunday' rule and many club constitutions, at least until the inter-war period, incorporated instructions like that of Warrington Golf Club in 1904 which 'closed the links absolutely on Sundays both for play and promenading'. The inter-war period saw a great extension in Sunday play and a relaxation in attitudes towards it[40] which became further liberalised during and after the Second World War when there was a widespread feeling that events should take place on days when work was not general such as Saturday afternoons and Sundays, whatever the Church might think. In 1944 a long-standing convention was broken when the Football Association sanctioned Sunday soccer. As society became progressively more democratic and secular, individual clubs balloted members concerning play on Sunday with the majority receiving, like the Trowbridge Recreation Club in May 1946, the go ahead with the proviso that 'there would be no bar and no tea making facilities'. The trend towards a complete secularisation of society continued throughout the modern period and the last vestige of Sabbatarianism was removed in 1994 when Bills allowing shop trading and horse-racing on Sunday passed through parliament.

One factor which often exercised the Lord's Day Observance Society as it monitored recreational activity on the Sabbath was the participation of women, which was considered particularly harmful to the growth of family life. Prior to 1700 or so it was most unusual to find women taking part in sport of any kind, exceptions being hawking and horse-riding for the genteel class and feast day activities like smock-racing for the labouring class. But during the eighteenth century when country moved to town, commercial activity increased and the old social order began to break down, the more prosperous woman took tentative steps towards sporting emancipation. This first happened in the hunting field, but not without adverse comment as in James Thompson's epic poem of 1730 *The Seasons*, in which he criticises the ladies' 'uncomely courage and unbeseeming skill with which the winning softness of their sex is lost'. A century later, however, Surtees in his *Analysis of the Hunting Field* confirmed their acceptance by acknowledging 'some uncommon performances by women that would put nine tenths of men to the blush', and by the late nineteenth century Lady Augusta Fane had become one of the most prominent figures in hunting. The construction of many artificial lakes at country houses throughout the land encouraged ladies in the genteel pursuit of boating away from the main water courses through which much commercial traffic continued to flow. Much later, following the emancipating influences of the Women's Property Act of 1870 and the Matrimonial Causes Act of 1878, it was felt that 'now that everything is changed it is essential that every English girl should learn to row'.[41] This advice to the lady of leisure came at least a century after it had become obvious that women could row perfectly well, as evinced by crews of fisher-women at Saltash Regatta in Devon, but it remained contemporary wisdom that women, certainly gentlewomen, could not sustain the effort of maturing physically whilst indulging in strenuous mental or physical activity.[42] As the women of Devon took to boat racing, the women of Sussex took up the cricket bat, for during the 1780s and 1790s the Bury Common women's team became so famous that it challenged the All England eleven (without response). Unlike their aquatic colleagues, however, their involvement was not emulated by their more genteel sisters for whom cricket first became a sport in the twentieth century at the all-girl public schools. The general attitude to women in cricket was that they made excellent teas[43] but that the 'pavilion was the temple undesecrated by the foot of woman, one of the last asylums of the merely male in an epicene world'.[44] Despite this the 1930s saw many women's cricket clubs established, like that in Bolton where it was generously 'allowed to use the men's ground on one day a week only'.[45] The next sport in which women were to make their mark was archery and as early as 1821 the Mersey Archery Society was made up of 29 men and 21 women who regularly shot together; and the Staffordshire Society which had failed as an all-male club was resuscitated most successfully in 1863 as a mixed association with Lady Edwards as Patroness and Eleanor Sneyd as President.

6. Lady Greville in her *Gentlewomen's Book of Sports* of 1880 opined that it was 'essential that every girl should learn to row since now that everything is changed it is seen to be the very best thing for her'. Most girls would start in boats like these and graduate to racing skiffs, in which they began to contest regattas during the Edwardian period despite the attitude of the Skiff Association which continued to maintain that it was 'unladylike'.

Although women's ability in shooting was the equal of their male colleagues and their numbers in many societies greater than men's (or perhaps because of it) the sport never attained truly popular status and remained what *The Times* rather dismissively called a 'primitive, decorative kind of amusement admirable for displaying the female form and productive of social pleasure and friendly rivalry'.[46] Women's sport developed in isolation in schools and colleges and elsewhere came to be rooted in a new kind of suburban culture centred in the family garden and private club where 'the majority of middle class women remained in a kind of psychological and physical bondage'[47] and into which during the 1850s were introduced croquet, badminton and later lawn tennis, all of which were designed with women players very much in mind. Tennis had evolved from the all-male royal tennis through the rather rough and ready field tennis to the unisex 'lawners' in response to a suburban demand for a low skill, convenient and social diversion, and during the last quarter of the nineteenth century the growth of lawn tennis clubs was meteoric, particularly in the commuter belt around London. Many of these clubs had women in the majority as members, as at Dunmow Park in Essex where in 1896 there were 18 women and 9 men members, and whose facilities were used almost exclusively by women at least during the week so that special arrangements had to be made for 'week day' men, as at Walthamstow where a rule of 1897 advises that two courts should be set aside for the use of gentlemen only on Tuesdays and Thursdays.

Another exclusively middle-class sport for women was golf, but here the men were far less inclined than their brothers in tennis and archery to allow female incursion and only permitted their womenfolk to 'play upon such days and subject to such restrictions as the committee shall from time to time determine'.[48] However, at a time around the turn of the century when there were one million domestic servants and wives had more leisure time to fill than their husbands, it was inevitable that their influence should be felt. Hence ladies' participation was tacitly endorsed in most golf club minutes, and they were accepted as *ipso facto* members without any executive or voting powers. Eligibility for membership in the larger clubs remained restricted to adult males but in more remote areas clubs were established with the intention of incorporating women as full members, such as Appleby in Westmorland where the club began in 1894 with 43 men and 33 women subscribers who financed a clubhouse with equal but separate accommodation. In many areas where golf was particularly popular it was impossible for women to integrate in this way as their very presence threatened the smooth running of clubs already fully subscribed with men, but at Sunningdale this situation was to some extent mitigated by the inauguration in 1906 of a Ladies Golf Club which negotiated with the well-established men's club a rent and affiliation fee which produced mutual satisfaction.[49] The growth of women's golf and the difficulties which inevitably attended it gave rise to the Ladies Golf Union in 1893 which facilitated the improvement in playing conditions for women and organised a Ladies' Championship, the first of which was held at Lytham and St Anne's that same year. Considering the huge popularity of both tennis and golf amongst a certain class of socially well-connected women, perhaps it is not surprising that it was in these two sports that women first competed at the Olympic Games in 1912, since it was considered that they were essentially ladylike, not too strenuous and could be satisfactorily accomplished fully clothed.

The prudery with which much women's sport was often contemplated gave rise to strict regulations with regard to appropriate dress which must have made certain activities extremely difficult. In boating the first rules of the Oxford University Women's Boat Club in 1906 stipulate that 'girls shall have a draw string in their skirts so that no ankle is exposed', despite which the Skiff Racing Association still complained in March 1907 that 'the costumes worn by the ladies were unnecessarily scanty', and even as late as 1936 the Alpha Ladies Club members were advised to clad themselves 'most circumspectly' in long blue stockings (white suggested underwear), black shorts, tops which covered the arm pits and berets to cover long hair. In hockey the 1898 rules of the Kendal Women's Club stated that 'skirts must be no more than six inches above the ground all round', to be accompanied by a green blouse, white collar, white tie and green Tam O'Shanter. In swimming Councillor Margaret Ashton of Manchester Corporation thought that 'men were allowed to witness women's swimming competitions in a manner quite indecent'.[50] Such prudery was not universal, at least in swimming, and in the 1914 mixed bathing debate in Manchester inquiries were made as to the practice in other towns, with the result that 18 replies were favourable and 26 not so with all those favourable being in the London area, and since Manchester feared falling behind the capital mixed bathing was given the go ahead forthwith. Swimming clubs had long incorporated ladies' sections which met apart from the men, sometimes as in Stockport in baths built specially for them. Ladies' galas were held in Netherfield, Tyldesley, Stockport and Warrington throughout the 1870s, which considerably boosted recruitment with the Netherfield club in 1890 having 55 men and 53 women members, and similar parity existed in most of the clubs in the greater Manchester area. In 1905 an independent Nottingham Ladies Swimming Club was established and in 1914 the Park Swimming Club in Tottenham had 77 men and 77 women fully subscribed.

Whereas in swimming the mixing of the sexes took until the First World War to accomplish to any degree, in cycling it was immediate and proved extremely important in providing all classes of women with opportunities for shared physical recreation already available to the leisured class in hunting, archery, croquet and tennis. The membership of the Cycling Touring Club in 1890 was 60,000 of whom over 20,000 were women and women were important members of clubs up and down the country, providing, for example, five out of nine committee members in the Bristol Cycle Touring Club in 1912 and organising all 14 summer runs in 1914 for the Darlington Cycling Club: positions of influence which were strengthened immediately following the First World War.[51]

Despite strenuous efforts on the part of many people to encourage women to participate more fully in sporting activity, it was only in the relatively leisured class that any real progress was made. One of the few sports that attracted other classes was athletics and the Women's Amateur Athletic Association was established in 1922 with support mostly from the lower middle and working class amongst girls who would also take part in cycling and hiking, both of which were positively encouraged by the Youth Hostel Association formed in 1930 (also known as 'your husband assured'). However, the vast majority of working-class women simply refrained from any sporting activity and were far more likely to be involved in 'going to the cinema, dancing, drinking and promenading'.[52] A situation which existed throughout the Second World War, during which public houses in working-class areas continued to do excellent business day and night and when women in particular condemned sport as a 'criminal waste of time'.[53] It is not surprising that working women chose a passive rather than an active role with regard to recreation, for not only did they expand sufficient energy in their normal daily routine but were also perfectly aware that a cultural barrier separated them and their menfolk from activities largely carried on in private members' clubs. Many of the recreational activities which we have discussed in the present chapter, and the forms that they took, provided the well-to-do with further opportunities to confirm their social superiority by demonstrating a leisurely lifestyle. This was calculated to betoken a gentility which was exemplified in the amateur ethic and institutionalised in the amateur club, and it is in the evolution of both that we shall turn in the following chapter.

NOTES

1. R. Rees, 'The development of physical recreation in Liverpool' (M.A. Liverpool University, 1968): 'towards the end of the eighteenth century there was a recreational life which included boating, cricket and bowls'.

2. Edward Harbottle Grimston, *Cricket Diary for 1824* which itemises 55 games attended during the season ranging from Sheffield to Sussex.

3. Report of one man's gambling on cock fighting at Belford, Northumberland, between 23 March and 25 May 1785 indicating an overall loss of £18 12 0d.

4. See the *Cumberland and Westmorland Wrestling Society in London* notes for 1871 citing wrestling had taken place at the Angel at Islington from 1775 and latterly at Islington Agricultural Hall. Cumberland and Westmorland 'back hold style' supplanted the Cornish 'all in' style which degenerated into brawls.

5. Conspicuous consumption and social advancement are particularly evident in the stress laid by club members on correct dress. Some examples follow: *The Staffordshire Bowmen* of 1791 dressed in single-breasted green frock coats, white waistcoats, white trousers, white silk stockings, white neckerchief, dark fur hat, a buff girdle with a green worsted tassle.

   The *Lambton Tally Ho Club* of 1790 had an undress uniform of a plain scarlet coat with white buttons and a dress uniform of a black coat with gilt buttons, with a white upper waistcoat and a scarlet undercoat.

   The *Dresden Boat Club* of 1839 used a plain blue flannel jacket, broad brimmed straw hat and a dark blue and white bird-eye neckerchief.

   These and many others helped to advertise the social distinctiveness of their wearers. The etiquette of dress was further formalised in the public schools where fines were levied for 'improper dress' and when pupils graduated to Oxbridge they took this affectation with them into the sporting clubs of college life. Thus endorsed and confirmed it found its way into the rules and regulations of those clubs established by the Oxbridge men when they returned to their home towns.

6. Particularly on the River Thames the demand for boats became a craze towards the end of the century. Rowing tours from Oxford to London became fashionable and in 1898 the Thames Conservancy figures show that 10,482 pleasure boats were registered. A similar trend is discernible elsewhere around the country at Huntingdon, Gloucester, Lincoln, etc.

7. Statement to a public meeting at the Corn Exchange, Worksop on 10 Nov. 1863.

8. T. Wright, *Some habits and customs of the working classes by a journeyman engineer, 1867* (Kelly, NY, 1967). The Christian ethic found expression in many other recreational activities including the formation of football clubs, e.g. Aston Villa (Wesleyan), Bolton (C of E), Everton (Congregationalist) and J. Golby and A. Purdue in *The Civilization of the Crowd 1750–1900* (Batsford, 1984) note the Christian origins for walking tours, rail excursions (p. 98) brass bands and choral societies (p. 106).

9. A. White, *Efficiency and Empire* (Longman Green & Co., 1901), makes the point that of 10,000 offering to join up in October 1899 in Manchester alone, 8,000 were found to be unfit for active service and only 1,200 attained even moderate military standards of physical fitness.

10. Durham branch of the *National Playing Fields Association*, inaugural minutes, 8 Feb. 1927.

11. Bolton branch of the *National Playing Fields Association*, inaugural minutes, 17 Aug. 1927.

12. See a detailed analysis of the effects of rail on the development clubs and regattas in N. Wigglesworth, *The Social History of English Rowing* (Frank Cass, 1992), Chapter 7.

13. *The Greville Memoirs*, ed. Fulford (Batsford, 1963), entry for 18 July 1837.

14. *Thames Rowing Club* minutes, Notice for March 1861: 'The rowing train leaves Waterloo at 6.34 p.m.; crews will be formed at 7 p.m.'

15. *Society of Staffordshire Bowmen* minutes, 2 June 1864 and 25 Aug. 1870 shoots at Uttoxeter and Alton Towers dependent on the trains to transport the 90 and 200

participants respectively.

16. For example, *Fambridge Yacht Club of Essex* list of members for the years 1898 to 1914 shows that 50 per cent of subscribers with boats moored at Fambridge were domiciled in London EC or NW. The other 50 per cent were retired and lived locally.

17. *Warrington Anglers' Association*, Rules for 1903 include rule 29 'Membership cards to be shown when applying for cheap tickets'; Annual Report for 1911: 750 cards were applied for.

18. *The Times*, 15 Feb. 1870 (4d), Skating and Cricket on Mere Fen. Special trains from Cambridge with skating for cash prizes.

19. For example, the Diary of the Master of the *North Staffordshire Hounds* 1906–1907 and 1926–1927. There were also bad days: 8 Nov. 1926 'Awful day, no scent, no foxes and soaking wet'. Despite the barren days the hunt managed to average one kill per outing: 86 for 1906/7 and 67 for 1926/7.

20. *Vale of Derwentwater Angling Association* minutes, 30 Aug. 1851 and a balance sheet showing 46 members at 2/6d, 20 at 5/- with several gentlemen donating £7, £5, £2 and £1.

21. A point worth making here is the community of membership which existed between the various clubs and societies. With specific reference to the Mutual Improvement Society formed by Richard and Charles Tuson and Joseph Hesketh all three of leading local families, we find that these three had a hand in establishing several other societies in Preston and were members of many others. Similarly in Warrington club records show common membership of bowling, cricket and rowing clubs and again in Lancaster with the Literary and Philosophical Society, Cricket and Rowing clubs and so on wherever membership lists exist.

22. See a 'Chapter of Autobiography' in the *Fortnightly Review* by Charles Wordsworth, Vol. 40, 1883, pp. 50–97.

23. F.V. Morley, *The River Thames* (Methuen, 1926).

24. It is interesting to note that one of the latest exercise machines, the rowing ergometer, is now the subject of national, international and world championships.

25. *Bolton Rugby Union Football Club* minutes, 9 May 1904.
    Trowbridge Recreation Club minutes, 7 Oct. 1913.
    Warrington Public Parks Bowling League minutes, Constitution, 1929.
    Sunningdale Ladies Golf Club minutes, 7 March 1932.
    Mass Observation Archive, Survey of Worcester, October 1940.
    This last source also makes the comment that unusually 'a characteristic of this war is that people do play games without a sense of guilt or fear of the white feather'.

26. The entry free for the club was designed simply to pay back the purchase price of the boat which remained the property of the 'primitive members' who paid the club's expenses monthly on an equal basis. *Dresden Boat Club* rules for 1839.

    The original 'one boat' clubs were so popular because they so conveniently catered for small social groups, usually five, seven or nine. Indeed the Lancaster Rowing Club owed its very existence to the dissolution of Lancaster Cricket Club since the group of friends who had formed it regularly failed to find a full eleven to play and so disbanded to establish a rowing club where as few as five would suffice. *Lancaster Rowing Club* minutes, 20 Sept. 1842.

27. *Society of Staffordshire Bowmen* minutes, 25 Aug. 1870.

28. *Alcester Cricket Club* for April 1861.

29. *The Times*, 19 Oct. 1846 (5a).

30. A good example of Greville's attitude is to be found in his diary for 17 Sept. 1823 where he writes 'what concerns me most is winning and losing since I am a very considerable loser by this year and getting H with child' (Lady Graham, wife of a friend). *The Shooting Diary* of Charles Shaw MP for 5 Sept. 1785 mentions 'dining with the Justice and learned of Jenny who lived with Mr. Hewitt [Shaw's best friend and shooting companion] drowned in the river being with child and forced by the severity of her family to take this desperate step'. Such excerpts, featuring another of the gentry's favourite recreations, indicate differing social attitudes: Lady Graham's child although identified was brought up along with her others whilst Jenny as a woman of no status

would have received little or no support from Hewitt or anyone else.

31. *Gatewood Fox Hounds* list of subscribers for 1836 includes five Lords, one Lady, one Knight, two Earls and two Honourables.

The *Norfolk Fox Hounds* were established in June 1830 to give local gentry the opportunity to hunt without having to travel far. It was formed under the patronage of the Marquis Cholmondeley who allowed extensive drawing of coverts on his land to encourage the growth of the fox population – minutes, 8 June 1830.

32. *Greville Memoirs*, ed. Fulford (Batsford, 1963), 22 Nov. 1845.

33. The incidence of church support for sporting clubs is astonishing. Of the 120 associations looked at in the present survey, 86 had priests as officers, committee, patrons or president.

34. *Public Notice* of a meeting at the Guildhall, Walsall, 2 June 1846.

35. For example, the Middlesbrough Temperance Society found that on Sundays four times as many people went to the public house as to church. Quoted in *At the Works*, Lady Bell (Arnold, 1907).

36. *Isle of Wight Observer*, 29 Dec. 1877.

37. This (p. 64) and much else relevant to the topic quoted in M. Quinlan, *Victorian Prelude, A History of English Manners 1700–1830* (Columbia U.P., 1941).

38. So momentous was this that 'The First Sunday Outing' was captured in oils by Arthur Spooner; this was kept by the club and sold in 1984 for £90,000 which secured the club's future.

39. For example, *Walthamstow Cycling Club* rule 3 1878 and *Worcester Tricycle Club* rule 5 1884; participation for Sunday runs for the Tricycle club in 1884 were 56 in April, 18 in May and 42 in June, averaging nine per outing.

40. Even a stalwart of the Establishment like Arthur Conan Doyle wrote to *The Times*, 23 May 1924 (15d), to advocate the opening of the Empire Exhibition at Wembley on Sundays so that 'the poorer people might have a chance of seeing the show'.

41. Lady Greville, *The Gentlewomen's Book of Sports* (Spalding, 1880).

42. M. Maudsley, 'Sex in Mind in Education' in *Fortnightly Review*, Vol. XV, pp. 446–83.

43. There was always fulsome praise for the ladies' 'untiring labours in the tea tent' in Annual Reports. This quoted from *West Kent Wanderers Cricket Club*, 24 Nov. 1913.

44. *The Times*, 7 Sept. 1929 (6a).

45. *Bolton Cricket Club* minutes, 12 March 1936.

46. *The Times*, 2 Sept. 1939 (IId).

47. See, for example, 'Sport at Oxbridge Women's Colleges to 1914', K. McCrone, *British Journal of Sports History*, Vol. 3, No. 2 (September 1986) – primarily lawn tennis, hockey, golf, rowing and bicycling.

48. A universal rule here quoted from *Lancaster Golf Club* Annual Report for 1913.

49. The reason for this appears to be that Sunningdale Ladies Golf Club was made up almost exclusively of wives of Sunningdale GC committee members, namely Mrs Raymond Atherton, Mrs Dudley Charles, Mrs John Fleming, Mrs Sydney Marsham, Mrs Edward Villiers, etc., all of whom were co-operatively non-feminist. The earliest women's club was St Andrews (1867) followed by Mussleborough and Westward Ho! (both 1872).

50. *Manchester Guardian*, 12 May 1914 (7e), 'Mixed bathing in Manchester'.

51. *Darlington Cycling Club* minutes, 11 March 1919. *Bristol Cycle Touring Club* minutes, 4 Feb. 1919.

52. E. Roberts, *A Woman's Place – an oral history of working class women 1890–1940* (Blackwell, 1984).

53. *Mass Observation Archive*, University of Sussex, 'Report on the attitudes to the continuation of sport in wartime', April 1942.

6
Amateurism

No manner of artificer or craftsman be allowed
to play on pain of 20 shillings fine ... every
nobleman and other landowners might play
without penalty.

(Act of 1541 concerning unlawful sports)

To allow a mixing of professional and amateur
is as senseless and impractical as the negro
fraternising with the refined and cultured
members of the civilised world.

(Caspar Whitney, *Sporting Pilgrimage*, 1894)

Amateurism derived from an eighteenth-century connoisseurship of
fine and polite arts by gentlefolk who dabbled nonchalantly and
without desire for excellence of performance. This explained their
disdain for those who strove mightily for precisely this, namely the
professional and quasi-amateur who by definition therefore could not
be gentlemen. Trollope conveys this disdain perfectly in his *British
Sports and Pastimes* of 1868 where he says that playing billiards is the
amusement of a gentleman but to play billiards eminently well is the
life's work of a man who in learning to do so can hardly have continued
to be a gentleman 'in the best sense'. The prejudice against such
performance was underpinned by a similar distaste for trade learned
from a classical education which stressed the Athenian concept of
a social class of people born to rule which was developed by the
Victorians into a religious orthodoxy extolling the benefits of a strict
social hierarchy. This in turn produced an amateur ethic which
preached the exclusion of the professional at any cost, an exclusion
which was facilitated by the peculiarly feudal nature of English
society. The social and cultural apartheid based upon the ownership of
land had constituted English society for centuries when the rise of
mercantilism threatened to undermine it in the eighteenth century.
Despite gross social, political and economic inequalities, the ruling

class in Georgian Britain remained entrenched and immune from contemporary revolutionary trends, a situation explained by the deferential nature of the English character, the flexibility of the ruling class and the prospect of social mobility opened up by pioneering industrialisation.[1] The rulers consolidated their positions by virtually taking over the great public schools: in 1700 only 17 per cent of peers were at Eton, Harrow, Winchester and Westminster while in 1780 there were 72 per cent. By 1807 the peerage controlled the election of a third of Members of Parliament, with other sons taking up top jobs elsewhere through patronage and purchase.[2] This class had a daily round of amusements which supplanted the traditional gentlemen's pursuits of dinners, playhouse and gambling, and in sporting terms were the first people to make active sport a gentlemanly activity by appropriating some activities like bowling, cricket and rowing at school and coffee house levels.[3]

This appropriation signalled a gentrification of the sports involved and so the rules and regulations in force were refined to meet the supposed higher moral standards of those newly participating. The 'New Rules and Orders to be Observed' at the Rugeley Bowling Green in 1776 contained no fewer than 45 laws, including sanctions against betting, blaspheming or any activity 'likely to be unsuitable for civill company'. As the activity became fashionable in town at coffee houses, 'Rules and Instructions for the Art of Bowling' was published in 1786 by a Society of Gentlemen which sought to 'remove doubts and prevent disputes becoming necessary'. The boat clubs of the Star and Robin Hood coffee houses contended with similar clubs on the Chelsea reach of the River Thames in 'straight away' racing which placed scientific oarsmanship above the fouling manoeuvres current in watermen's races popular at the time; and in cricket the gentle concept of fair play overriding a winning approach can be seen in the advice given in the Hambledon Club's minutes of May 1774 'that every cricket player that gets thirty runs shall be obliged to give up his batt for the innings'. As the eighteenth century wore on and the number of public school graduates increased, the greater became the desire to exclude socially unacceptable elements from the field of play. In cricket there was mounting disapproval of those gentlemen who played with those 'not compatible with their rank and station'.[4] In rowing the professional steersmen were gradually ousted, and in horse-racing the Newmarket stewards began their successful campaign to dominate the sport by winning the legal right to 'warn off' any undesirables from the Heath which nevertheless continued to be open public land.

Despite the growing inclination to exclude those not considered

suitable from their sporting activities, the gentlemen maintained an attitude of *noblesse oblige* in patronising the sporting endeavours of their social inferiors, with much of their wagering on tradesmen's 'wrangles' being praised as 'finding employment for the labouring mechanic'.[5] This was the contemporary urban equivalent of an age-old feudal obligation placed upon aristocratic landowners to support tenants in time of need which also customarily extended to sponsorship of local sporting events.[6] It is, however, difficult to escape the conclusion that the new class of public school educated gentlemen adapted age-old customs solely to develop their own social exclusivity rather than to meet any social responsibility. Although the desire to keep the lower orders at arm's length derived partly from sheer snobbery, it was also regarded as a necessary form of social containment and control in an era of revolution and unrest at home and abroad. A breakdown in class structure was seen as the precursor of anarchy and many thought that the demand for an extension of the electoral franchise following the Napoleonic Wars which was granted in 1832 was the beginning of the end of civilisation as they had known it, even though the reform maintained the vote in the hands of the materially prosperous. A letter in *The Times* of 13 April 1840 signed by 40 clergymen expressed the fears of the establishment in all its forms in noting the 'fearful progress of socialism, a system which tramples all decency underfoot and sets lawful authority at defiance bringing bloodshed, anarchy and ruin'.[7] Set against this background, the amateurs' fight for survival must have seemed to those involved a struggle for a civilisation based upon 'hereditry, rank and nobility of blood as the essence of christian privilege' against those who 'honoured no one except for his own merit and his own deeds'.[8] Very soon more social progress further threatened the position of the gentleman amateur: the Ten Hours Act of 1847 freed workers on a Saturday for the pursuit of greater leisure, the Reform Acts of 1867 and 1884 extended the franchise to various classes of working men, the Union Chargeability Act of 1876 allowed a greater mobility of labour, the Labour Representation Act of 1869 promoted working class Members of Parliament, and the Education Act of 1870 extended the educational franchise deep into the lower classes. By 1888 Mrs Beeton, that keen observer of the domestic scene, could comment with some truth that events were day by day 'removing the landmarks between the mistress and her maid, the master and his man'.[9] But it was precisely these landmarks that the gentleman was determined to maintain in his sporting life.

The initial battle was joined not with the out and out professional

who emerged later in the nineteenth century but with the quasi-amateur who may or may not have taken payment for his on-field activities but was most definitely regarded as socially inferior. The genesis of this approach lay in the perceived link between popular recreation and civil disturbance which threatened the status quo and reached back through the centuries to the times of prohibited and unlawful sports. Working men and women took full advantage of the long-established holiday sports and such commitment allied to the ever-present availability of alcohol resulted in normally good-natured but excessively boisterous behaviour. However, in the context of the social unrest which continued for many years after the battle of Waterloo, many such sports were curtailed or barred entirely by the authorities as possible sources of revolutionary fervour, one example of which occurred at Berkamstead Common in 1819. The sports here as elsewhere had taken place 'time out of mind' but in this particular year Lord Berkamstead directed his steward to caution all persons from attending under pain of prosecution. The local constable inquired why he was taking this attitude, only to be told that the Lord of the Manor feared mass trespass by 'idle people' but was finally prevailed upon to allow 'cricketting as usual' by a prominent local resident whilst maintaining his ban on 'women bruising for a prize, trap ball, quoits and Dandy Horses' and prohibiting any extension of licensing hours.[10] During this post-war era it was therefore a small step in the imagination for the new class of gentlemen to extend a presumed guilt by association from working people at rural sports to tradesmen at organised sports. It was this synthesis which provided them with a Christian and patriotic justification for actions which they were inclined to take in any event for social and cultural reasons. This is exemplified in the attitude taken by the Warrington Regatta secretary when he complained in 1844 that 'the public notice of rural sports with my name on it (erroneously) will militate against the good opinions of regatta subscribers who heartily disapprove of them'.[11] If we stay with rowing for a while since it was in this sport that a particularly rigorous social apartheid was enforced, we can see the individual application of personal antipathy to members of the despised class of quasi-amateur in the form of the crew of The Wave at the Lancaster Regatta of 1844. Having been accused of fouling, this crew of 'mechanics' was refused the prize of their event to which their captain took considerable exception, explaining in a letter to the organising committee 'that compared to you I am but a humble individual but there was great dissatisfaction that the prize for Amateurs was 20 guineas whilst that for the poorer class was but £3 showing anything but a liberal spirit

towards those in a lower sphere of life'. No reply was sent but the minutes of the regatta for 30 September contain the committee's disdainful response: 'No notice whatever was taken of this most despicable attempt to discredit the regatta which has been conducted in every respect to the satisfaction of all'. Henley Regatta, the leading event, managed to maintain its gentlemanly character by dispensing with the aid of taverns or public houses;[12] and the leading club, London Rowing Club, secured its social purity by making a strict division between gentlemen amateurs and tradesmen amateurs and ensuring that 'the barriers between them were not broken down'.[13]

In cricket the tone of the game had been set by gentlemen since the late eighteenth century at least, so that by 1853 *The Times* was able to praise the past season as played more closely in the true spirit upon which the health of the game depended, knowing that this had been achieved by the imposition from above of an etiquette and hierarchy entirely consistent with its own prejudices. This had not been brought about without some dissent and undesirable elements were excluded from participating, and on occasions from even watching, which was made easy by the early enclosure of cricket grounds. In Newcastle in 1858 hordes of working men were denied access to the cricket ground on the pretext that they were 'not respectable',[14] and it is significant that of all sports it was cricket that last dropped the distinction between players and gentlemen in 1963.

The *Saturday Review* of 20 April 1867 stated very clearly the view taken by gentlemen: 'The facts of his being civil and never having competed for money are NOT sufficient to make a man a gentleman as well as an amateur', and as we have seen gentlemen amateurs could and did compete for money without prejudicing, at least in their own eyes, their amateur status. The argument sometimes employed to explain the exclusion of the quasi-amateur, semi-professional and professional was his higher level of expertise which would render unfair any competition with him, and yet at the same time many amateurs openly boasted of triumphs over the professional and there is plenty of evidence for this in cricket, rowing and horse-racing.[15] The inescapable conclusion is that social prejudice alone informed the Victorian attitude towards the working man and all his activities, but his very exclusion only encouraged the growth of alternative forms of sport which futher threatened the amateur ethic. The truly amateur tradesman, not only feeling that he might as well be hanged for a sheep as a lamb but also seeing his social superiors winning prize money, became more, not less, inclined to supplement his wages with sporting earnings and an increasingly competitive leisure market eventually produced the full-time professional. 'The curse of gate money which enabled the man of lower rank to earn large salaries'[16] was often cited by governing bodies as evidence that the priority given to spectators ('Spectatorism') was undermining the true nature of sport ('Corinthianism') and encouraging greater numbers of working men than ever before to contemplate sport as an occupation.

The first move towards this came with the demand for 'broken time' payments, for although payment in the past had often come in the form of prizes, compensation for lost working time was seen as the equivalent of wages and as such was vigorously opposed by the amateur governing bodies. Such payments had been made in cricket since the middle of the nineteenth century at least, were formerly sanctioned as wages in association football in 1885 and began to appear in rugby union football during the 1870s when local derbies in the north of England were drawing crowds of 6,000 compared to 4,000 at international matches in London. The men who played in the north were miners, mill hands, foundry workers and tradesmen who earned perhaps 25s for a five and a half day week and who could ill afford to lose half a day's pay to play football. The gentlemen in charge of sports like rowing, tennis and golf found it relatively easy to marginalise the artisans since both financial and social strictures excluded them at club level and in association football and cricket they had been largely incorporated at appropriately subservient levels,[17] but in rugby, whose overwhelming popularity lay in the north, it proved impossible for gentlemen in London to enforce their will. These gentlemen of the Rugby Football Union disapproved of nationwide cup or league competitions but allowed various county committees to exercise their jurisdiction, with the result that the Yorkshire committee established the Yorkshire Challenge Cup which became an obsessive focus for teams and set a northern precedent which encouraged fierce competition, huge crowds and, inevitably, substantial payments to players for expenses and broken time. This led to stringent rules concerning the transfer of players being introduced in 1888 which were ferociously applied in the north by the reverend Frank Marshall, headmaster of Almondbury Grammar School, Huddersfield, and in 1893 a bye-law which stressed the amateur nature of the game and the confirmation of its headquarters in London 'where all general meetings shall be held'. Representatives of several northern clubs placed a motion at one of these general meetings on 20 September 1893 asking that 'players be allowed compensation for bona fide loss of time', only to be rebuffed with the reply that 'the above principle is contrary to the true interest of the game and its spirit' which was endorsed by 282 votes to 136.

7. Taken from *The Yorkshireman* magazine, this cartoon illustrates the contentious issue of broken time payments for northern rugby players. The Reverend Frank Marshall, witch-finder general for the Rugby Football Union, and James Miller of the Yorkshire Committee and champion of working-man rugby are but thinly disguised.

Further, more punitive anti-professional bye-laws ratified in 1895[18] led to the famous meeting at the George Hotel, Huddersfield on 29 August, when a Northern Union was established which nevertheless 'repudiated any idea of professionalism and was determined to punish any departure from this principle'[19] whilst at the same time making such departures inevitable by inaugurating a northern league and two further cup competitions. It was such behaviour that led amateur gentlemen to conclude that there was 'an inclination to kick over the traces in the provinces where some very crude notions of amateurism and sport still prevail particularly in athletics, cycling and football'[20] and led them to redouble their efforts to retain overall control. At first the Northern Union took infinite pains to exclude the true professional from its activities, and recourse to its minutes shows a remarkable conscientiousness in identifying those players not conforming to the principle of payment for broken time only.[21] Nevertheless, the sheer scale of the task was beyond its limited administrative and financial capacity so that by 1900 the regular weekly issue of permits to play fell by the wayside to be replaced by the occasional prosecution of particularly blatant examples of professional behaviour.[22]

As far as the governing bodies were concerned this kicking over the traces had the effect of damaging the very nature and spirit of sport as they understood it and was held responsible for the decline in British sporting fortunes. This was first remarked upon in cricket when the national team lost to the Australians in 1882, a mortifying defeat notified in the obituary columns of the *Sporting Times* of 6 September and to be recalled some years later when Leander Club lost to Harvard University at the Henley Regatta of 1914 by an insertion in *The Times* of 6 July which commemorated 'the memory of British rowing which passed away at Henley on July 4th'. This sporting decline, also noted in athletics, cycling, football, rugby and even bowling[23] was attributed to 'the accursed greed for gold' which diminished the available pool of truly amateur home-grown talent whilst strengthening foreign opposition which failed to adhere to strict Corinthianism. One of De Coubertin's prime motives in his promotion of a renewed Olympic Games following his study of English sport in the 1890s was to support the ideal of Corinthianism and combat the rise of professionalism, but unfortunately it was to have exactly the opposite effect. Disappointing British results at the Games of 1908 and 1912 led to further anxieties concerning the growth of Sunday play, fuelling feelings that sport had gone too far in pursuit of excellence and that it all reflected a horrible decadence in English society. This placed the governing bodies of sport in a cruel dilemma which left them a choice of taking up the foreign challenge by adopting less than amateur methods or with-drawing from international events altogether and satisfying themselves with lower quality domestic competition in which gentlemen could meet gentlemen on a level playing field.[24] The First World War inter-vened before any resolution of this dilemma could be reached but the war itself helped to harden the attitudes of many against any dilution of the true sporting spirit which was held responsible for victory over an underhand and unsportsmanlike enemy.[25] However, further depressing results at post-war Olympic Games resulted in a loosening of amateur principles, not only in the professionalisation of training methods but also in the acceptance that the payment of certain expenses was justified in pursuit of the best possible performances.[26] Immedi-ately following the war there was a temporary return to a purer amateurism in domestic competition due to demobilisation procedures keeping many professionals in uniform much longer than necessary, but the inexorable progress of professionalisation continued with renewed vigour during the depression years of the 1920s and 1930s.[27]

Given this trend it is not surprising that these years saw a re-assertion of amateur exclusivity that had begun in earnest at the beginning of the nineteenth century. As we have seen, this exclusion of undesirables was often of a physical nature so that at the Fulwood racecourse in Preston in 1805 we find that on 9 July a resolution was passed 'to keep the course shares from passing into the hands of those not approved by the members' so that 'none but noblemen and gentlemen should be admitted to the enclosure'. Later that same year there is evidence in the minutes that undesirables were ejected from the newly erected grandstand for 'foul language and improper behaviour' and that even a Mrs Brierley and her entourage were subject to an 'action of ejectment' for some unspoken, perhaps unspeakable, activity. Similarly in Darlington where the local society of archers used an enclosed shooting compound, it was relatively easy to exclude those thought unsuitable for genteel company, as on 8 July 1797 was a Mr Hodgson who was expelled for 'having made use of very improper language and abused and ill treated all the gentlemen present without an apology'. Such physical exclusions and expulsions were facilitated wherever enclosures were used so that the authorities in cricket, racing, early archery, bowling and even rowing at certain venues were able to police the entry of spectators and participants alike in order to maintain the tone and style of play to their satis-faction. But of course there were other subtler means of exclusion utilised by these and other sports. Certain forms of language and behaviour were considered compulsory for association members, as were very particular styles of uniform dress, and subscription levels precluded from membership all but the well-to-do so that membership cards became vital 'in order to prevent all objectionable persons entering under the plea of belonging to the club'.[28] Some clubs, like the Dresden Boat Club whose membership 'shall not exceed six on any consideration whatever', simply restricted affiliation to manageable proportions by word of mouth recommendation, but all the gentlemen's clubs operated a more or less strict black ball system of election in which any current member could retard or prevent future memberships.[29] Application for membership usually entailed filling out a form which required the applicant to provide several personal references, his banking details, and particularly in the latter part of the nineteenth century his occupation or profession, since at this time there were many well-to-do tradesmen clammering to join the more respectable clubs whose members generally wished to exclude them on social and cultural grounds.[30] This often caused considerable ill feeling amongst members who disagreed about the desirability of admitting applicants and many minutes show this in operation, for example those of the Astley Bowling Club for May 1905 which feature protracted discussions concerning the membership of Messrs Ashworth and Fletcher, the latter being denied entry due to his perceived social failings.[31]

Much mid-Victorian exclusivity derived from the uniqueness of public school culture which informed most amateur sport initially in the south of England but later throughout the country and was thus particularly strong in those areas which fed the schools. One such area was Blackheath, described by a youthful resident of the 1870s as a 'glorious place for children with safe residential roads fragrant with lime blossom and gardens full of flowering trees and shrubs',[32] and it is not therefore surprising that some of the earliest sporting clubs in cricket, hockey, football, rugby and running were established in this locality by boys returning from the public schools. It was in these areas that the code of amateurism embodied in public school games met and merged with the growth of affluent suburban recreation to form an alliance of wealth and birth which infused sport with a new idealism whilst segregating the elite from members of the lower classes participating in the same form of exercise. Exactly this fusion produced the Football Association in 1863 from a meeting of old boys' clubs in the London area which agreed upon terms of competition whilst endeavouring to restrict participation in the game to their own sort. Even rock-climbing, which is regarded today as the epitome of egalitarianism, began in a similar way in 1857 when the Alpine Club was established by Leslie Stephen, an Oxford professor, which led to a vogue in mountaineering amongst intellectuals but continued to exclude those in trade until well into the twentieth century.[33] Whilst it was relatively easy to employ exclusion tactics at club level, it became virtually impossible to do so in competition where tradesmen amateurs could not be fairly excluded from open competition with gentlemen amateurs. The sporting governing bodies sought to overcome this difficulty by continually redefining amateurism in increasingly exclusive terms, so that by the 1870s the Amateur Athletics Association had finally decided that an amateur was 'any person who has never competed in any open competition or for public money or for admission money or with professionals for a prize and who has never taught or assisted in the pursuit of athletic exercises as a means of livelihood'. This definition was adopted by other governing bodies of sport as a basis for their own strictures and *The Times* spoke for them all in a leading article of 26 April 1880 when it proclaimed that 'the outsiders, artisans, mechanics and suchlike troublesome persons can have no place found for them. To keep them out is a thing desirable on every account and so no base mechanic arms need be suffered to thrust themselves in here'. Guilt by association was a dominant theme at this time so that any player competing with a quasi-amateur or professional would himself become contaminated; even the acceptance of genuine expenses was sufficient to exclude players and teams from strictly amateur events. Americans were particularly prone to come unstuck on this point with both the American lacrosse team of 1885 and the Vesper Boat Club of 1905 being banned for 100 years by the English Lacrosse Union and Henley Regatta respectively for receiving commercially raised funds for travelling expenses. Both exclusion orders were rescinded when English governing bodies themselves began to sanction such expenses within their own organisations during the 1920s and 1930s, and in modern times it has become commonplace for such bodies to provide expenses to foreign associations to encourage their participation in domestic events.[34]

These rigorous definitions of amateurism allowed event organisers to demarcate competition into several categories, thus enabling the gentleman amateur to maintain his distance from open competition when he thought appropriate. This divisiveness affected every form of sporting competition, even down to the level of rural sport like those at Linton in Cambridgeshire where in 1891 the events were segregated into those for tradesmen, cottagers, labourers, labouring boys and amateurs. At club level there was a heightened awareness of social acceptability so that, for instance, the new Blackheath Harriers established in 1868 stipulated acceptance of 'gentlemen only' as befitted its location and function as a source of winter training for rowing club members, and not surprisingly it provided the Amateur Athletic Association with its first secretary in 1880. Clubs even changed their names to indicate a move away from questionable activities and towards respectability as outlined by their governing bodies; so we find the Eccentric Bicycle Club renamed as the Walthamstow Bicycle Club in 1878 and the Jolly Anglers becoming the Warrington Angling Association in 1891, and hordes of clubs added the word 'amateur' to their titles during the 1870s and 1880s to underline their bona fides. Many golf clubs inserted into their rules the information that 'the etiquette of golf as laid down by the Royal and Ancient Golf Club has been adopted as a bye-law' to reassure potential members of their social credentials, and some clubs even went so far as to specify suitable occupations for members, although neither was strictly necessary as the cost of the game was quite sufficient to limit membership.[35] Sailing clubs found themselves in an awkward position as many followed a centuries-old tradition of allowing professionals to take the helm in offshore races, something which became increasingly unacceptable during the middle of the Victorian era and was positively frowned upon after the barring of those 'in and about boats' by the Amateur Rowing Association in 1883. The Warrington Sailing Club in 1886 consisted of 'amateurs only' and rule two excluded all help from watermen who were defined as 'persons who had at any time earned their living on trading vessels'; but the Fambridge Yacht Club in Essex tempered this exclusion by stipulating yachts must be 'steered by members of the club and no paid hand in any race shall touch the tiller after the first gun'.[36] No sport was exempt from rigorous self-appraisal in the pursuit of amateur purity and even the small provincial clubs generally followed the line laid down by their masters in London: the Tyldesley Swimming Club of Lancashire in 1877 disqualified 'those coming under the term professional' from any club competition after the establishment of the Metropolitan Swimming Clubs Association in 1869; the Warrington Bowling League blacklisting 21 players following the inauguration of the English Bowling Union in 1903; and the Cestreham Bicycle Club in Buckinghamshire immediately adopting the regulations of the National Cycling Union in 1878.

The exclusion of the quasi-amateur from sport organised by the gentlemen of metropolitan-based governing bodies had the effect of fragmenting the domestic sporting scene into separate factions, nowhere more obviously than in rugby football which split into amateur and professional producing the Rugby League in 1922. Elsewhere there was similar evidence of sporting apartheid. In rowing the intran-

11th Race. Single-handed. Professional. 3rd Aug 1889.

8. Professionalisation was not confined to the major team games and here is an example of a yachting race for professionals on Lake Windermere. Most of the helmsmen would have been Morecambe Bay fishermen hired to represent local businessmen who would back them for large sums of money as a weekend diversion.

sigence of the Amateur Rowing Association in banning working men from affiliated clubs and events led to the establishment of the National Amateur Rowing Association in 1890, which catered for all those excluded by the strict code of amateurism then in force and enabled rowing to flourish in the north of the country where it was in danger of being restricted to gentlemen only. In cricket the Lancashire and Yorkshire professional cricket leagues were established during the 1870s to suit the needs of factory workers, attracting large crowds and producing some very fine players despite the contempt in which they were held by the grandees of the MCC. In athletics the northern clubs formed themselves into the Northern Counties Athletic Association and concluded that 'they could very well do without the South and hoped that the Northern members will treat the Southerners with silent contempt' for their metropolitanism.[37] In swimming the same southern arrogance produced the Northern Counties Amateur Swimming Association when representatives of 27 clubs met at the Commerical Hotel in Manchester in April 1889 in response to the Amateur Swimming Association's indifference to supporting events outside London. The Northern Cross Country Association established in 1882 encouraged the participation of quasi-amateurs in direct contravention of Amateur Athletic Association laws and harrier's conventions; and the London-based National Cyclist's Union had an outright ban on trialling and road racing which only encouraged the growth of professionalism, particularly in Manchester.

The north–south sporting split reflected a social, cultural and economic apartheid apparent elsewhere in society in living standards, political affiliations and daily custom, which became ever more pronounced over the turn of the century, through the First World War and into the 1920s. The General Strike of 1926 was a symptom of 'the post war class cleavage from which the country suffered'[38] and the exclusion of working people from full participation in organised sport was only a reflection of their routine exclusion from social and economic benefits enjoyed by others. With this in mind it was hoped that a general socialisation might have followed a debate on the relaxation of the amateur rule in sport held in the House of Commons,[39] but this had to wait until a Labour government took office in 1945.

Despite the class cleavage and the cultural and geographical divisions, there were bastions of amateurism in the regions and these were usually centred upon particular clubs constituted of the right class of person: for example the Manchester Cricket Club, the Royal Chester Rowing Club, the Northern Lawn Tennis Club, Gosforth Rugby Union Club, the Warrington Swimming Club and the Royal

Lytham and St Anne's Golf Club. These organisations administered sport in their areas with a strictness which commended itself to the governing bodies in London and were often rewarded for their zealousness with prestigious events such as international rowing trialling on the River Dee, the Northern Lawn Tennis Championships modelled on Wimbledon, and Olympic swimming trials. Such happenings only served to expose the malaise of much grass-roots sport caused by unsympathetic governance from London, and many sports complained bitterly of harsh amateur rulings pointing out that these caused support for their events 'to leech away to more popular branches of athletics'.[40] As we have seen before, the unbending attitude of the gentlemen tended to force many participants into the opposition camp which gradually became sufficiently powerful to modify or ignore the less sensible amateur regulations. Many clubs sought protection from creeping professionalism by affiliating themselves to an increasing number of governing associations, a process initiated by the aristocracy who formed the Jockey Club in 1750 and to which all the major sports had acceded by the 1880s, leaving minor sports like rambling (1891), skiff racing (1901) and bowling (1903) finally to endorse by establishing their associations.[41]

The new amateur rules percolated down from the first governing bodies often through regional associations to the clubs at grass-roots level, at every stage increasing the growth of central control. The Jockey Club sought to curb what it regarded as licentiousness by establishing the new Rules for Racing in 1832, which although only applicable to Newmarket were recommended to stewards of other courses for the sake of uniformity and certainty. Soon after this race authorities adopted the new rules and public notices advertising the meetings would usually stipulate 'All Rules and Regulations at Newmarket will be adhered to',[42] since without such adherence the Jockey Club refused to arbitrate in any disputes arising from the events. A similar function for cricket clubs was provided by the Marylebone Cricket Club and many new clubs stipulated their allegiance to 'the Laws and Regulations of the M.C.C.' or their closest area representative; so we find, for example, the Huyton Cricket Club basing its rules on those of the Liverpool Cricket Club which like those of other MCC-approved clubs regulated general conduct such as time keeping, appropriate dress and acceptable language.[43] Catford Cycling Club became stalwarts of the National Cyclists Union, joining up at its inaugural meeting in 1886 with each member paying the capitation fee, and later it joined two further governing associations which confirmed its amateur and recreational status.[44] In rugby football it became of paramount importance to demonstrate amateur credentials and the Rugby Union, usually through its representatives at county level, often fined clubs which broached amateur etiquette and pressurised them to initiate or maintain affiliation, particularly at times when subscription levels increased to meet greater administrative costs. Following one such chastisement consequent upon virulent internal disagreement, the Sharpness Rugby Union Football Club finally came into line on 10 August 1895, recognising unanimously 'the benefits to the amateur game of belonging to the County Rugby Union'. Similar sentiments were expressed with perhaps more reason by the Bolton Rugby Union Football Club which took the unusual step of affiliating directly to the Rugby Union in London and the Lancashire Rugby Union in Manchester.[45] Even bowling, that most sedate of sports, suffered its schisms as the crown green game in the north developed by attracting quasi-amateurs to its sponsored league competitions; and clubs like the old established Headingley Bowling Club sought to strengthen the district Amateur Bowling Associations by taking 'a very particular and active interest in proceedings';[46] and even in the south there were clubs which refused to play others because they remained unaffiliated to the local amateur association.[47] In similar vein the Warrington Swimming Club joined each governing body as it became available: the Swimming Association of Great Britain in 1882, the Northern Counties Amateur Swimming Association in 1893, the Amateur Swimming Association in 1894 and the Lancashire Water Polo Association in 1896, all of which sought to uphold the sport for the 'best class of amateur'. Boxing, one sport which had been thoroughly professionalised, nevertheless continued to be popular at grass-roots amateur club level due to a bewildering array of club, local, regional and national bodies which provided administration and personnel to facilitate the smooth running of matches at every weight and age. As in previous periods of economic depression, there was a predictable rise in participation even in the amateur code during the 1930s as the Amateur Boxing Association sought to encourage youngsters to take to the ring for recreational purposes only, and its annual report for 1938 cites an increase in membership in the Northern, Midland and Western County Amateur Boxing Associations and a staggering 438 inter-club tournaments in the London Division alone.

Although all these organisations took their lead from the metropolitan governing bodies many implemented their regulations in the light of local conditions and this often led to confusion as communication between the centre and the regions broke down. It resulted in many anomolous situations in which amateurs appeared to act like professionals and vice versa: negotiations between the amateurs of the Northern Rugby Union and the Amateur Athletic Association concerning rugby players taking part in amateur athletics 'proved unsuccessful'[48] and yet Alfred Tysoe of Salford Harriers, who like his club mates was familiar with Harry Hardwick's sponsored sports on Kersal Moor, gained Olympic selection and won the 800 metres in the 1900 games. The so-called 'professionals' of the Northern Union were not allowed to make or receive 'any payment for playing football during the duration of the war'[49] and Barrow Rugby Club was not even allowed to present medals to its successful team of 1918. The Northern Union could not decide whether to accept a man suspended by 'the English Rugby Union' and eventually decided against doing so on the grounds that it would jeopardise its amateur status. The Football Association refused to reinstate Jack Sharp, a professional player, as an amateur so that he could become a director of a club, even though he had for many years played country cricket as an amateur.[50] Such anomalies were legion and only served to bring the management of sport into disrepute amongst a general public increasingly interested in watching the best possible sporting performances regardless of players' credentials. Such confusion assumed international significance when sport on the continent, which had always been regarded by the English governing bodies as less than fully amateur, produced supranational governing bodies. So, for example, the Football Association which had for decades presided over an overtly professional game refused to join the Fédération Internationale de Football Associations in 1904 until its regulations were brought more into line with English custom, whilst at the same time the Amateur Football Association was established in 1908 by clubs offended by the level of professionalism allowed in the English game. Similarly the Amateur Rowing Association refused to join the Fédération Internationale Sociétés d'Aviron which had been formed in 1892 since it regarded English amateur status as far superior to that of foreign associations which allowed tradesmen to compete with gentlemen. This caused the domestic body acute embarrassment when preparing the Olympic Regatta of 1948, when it found that membership of the international governing body was an absolute requirement of the International Olympic Committee.

Preparation for the Olympic Games of 40 years earlier had precipitated the establishment of the British Olympic Committee in 1906, whose prime mover was the Baron Desborough, at that time President of the Marylebone Cricket Club, the Lawn Tennis Association, the Amateur Fencing Association, the Amateur Wrestling Association, the Amateur Athletic Association and a steward of Henley Royal

Regatta and whose amateur credentials were therefore impeccable. The English Olympic effort until this point had been less than enthusiastic: in the first games of the modern era in 1896 there had been barely 100 competitors all told with British individuals taking a purely recreational part in cycling, fencing, shooting, rowing, swimming, gymnastics, tennis and athletics.[51] In 1900 and 1904 there were still no official British teams and so when the 1908 games were awarded to London it became a matter of national prestige to produce an effective and united response, but the first impressions gained by the new British Olympic Committee were not encouraging. No financial resources were available and so a Franco-British exhibition was arranged to raise funds to build the Olympic stadium, the White City, at Shepherds Bush, a commercial involvement echoing that of the Louisiana Purchase Exposition which supported the 1904 Olympic Games. The government steadfastly refused to offer any financial aid to the organising committee and no grants were made for the entertainment of foreign athletes, although according the *The Times* it had 'always been in favour of putting international hospitality on an organised basis'.[52] These first games in Britain were the last at which the host country had full jurisdiction over the sports as there were so many protests from the visitors that international bodies were soon formed to iron out the various problems of rule interpretation and amateur status. The atmosphere was badly marred by the antagonism between the British and American teams, as the latter accused the host judges of discrimination against the professionalism of their approach with the result that the British for the first and last time managed to win the most medals. Despite this numerical superiority it was felt that the home teams had under-performed, but whilst some considered the amateur approach to be at fault, others denigrated 'those who make a business of sport. We shall not go too far wrong in the cause of true sport if we stick to our antiquated methods.'[53] Unfortunately, for those in the English sporting establishment who upheld the cause of true sport, the international trend was turning increasingly towards a more professional approach and failure at the Stockholm Olympic Games of 1912 caused widespread consternation as some of the British team bemoaned 'the way in which affairs have been managed has been a mere farce made more ridiculous by contrast to the perfect organisation of the Americans'.[54] There were calls for a professionalisation of the training, organisation and funding of British teams abroad, but by 1920 and the Games at Antwerp a leading sports administrator was seriously advising withdrawal from the Olympic movement altogether, whilst this was repudiated by the secretary of the British Olympic Committee and significantly by 45 of the British team who considered that the professional approach was the only way to success.[55] This approach reached its pre-war zenith at the Berlin Olympics in 1936 where the Third Reich registered its overall sporting domination using techniques of training and selection later adopted and improved by the eastern bloc countries, some of which were ethically and morally highly questionable.[56]

The inflexibility of the governing bodies over the definition of amateurism allied to the traditional xenophobia of the English gentleman combined to produce an unhelpful tension in international sporting relations which continues to have repercussions today and to which we shall return in Chapter 8. On the domestic front, the continuing application of the amateur ethic, particularly during the nineteenth century, was directly responsible for the formation of hundreds of clubs throughout the country which were established either for the purpose of maintaining social exclusivity or providing those excluded with the means of carrying on organised activities. It is to the fortunes enjoyed by these clubs that we turn in the following chapter.

NOTES

1. These and further explanations concerning England's relatively smooth progress to the modern era in I. Christie, *Stress and Stability in late eighteenth century Britain* (OUP, 1985).
2. J. Channon, *Aristocratic Century* (CUP, 1985).
3. The first rowing clubs in the 1790s were the Isis Club at Westminster School and the Monarch Club at Eton College; at coffee houses they were the Star and Arrow clubs which amalgamated into Leander Club in 1818. In cricket, Westminster School graduates were instrumental in founding the White Conduit Club in 1782 and bowling became a fashionable pastime at coffee houses during the 1780s.
4. *The Times* (9 Sept. 1788; 2 Sept. 1790), 'The state by cricket rules discriminate the Great and on either side the great game is played'.
5. A contemporary account of 1775 quoted in M. Sands, *Invitation to Ranelagh* (Westhouse, 1946).
6. Wray Vamplew, in *The Turf: A social and economic history of horse racing* (Allen Lane, 1976), makes the point that there had always been an aristocratic obligation to patronise their local meeting and their participation at other mmeetings was 'a self imposed requirement of Society's social diary'.
7. Establishment fears grew in the following years: *The Saturday Review* (5 July 1862), 4b, maintained that the great working class 'as a body becomes every day a firmer phalanx not really impressible or subject to change', and a few years later Robert Lowe MP came to the conclusion that 'one class may swamp the other' – *Hansard* (26 April 1866), c2099.
8. The warden of Radley College in 1849 quoted in G.L. Guttsman, *The English Ruling Class* (Weidenfeld and Nicholson, 1969), p. 207, 'A gentleman both knows and is thankful that God instead of making all men equal has made them all most unequal . . .'

9. Mrs. Beeton, *Book of Household Management* (Longman, 1888), p.453.

There were other assiduously erected or maintained 'landmarks' in other walks of life: In the Theatre beginning in 1865 the managers abolished the low priced pit and introduced complex booking rituals, made and provided separate doors for stalls entrances with the overall intention of making the theatre more refined. See J. Pick, *The West End – mismanagement and snobbery* (Offord Publications, 1984).

In the professions for which at the beginning of the nineteenth century there were only seven qualifying associations a number which escalated to 40 by 1900 including those for solicitors, architects, builders, pharmacists, actuaries, librarians, bankers and eight types of engineers. See H. Perkin, *Professionalism, Property and English Society since 1880* (University of Reading, 1981).

In racism where despite the anti-slavery movement the Victorian attitude towards black people hardened in the middle of the century because the social and political climate forced middle class Victorian in upon himself 'as perceptions of class shifted so Victorian racism intensified. See D. Lorimer, *Colour, Class and the Victorians* (University of Leicester, 1978, p.47).

In religion where middle class people worshipped in the Church of England, Congregational or Wesleyan parishes and the lower orders were catered for by the more robust Free Methodists, Christian Brethren and Salvation Army.

In language where the terminology of class altered from an objective/economic statement to a subjective/cultural interpretation, that is from Middle Classes–Lower Classes to Middle Class–Lower Class, a shift which became widespread in the first quarter of the nineteenth century. See G. Himmlefarb, *The idea of poverty – England in the early industrial age* (Faber & Faber, 1985), Chapter 13, 'The language of class'.

In education where the *Taunton Commission of 1864* proposed that the upper middle class would have limited entry to public schools, proprietary boarding schools and grammar schools; the middle class would be educated in second grade schools up to the age of 16 and the lower middle class in third grade schools until the age of 14 with the differentials between them maintained by appropriate fees.

10. *Public Notice* (26 May 1819) banning the Berkhamsted Sports. *Letter* from the constable (27 May 1891) asking Why? *Letter* from Mr Bailey, a prominent local resident (29 May 1819), 'It has been a commonplace from time immemorial to hold sports ...'. *Letter* from Lord Berkhamsted (30 May 1819), 'I do not object to cricketting as usual if confined to that but if it extends to greater evil that must likewise be stopped'.

11. *Warrington Regatta* minutes (14 Aug. 1844).

12. *Henley Regatta* minutes (18 May 1859).

13. *London Rowing Club* minutes (20 March 1872).

14. *Newcastle Daily Chronicle* (4 June 1858).

15. For example, victories in the Gentlemen versus Players cricket matches; evidence from 'Guts' Woodgate concerning victories (in training only of course) against professional crews, quoted in W.B. Woodgate, *Reminiscences of an old Sportsman* (Nash, 1909) and in horse racing where twelve Grand Nationals were won by amateurs between 1871 and 1885.

16. *Rowing Almanack* for 1901, 'Review of the Season'.

17. This calls to mind the fourfold means of repression of popular activities quoted in E & S Yeo's *Popular Culture and Class Conflict* (Harvester, 1981), namely (i) by joining and taking them over; (ii) by organising rival activities; (iii) by licensing them and pricing them out of reach; and (iv) by outright banning.

18. 'Rules as to Professionalism' (July 1895): definition of a professional as anyone receiving a medal or monetary reward as a secretary, treasurer of a club or playing with a professional.

19. As recorded in the *Wigan Observer* (31 Aug. 1895).

20. *Rowing Almanack* for 1897.

21. For example *minutes* for 15 Sept. 1899. Joshua Platt was reported for a breach of the Professional rules as he had played football on a Saturday although he had not been working during the week and could not therefore legitimately claim broken time pay-

ments. Also *minutes* for 3 Nov. 1899, '66 special permits granted to play in tomorrow's matches some conditional on working Friday and Saturday'.

22. For example, *minutes* for 14 Oct. 1904. The case of W. Voisey of Wigan RFC charged with playing football while out of employment (and many others at various times).

23. For example, *The Yorkshire Association of Bowling Clubs* considered that 'there was a certain slackness these days in the sporting spirit of our clubs', spoken by the club representative on the Association and quoted from *Headingley Bowling Club* minutes (8 March 1917).

24. The Football Association for instance recalled the halcyon days of the FA Cup when the first seven finals were contested by only four clubs whose social backgrounds were unmistakable: the Royal Engineers (all officers), the Old Etonians, Oxford University and The Wanderers (all ex-public school).

25. Difficult though it is to believe at this distance removed from the conflict there was an element of English society, usually public school educated officers and gentlemen, that regarded the war as 'a sportsman's game and our men played it even with our enemies' (*Yorkshire Observer*, 13 June 1923, 12c, on unveiling Bradford Rowing Club's War Memorial). It was common for such officers to lead charges against opposition emplacements by punting a rugby or soccer ball towards the machine guns. One such, the England international rugby player E.R. Mobbs was killed in 1915, is commemorated annually in the Mobbs Memorial Match.

26. The British Olympic Association sanctioned for the first time in 1929 payments for broken time on behalf of the national football team.

27. An example of the temporary revival occurred in cricket when in 1919 the counties fielded largely amateur sides; when Somerset tied with Sussex in May 1919, 14 of the 22 players were Gentlemen. The quality of play evidently suffered however: Mr Heygate of Sussex suffered so badly from rheumatism that it took him fully two minutes to reach the wicket, a tardiness for which he was dismissed.

28. *Alcester Cricket Club* for 1871 which also included 'no selling of beer on the ground and no abusive or improper language'. Subscription levels varied in the early nineteenth century but in particularly exclusive sports like archery and later golf they were several guineas which resulted in a refined membership of doctors, clergy, 'esquires' and their ladies.

29. 89 out of 120 clubs and associations looked at in the present survey used the black ball method. The strictest was the Moseley United Quoit and Bowling Club which in 1867 stipulated 'one black ball to exclude' whilst most others satisfied themselves with a proportion such as 'one black ball in three'; the most democratic club was the Darlington Billiard Club of 1863 whose members were elected by a simple majority of present members. Of course, the most exclusive clubs and associations like the Jockey Club, the Marylebone Cricket Club and Henley Royal Regatta refrained from any kind of election and organised membership by recommendation and invitation only. Admiring this approach, De Coubertin recreated it in the election procedures for the international Olympic Committee which remain in force today.

30. 45 of our sample required to know the occupation of the applicant, e.g. not surprisingly the *Moseley United Quoit and Bowling Club* (18 March 1880) and the *Fambridge Yacht Club* whose minutes of 1 Oct. 1898 tell us that the Chairman Sir Samuel Pechell and the Committee arrogated to themselves 'the power to select other members of the club'.

31. Such exclusions could have surprising consequences: the Lord Mayor of Chester having been excluded as a plumber's mate as a youth from competing at Chester Regatta took considerable satisfaction in declining the Presidency of the event in 1934. For further coverage of this incident see the *News Chronicle* (30 July 1934), 7a, 'Snobbery in the Rowing World'.

32. *The Times* (15 Aug. 1936), 6e, 'Blackheath in the 1870s'.

33. The well known climber Alfred Mummery was blackballed in 1880 by the Alpine Club because his father was in trade. His famous and well publicised ascent of the Grepon in the French Alps was his well orchestrated response.

34. For example, £5,000 provided by the Henley Stewards towards the travelling expenses

of the Russian international squad to the Henley Regatta of 1987.

35. For example, *Beccles Golf Club* which in addition to the obviously genteel class of person already accepted for membership designated Naval and Military Officers, Clergy and Masters of Endowed Schools as potential members (*Rules for 1899*). The cost of the game was several guineas for membership and annual subscription and as much as thirty shillings for a round for two which represented an average weekly working wage even until the Second World War.

36. *Fambridge Yacht Club Rules* as agreed on 1 Oct. 1898 (Rules 23). Sailing clubs were particularly hierarchical and followed the naval pattern of command: Commodore, Vice Commodore, Captain, Lieutenant down to 'private members' and of course had 'distinctive uniforms and badges for the officers' (*Corinthian Sailing Club*, Hammersmith, *minutes* (22 Jan. 1895).

37. Editorial in *Athletic News* for December 1895.

38. *The Times* (2 Nov. 1926), 12b.

39. *Hansard* (7 April 1937), Vol. 322, pp. 236–7, 'A man who earns his living by his hands is not eligible as an amateur. There are many Honourable Members in all parts of this House who would like to see that rule revised.'

40. *Cumberland News* (17 July 1909), 5e, on the decline of traditional events like wrestling at the Talkin Tarn Sports.

41. All such associations before these dates and since were established in the words of the *Skiff Racing Association* 'to maintain the standard of amateur sport', *minutes* (10 March 1910).

42. From the Race Notice of Stafford Races (28 Sept. 1838); also prominent are those for Walsall, Stone and Lichfield in the same year.

43. *See Huyton Cricket Club* rules for 7 May 1860; *Stansted Park Cricket Club* (7 April 1864); *Walsall Cricket Club* (1 July 1847) and of course many others.

44. *Catford Cricket Club* minutes for 20 Jan. 1913, 'good attendance and an interesting discussion took place on important matters including our membership of three governing bodies'.

45. *Bolton Rugby Union Football Club* minutes (15 Sept. 1904).

46. *Headingley Bowling Club* minutes (8 March 1917).

47. See, for example, minutes of 5 June 1937 of the *Moseley Bowling Club* which records the cancellation of 'all fixtures with the Salisbury Club as they do not play to any recognised rules' and were unaffiliated to the Wiltshire Amateur Bowling Association.

48. *Minutes of the Northern Rugby Football Union* (3 July 1899).

49. *Minutes of the Northern Rugby Football Union* (8 June 1915) '... this came about partly because there has been widespread disapproval of the Football Association's decision to allow continuation of professional activities during hostilities'.

50. *Professional Footballers' Association* minutes (23 Aug. 1920).

51. Typical of the English approach was the participation of the men's doubles in the tennis tournament which came about as the only way in which some English players who happened to be there could secure a court to play on as all the courts had been block booked by the Games Committee.

52. *The Times* (7 July 1908), 9c.

53. *The Times* (27 July 1908), 10a–d.

54. *The Times* (19 July 1912), 12f.

55. *The Times* (14 Aug. 1920), 6c. A letter from Theodore Cook worth quoting in detail: 'This country has made it perfectly clear that the whole Olympic Games movement has become entirely alien to English thought and character. England has utterly refused to give our representatives sufficient money to give them any chance of showing their best form. The Secretary to the British Olympic Committee should inform the International Olympic Committee that this country will not be represented at any future games and so say farewell to the Olympic movement as it is presently conducted.'
    This was generally interpreted as a cry against the creeping professionalism of the Games and the consequent worsening of international relations brought about by cutthroat competition. This isolationist attitude was repudiated with some force in letters

of 19 Aug. 1920 (6d) and 27 Aug. 1920 (6d).

56. Some insight into the German approach to the Games of 1936 may be gained in their treatment of Jack Beresford and Leslie Southwood the British entry in the Double Sculls event at the Olympic Regatta. Their boat was shipped to Germany some weeks before the regatta so that they could practise on the event course but it was lost somewhere on the German rail system, but fortunately another boat became available and the pair won the gold medal. Only recently (1994) it has come to light from an ex-East German rowing coach who was a junior assistant with the German Olympic rowing team in 1936 that an order was given that the British boat should be 'lost'. It was found many weeks after the regatta in an obscure siding several hundred miles from Berlin.

7

Club Fortunes

John O'Gaunt Bowmen, established 1604, revived
1788, 1820, 1869 and 1977
(From the facing page of the current minute book)

All sport brought to a halt
(Headline in the *Daily Mail*, 4 September 1939)

Taken over a period of several centuries it is apparent that club
fortunes have been affected by an enormous variety of factors. The
range extends from the obvious considerations of geography and
environment, through those of social culture, politics and economics
to club constitution and administration, each of which had its effects
on advancing or retarding club progress. During the eighteenth century,
for example, Manchester and Liverpool 'sucked in such a mass of
population from other regions that the whole demographic balance of
the country was upset',[1] with the result that many rural sports were
introduced to an urban environment for the first time outside London.
More convenient travel stimulated growth outside the metropolis and
significantly the word 'provinces' only came into the language in the
1780s, serving to identify the divide which already existed between the
country and the capital city which had always been criticised for
monopolising commercial activity to the detriment of elsewhere in the
country. Certainly during the 1870s it was obvious that the 'provinces
were asserting their claim to a more important place in the national
development'[2] and that much of this assertiveness came from working
people who had been awarded a free Saturday afternoon by the Factory
Act of 1878 and filled it with recreational activity of all forms including
sporting participation and spectatorship. Some employers, like Beyer
Peacock of Gorton in Manchester, encouraged the formation of
works' clubs and joint championships were organised, many of which
became traditional annual events such as the Manchester Business
Houses Cross Country Championships held in Heaton Park regularly
until the 1930s. It was the development of such grass-roots organisations

that led in turn to the regional associations and leagues which gradually replaced the metropolitan agencies as the focus of much sporting activity.

As we have seen, it was during the 1870s that a stricter codification of social class came into being and the easier identification of a working class only served to isolate the growing middle class which chose to live out of town in the new 'suburbia'.[3] In sporting terms the new money of this class facilitated the spread of recreation shown by the enormous increase in the number of sports clubs in suburban areas used by the youth of the new bourgeoisie who had the time and money to join them.[4] Whilst the growth of middle-class sport was noticeable in membership levels at clubs, in working-class culture it was more evident in increasing levels of spectatorship, perhaps as a result of working people's disinclination to tire themselves further with physical efforts but also because until 1902, unlike their social superiors, they had no physical education which might have encouraged them to participate in greater numbers.

Just as economic prosperity was responsible for an increase in recreational activity, so economic depression resulted in commensurate decline. Many of the first sporting associations, established as they were by friends contracting to purchase shares in the new venture and to bear any subsequent liabilities, were often badly affected by economic fluctuations. Each of the 20 original subscribers to the Fulwood Race Course near Preston were asked to subscribe £15 in 1786 but were very soon prevailed upon to add a further £10 to cover substantial losses of over £300 in 1790. By 1794 the races had been cancelled but by 1803, when the worst of the financial and economic problems caused by the Napoleonic Wars had been overcome, a dividend of 30 per cent was paid out to each of the remaining subscribers. During the same period a similar fluctuation can be seen in Darlington where the local archery society was compelled to add a surcharge of 5s to ensure the continuation of the society, which only began to show a working profit in 1809. Later on in the century, further decline set in during the 1870s when a great industrial depression began which lasted with minor upturns until 1896. The Staffordshire Bowmen were constrained to reduce their activities from three shoots a season to two shoots since otherwise 'expenses would be rather heavy',[5] whilst the Headingley Bowling Club suffered a catastrophic reduction in membership from 112 in 1873 to 54 in 1876, which improved between 1880 to 1882 and 1886 to 1889 thus reflecting temporary upturns in local economic fortunes. The Astley Bowling Club was for several years in the 1880s unable to pay the rent on its ground due to arrears in subscriptions brought about by unemployment, and during the late 1870s the Tyldesley Swimming Club was forced to abandon its annual festivals 'due to the disastrous state of trade'.[6] Many clubs like the Tyldesley Cricket Club in 1889 appointed a collector of subscriptions on 10 per cent commission, but even this drastic action often failed to save clubs from extinction and many like Irthing Vale Cricket Club in 1874 decided to cease activities and to re-establish at some later date when the economic climate became more propitious. Some clubs struggled through the bad times with a much reduced level of membership and competitive activity, one such being Appleby Golf Club in Cumberland which suffered a serious decline in membership during the 1890s so that by 1899 it could boast only 15 women and 20 men subscribers. Like many other clubs it managed to continue by effectively amalgamating with a neighbouring club, thus securing vital cost and efficiency gains.[7] The new century failed to produce greater prosperity with a brief upturn immediately followed by the Great War, which in turn was followed by two decades of economic depression and stagnation, all of which was reflected in club development. The Lancaster Golf Club in 1912 regretted the 'falling off of visitors to the amount of nearly 50%' and record resignations;[8] Bolton Rugby Union Club was forced to disband 'owing to the extreme difficulty of raising a team' due largely to the personal costs involved in playing;[9] and Kendal Ladies Hockey Club could no longer afford to rent their field and folded in 1911. The 1930s saw a continuation of the same so that the Park Swimming Club of Tottenham bemoaned the financial depression which affected its galas during this era, as did the Kendal Swimming Club which was brought close to extinction by the reduction in funds from this prime source of income. The South Saxon Archers, even though sited in the relatively prosperous Sussex, were forced to admit defeat in 1932 due to the 'altered economic circumstances', and at the other end of the social and geographical scale the Warrington Anglers' Association experienced its 'worst ever season in respect of unemployment' with the result that it 'waived subscriptions for any genuine case'.[10] Such unemployment did, however, have some benefits for sport since the 1930s was undoubtedly the golden age of boxing as floods of new talent flowed from the dole queues into very often dubiously managed commercial bouts in the larger industrial cities, particularly Manchester which excited great interest from increasingly sophisticated audiences.

The growth of industrialisation and of massed populations was facilitated to a large extent by the existence and continued extension of the rail system throughout the country. That which encouraged the growth of urban centres also allowed the rapid distribution of pleasure-seekers from such centres into the country at large, and relatively early in the development of rail travel we can see the effect that such ease of movement had on the growth of sporting events. In rowing outlying aquatic venues were brought into the regatta and club circuit as the iron road reached them.[11] In hunting it became possible to spend easy weekends hunting in Oxfordshire when the railway first opened up the Thames Valley and Birmingham routes in the 1840s, to be followed in the 1850s by Leicestershire, much frequented by Anthony Trollope who began to hunt there in 1851 when the first convenient train service began.[12] We have seen how the new rail service to Liverpool in 1837 was commended by Lord Greville for its convenience in transporting him to the races, and reference to the Racing Calendar for any date in 1840 shows an enormous spread of meetings, the overwhelming majority of which had recently become accessible by rail from London.[13] At a more parochial level, 'derby' games were greatly enhanced by ease of player and spectator access brought about by local rail connections so that, for instance, the Whitfield Cricket Club in Northumberland only needed to catch any train on the Tyne Valley line to travel to all its 15 away fixtures at places like Haydn Bridge, Allenhead and Haltwhistle, with return matches similarly facilitated.[14] Elsewhere other forms of transport made life considerably easier for local sport: the new Bolton Union Football Club established in 1904 chose its playing field for its proximity to the local tramway terminus and therefore its accessibility to all likely members. Later in the century when cars became common, at least for the well-to-do, we can see their application to the sport of golf since many of the new courses were sited well beyond the range of any municipal transport. Hunting, according to Lady Augusta Fane in her book *Chit Chat* published in 1926, was spoilt by motor cars since they 'enabled a crowd of strangers to hunt where they do not live and where they consequently spend no money'. Nevertheless they did have their uses in transporting hunt members to the more remote meets and in providing hunt followers with a speedy and comfortable means of keeping up with the chase. This could often be useful, as it was for the North Staffordshire Hounds in January 1927 when one rider fell heavily off his mount 'and had to be taken to hospital by car'. Until cars became common for all in the post-war period, most sporting club outings were likely to be transported by charabanc and Netherfield Swimming Club in Kendal epitomised such usage in its Monday trips to Lancaster baths for training, leaving at '6.30 p.m. and returning at 9.00 p.m. sharp; 1/– for seniors and nothing for the juniors'.[15]

Many of the factors determining the fluctuations in club fortunes were specific to the particular sport. A Public Hand Bill published in the Birmingham Gazette of April 1790, for example, illustrated how the Wolverhampton Hunt suffered in a way which has become peculiar to hunting. A local smallholder, Mr Gough, aggrieved that the hunt had ridden rough shod over his property 'lay a foil and drew a Drag over his grounds' to entice the hunt into a compound where he endeavoured 'to destroy the hounds with a large stick'. Naturally he failed to do so and the huntsmen published the Hand Bill to publicise their judgement on Gough as 'contemptible in the Field as he is in every other part of his character', which was not surprisingly one of antipathy towards the perceived establishment in all its forms. Although the role of hunt saboteur remained undeveloped until after 1945, the hunting fraternity had plenty of other problems to confront, not least of which was the destruction of habitat and over-culling that led to totally fruitless days in the field. The Stayley Hunt at a General Meeting on 14 September 1904 decided that it should disband 'due to the over killing by non-subscribers of the hunt who used lurchers'. Elsewhere urban encroachment drastically curtailed the scope for hunting, perhaps the first example of which was quoted in Cosmo Gordon Lang's 'Sermons' in 1913 when towards the end of the eighteenth century Lord Berkeley's huntsman found a fox at Worm-wood Scrubs only to lose him in the newly built Kensington Gardens where pursuit became impossible. The general availability of foxes in particular was maintained by assiduous planting of coverts for their protection wherever the hunt may have endangered their survival. Throughout the nineteenth and early twentieth centuries, where records exist, we can see that seasonal totals of foxes killed did not vary a great deal; however past and present saboteurs would be happy to note that many days in the field were 'awful – no scent, no foxes and soaking wet'.[16]

Horse-racing not only suffered from local economic depressions which effectively killed racing in places like Lancaster where subscriptions dried up completely in the 1850s, but like hunting was susceptible to the availability of suitable sites. Much of the bucolic racing of earlier times was restricted or terminated by the enclosures of land brought about in the eighteenth and nineteenth centuries and urban development also played its part. In Lancaster the old racecourse on Quay Meadow was developed in the eighteenth century into warehousing and the new course on Lancaster Moor suffered from a remoteness which together with a decline in trade brought about the demise of racing in the town in 1858. At Fulwood near Preston the original course of 1786 was substantially improved in its first years only to be bought out by speculators during the middle years of the nineteenth century and was soon thereafter covered with suburban Victorian villas. Similarly, the Newton course at Newton-le-Willows established in 1678 on Newton Common was moved by the descendant of the original owner to Haydock Park in 1897 when the Common became ripe for commercial development.

The costs attendant upon site and facility development often brought clubs to the point of bankruptcy and bore particularly heavily on those sports which were dependent on ground maintenance for their existence. Bowling, with its reliance on a well tended green, always suffered from periodic financial problems as the bowling surface needed replacing, rejuvenating or extending, and we can see this in operation in 1793 when the Didsbury Bowling Green committee employed Joseph Kelsall for 48 days to enlarge their green and were constrained to pay £36 12s 9d for maintaining it for that one season. Whilst this was an enormous expense proportionately, it was no greater than the £220 paid by the Trowbridge and Westbourne Recreation Club for the same task in 1921 which resulted in a similar increase in subscription experienced by the Didsbury members. In the early days of cricket it was common for the urban grounds to be enclosed with wooden panels at considerable cost in order to produce a secure arena, and even rural clubs would endeavour to enclose their grounds with canvas sheeting, partly to limit play and partly to control spectators with a view to charging entry fees. Such control continued to be necessary throughout the nineteenth century and even small clubs like Tyldesley Cricket Club in Lancashire required 255 yards of wood boarding at 8 feet tall to surround its ground in 1884 when it first began to compete in the local league and became responsible for large crowds of spectators. The Lancashire League also demanded a better playing surface at the club and so it relaid some 4,000 square yards at a cost only redeemable by the anticipated income from hundreds and occasionally thousands of spectators.[17]

Golf and tennis were also subject to the vagaries of facility provision, and the cost of maintaining golf courses and the greens particularly was often beyond the financial scope of smaller clubs. The Appleby Club, which eventually amalgamated with a neighbouring club, was helped on its gradual decline by this problem brought about by 'the farmer turning out his cattle which did great damage to the putting surfaces making them unplayable all summer'.[18] In tennis there were often problems with uneven grass surfaces and with the earliest artificial surfaces of rolled earth and crushed stone which were prone to ankle-turning corrugations. Bad weather brought this about and often caused great expense to smaller clubs who could ill afford it, such as the Dunmow Park Tennis Club which had exactly this problem caused by incessant rain followed by frost. The consequent expense of re-laying the surface, together with the problem of a reduced member-ship brought about by the dislocation of activity and the bad weather, forced the club to organise matches for the first time, which it did against local opposition at Saffron Walden, Ongar, Felstead and Chelmsford with the result that sufficient money was raised.[19] Such fluctuations never affected the Wimbledon Club, however, whose profits soared from 1s 10d in 1879 to £760 in 1881 as the championships became established. Despite the economic depressions which afflicted many clubs, it was able to afford a new pavilion costing £1,200 in 1899 when it was re-titled the All England Lawn Tennis and Croquet Club and continued to go from strength to strength, due in no small part to the inclusion of many members of the establishment on its subscription lists.

Whilst facilities could be considerable liabilities, their provision was also responsible for the growth of sport and in some cases its inception. Technological advances in cycle production followed by the construction of artificial tracks took cycling from a pure recreation into the realm of organised competitive activity, and another supply-led demand was evident in swimming. Consequent upon the Baths Act of 1850 which sought to encourage the establishment of public baths and wash houses, local municipalities were minded to provide not only baths for washing but also plunge pools for recreation. The growth of swimming clubs closely followed the opening of such pools; for instance in Manchester swimming grew in popularity enormously from the mid nineteenth century as the numbers of indoor pools increased. Early clubs like Mayfield and Osborne took their names from the baths they used, Mayfield opening in 1856 and Osborne in 1883. The opening of new baths in Warrington in 1893 was followed immediately by a public meeting called for the purpose of forming a swimming club, at which 17 persons were present and which resulted in 40 people subscribing to the new club at 2s 6d each. During the same year Stockport Council intended to 'provide a first class swim-ming bath eighty feet by thirty feet, a small swimming bath for ladies and some private baths for the labouring classes' which soon resulted in the establishment of swimming clubs for men and women.[20]

In the two major winter games of association football and rugby union football, internal tensions produced varying fortunes as the principle of amateurism which originally informed both codes was

9. Swimming as a therapeutic activity has been practised since mediaeval times but only became popular following its espousal by the aristocracy in the early nineteenth century. By the end of the century the bathing machine was a commonplace item of beach furniture, as here at Shanklin on the Isle of Wight. The provision of such swimming facilities at the increasingly popular coastal resorts encouraged demand for the construction of swimming pools, for more regular use, in the towns and cities of the country.

gradually eroded in both cases in the north of England. Rugby union first came to Lancashire, for instance, when a Mr Mather organised a match in Liverpool in 1857; and Richard Sykes, a former captain of Rugby School, established the first Manchester Football Club in 1860 with a ground on Kersal Moor. In Yorkshire early clubs like Headingley and Wakefield soon set the tone for amateur club development with ex-public school boys feeding the playing side which was further augmented by pupils from the old established grammar schools like Leeds Grammar and Queen Elizabeth Grammar in Wakefield. Smaller amateur clubs, like that at Bolton, were not as fortunate with their recruitment and attracted enthusiastic novices rather than school-trained traditionalists, and suffered competitively, socially and financially as a consequence. As a different social element began to play the game it became necessary to modify some of the amateur principles to accommodate working-class pragmatism, and the catalyst for the final split with the original Rugby Union came with the formation of the Lancashire and Yorkshire Leagues in 1892, leading to the establishment of the Northern Union in 1895. This had a devastating effect on the game, especially in the more industrialised Lancashire, as most of the strongest clubs left the Lancashire Rugby Union to join the Northern Union which was prepared to condone 'broken time' payments. The split only served to intensify the difference between the amateur and quasi-amateur elements in the sport and clubs identified themselves wholly with one or the other so that their geographical areas became known as 'league' or 'union' country.[21] As broken time payments became routine and eventually evolved into wages for part-time professionals, the financial inducements to 'go north' were overwhelming for poorly paid or unemployed union players, and particularly during times of economic depression there was a mass exodus of such players to the northern league clubs.[22]

In association football the professional element became more dominant than in rugby, and more quickly so, although its evolution followed closely similar lines. The Football Association was established in 1863 as a wholly amateur body with wholly amateur aspirations, and yet the growth of the sport in the northern industrial areas soon precipitated a rift with the governing body which declined to condone payment of expenses to players. County Football Associations were established in 1878 within which variations in conditions of play were allowed and as with rugby the parochial competitions of the north and midlands led to regular payments being made. Professionalisation came with the formation of the Football League in 1888 which was established by William McGregor, a member of Aston Villa Football

Club who, like many since, saw the commercial potential of a competition restricted to several major players, in this case 12 of the largest clubs.[23] A Second Division was soon added and other regional leagues sprang up, so that many clubs became substantial commercial enterprises for the first time. In 1899, for example, we can see how Tottenham Hotspur FC, not yet in the First Division of the Southern League, speculated on a 21 year lease on a ground behind the White Hart Inn. According to the Prospectus for Shareholders, the enclosure 'will be a very fine one capable of accommodating 25,000 spectators with 2,000 seated under cover' and 8,000 shares at £1 were offered of which 1,626 were sold in the first year. This was sufficient for work to begin and that same year over £7,000 was taken in gate receipts, which had to be set against nearly £4,000 in players' wages.[24] Such enterprise paid dividends and the club won the FA Cup in 1901, and despite the financial hardships of the First World War the seventeenth annual report of the club in 1915 professed confidence that 'there is no reason to doubt that the Company will continue to make subsantial profits in the future as it has in the past'. The Professional Footballers' Association, first established as the Players' Union of Association Players in 1898, complained that such profits should result in higher wages for the players, but the club chairmen essentially operated a cartel for their own mutual advantage and the maximum wage was only abolished as late as 1961. Meanwhile the huge gap between the professional and amateur sides of the sport, the latter now represented by the Amateur Football Federation, can be appreciated by looking at a typical village club, Kinson FC in Dorset, which at the time of Tottenham's first venture into big business was reducing its subscriptions from 1s 6d to 1s to encourage membership. The club had joined the Dorset Football Association in 1898 and debated the feasibility of affiliating to the Hampshire and Dorset Football Association for further competition and support, only to conclude that 'the club was hardly in a sufficiently forward position to embark on such a large venture'.[25]

Whether large or small, amateur or professional clubs of every sport continually suffered problems of viability which were often solved by amalgamation or association with others. We have already seen that the original Lancaster Cricket Club evolved into the Lancaster Rowing Club in 1842, and the process in reverse was accomplished by the Warwick Boat Club in 1927 when it transmuted into a tennis and bowling club which met more closely the needs of its members. The Appleby Golf Club was only one of many which joined with a neighbouring club in 1903 to maintain viability and we can see this in operation across the sporting spectrum. The Wood Green

Cricket Club amalgamated and effectively took over the Crouch End Cricket Club in 1865; whilst in 1884, following a move close to the bowling green, the Tyldesley Cricket Club joined with the local Lawn Tennis Club, charging 1 guinea for men and 5s for women. The same year Huyton Cricket Club arranged a mutually satisfactory association with the local hockey club. Very often the initial popularity of a game produced many clubs which later struggled for existence until rationalisation produced a viable organisation. This is well shown in Kendal where rugby football was introduced by J.W. Weston, an Oxford Blue in 1871: by 1881 there were eight clubs in the area which eventually merged to form the 'Hornet' and 'Town' clubs, which in turn joined forces to become Kendal Thursday Football Club in 1892. Wishing to preserve its amateur status at a time of creeping professionalism and to advertise the fact, the Thursday Club became Kendal Rugby Union Football Club in 1905. Remaining in Kendal for a moment, the local Ladies Hockey Club only staved off dissolution in 1900 by strengthening its links with the Girls' High School and saving money on field rental by condescending to mixed practices with the men's club.[26] Many clubs diversified into other activities in order to subsidise their core sport: Netherfield Swimming Club, also in Kendal, provided gymnastic equipment for the first time on 13 June 1877, and the Lewisham Hare and Hounds Club formed a cycling branch in 1886 holding joint handicap events, as did the Catford Cycling Club with Herne Hill Harriers to encourage support which was sweeping away from both clubs immediately prior to the First World War. The Derwent Rowing Club in its annual report of 1907 notes that 'the rowing club football club has proved to be the one thing necessary to form the connecting link between rowing seasons', and Blackheath Cricket Club found that hockey fulfilled exactly the same requirement.

Attachment to some more prosperous body was often the way in which a struggling club managed to continue in existence. Good examples amongst the clubs in the present survey include the Sunningdale Ladies Golf Club which enjoyed an almost symbiotic relationship with the host men's club; the Dunmow Tennis Club which moved to a more prosperous area at Olives in 1902; the Headingley Bowling Club which placed itself under the auspices of the Original Oak public house in 1908; and the Warrington Anglers' Association which joined the National Federation of Anglers in 1932 in order 'to give protection against any further attempts at interference from rival organisations'. Relations between clubs were, however, not always friendly: when a letter from the local Cricket and Athletic Club seeking support was read out to a meeting of the Catford Cycling Club on 18 March 1919, there followed 'an extremely unfavourable discussion and the matter was left over indefinitely'. This might have had something to do with a minute of 23 July 1914 which notes that a request to the very same club 'to reduce their charges to us was declined'.

To all the fluctuations of fortune and their causes outlined above must be added the element of changing custom which greatly affected participation in sport throughout succeeding generations. William Hickey justified his declining interest in rowing by explaining in 1773 that 'rowing ceased to be the fashion and was supplanted by sailing',[27] and Strutt a few years later in his *Sports and Pastimes of the People of England* mentioned that football although 'formerly in vogue has now fallen into disrepute and is but little practised'. Certainly during the nineteenth century there was a disproportionate increase in spectatorship at the expense of participation. By 1900 1 million people a year paid to watch First Division football alone, whereas many small amateur clubs struggled to field a team at all at the weekend.[28] This relative change from participation to spectating was particularly noticeable amongst the working class as sport became less of a recreation and more of an entertainment. At the same time the middle class actually increased its level of participation, evidence of which is significantly available in those sports most associated with them where the growth in club membership was nothing short of phenomenal. In 1850 England had one golf club but in 1914 it had 1,200 catering for an elite, amongst which it has to be said both snobbery and anti-semitism were rife.[29] In tennis there were 300 clubs affiliated to the Lawn Tennis Association in 1900 but 3,000 by 1937, an explosion explained by the construction of 3 million private suburban houses since 1920. In an era when football and rugby were beginning to attract large crowds, horse-racing was coming back into vogue, especially in the south of England, and new rules of racing were introduced in 1858 and revised in 1868 and 1871 to ensure fairer contests. So popular had the sport become that in 1883 checks were placed on the increase in the number of meetings since space in the calendar was fast disappearing. By 1880 cricket had also become a mass entertainment, with crowds of 15,000 or more attending county matches and many more for Test matches, the first of which was played between England and Australia in 1877 at Melbourne. *The Times*, in a leading article, contended that the Tests were a 'wholesome innovation' but deprecated the tendency of the spectators to regard matches as 'simply opportunities to observe displays of individual skill by cricketting stars'.[30] From the 1880s to the 1950s cricket was generally regarded as the national game and sustained mass attendances into the late 1940s, but with the advent of many other attractions these dwindled often to negligible proportions at county games by the mid-1950s. The popularity of one activity had a direct influence upon that of others: as with William Hickey's rowing and sailing we find the resurgence of wrestling in Cumberland coinciding with the decline of local race meetings during the 1820s; archery giving way to golf and tennis in the 1880s;[31] and cycling suffering a decline in competitive participation during the 1890s as swimming, boating, tennis and rambling all attained new heights of popularity. During the 1930s dog-racing became popular in the larger conurbations as an exciting and convenient alternative to horse-racing which had begun to suffer from an elitist image; the old street games of quoits and pitch and toss were gradually replaced by bowling as public houses added greens to their amenities; and fishing increased as the working man gained greater free time and easier access to the countryside.

There remains one last important determinant of club fortunes which bears upon all the foregoing factors and that is war. Wars alter the cultural and commercial climate, cause huge economic and demographic upheavals, curtail civilian movements, modify social and sexual stereotyping, and speed the rate of technological progress, all of which have an effect on sport at club level. In the eighteenth century sport was often described as 'manly, noble and patriotic' as it was understood that it prepared participants for military service. Pugilism was cited as evidence that the true-born Englishman had the determination and pugnacity to defend the realm against any foreign threat, and even the popularity of cock-fighting and bull-baiting were adduced as illustrative of the combative nature of the ordinary man in the street. Some activities were praised as particularly useful 'schools' for future conscripts, examples of which were archery up to and including the seventeenth century, rowing in the eighteenth century when Thames watermen were frequently 'pressed' into naval service,[32] and riding to hounds in the nineteenth century which was held to be invaluable training for the cavalry. The first hostilities to have a noticeable effect upon club culture were the Boer Wars at the turn of the nineteenth century, conscription for which showed up what was called 'the deterioration of the national physique'[33] – a view fully justified by medical tests such as those in Manchester during October 1899 which found 8,000 out of 10,000 volunteers unfit for military service of any kind.[34] Whilst educational reform sought to remedy these defects by introducing physical education into state schools for the first time, the National Rifle Association established in 1860 for 'the encouragement of Volunteer Rifle Corps' issued a memorandum on 16 January 1900 designed to promote the training of more riflemen. This resulted in a large number of applications to form local rifle clubs, conditions of membership of which were that each club must have at least 20 members and that rifles were to be issued on a ratio of one per ten members. The civil authorities exempted members from payment of firearms licences and the National Rifle Association Council believed that the whole scheme would be a 'fruitful source of valuable recruits to Her Majesty's forces'. Many of the new clubs passed on members to local rifle corps, which in turn supplied army units which had been reorganised in 1881 on a territorial basis. Most followed the pattern exemplified by the Casterton Rifle Club of Westmorland which was established 'to promote instruction and practice in the use of the rifle' and attracted 20 members at 1s entrance fee and 1s annual subscription.[35] Increased membership came prior to both world wars but by the end of the 1950s support collapsed and on 10 June 1965 it was 'unanimously agreed to wind up the club and members were advised to join the Sedbergh Rifle Club'.

The First World War, The Great War, the War to end all Wars, had as one might imagine an enormous effect upon English sport at every level. Immediately prior to the outbreak of hostilities the county cricket clubs changed from starting games on Mondays and Thursdays to Wednesdays and Saturdays in order to draw bigger crowds, for as *The Times* put it 'people in these mercantile days want a big return for their money and a quick decision of the game draws the money'.[36] A few months later Dr Grace wrote in the *Sportsman* that 'the fighting on the continent is very severe; I think the time has come when the County cricket season should be brought to a close for it is not fitting at a time like this that able bodied men should be playing day after day and pleasure seekers looking on'.[37] This abrupt end to professional cricket was replicated in the amateur game as members took the King's Shilling in their thousands, leaving juniors and veterans to look after the interests of clubs in their absence. At Irthing Vale CC in Cumberland a groundsman was employed to keep the square in trim but no play at all took place during 1916, 1917 and 1918; nothing at all happened at Huyton CC in Liverpool or at Durham CC or at Kempsford CC in Gloucestershire. Several years of inactivity on the field of play coupled with a continuation of social activities albeit at a lower level than usual, often resulted in a healthy financial situation in 1919 or 1920 when clubs returned to pre-war fixture lists. For example at Huyton, the fixture list was arranged as far as humanly possible using the same clubs and dates as in 1914 and 'everything was to be put in first class order as there were many new members likely to join' with the knowledge that the funds were there to do just that.[38] At Durham some 30 new junior members enrolled in 1919 and the annual report for that year records a substantial balance of funds in the account which was considered to be vitally necessary since 'the ground needed to be brought up to its pre-war condition'. At Kempsford in 1919 there were 34 new members bringing an income of £11 14s 0d which represented a considerable improvement on pre-war levels. In the early months of the war when the British forces were made up largely of volunteers and before conscription became widespread, sports clubs generally provided disproportionate numbers of men for front-line action and this is reflected in mortality rates commemorated on Rolls of Honour in every single club. At Huyton CC 56 members joined up and 10 died; at Durham CC 45 joined and 6 died; at Kempsford 20 and 4 and at Irthing Vale 10 and 2, representing a 17 per cent mortality rate, most of which was sustained during 1914–16. In 1917 Wisden published no less than 60 pages of obituaries, finally recording in 1919 the deaths of 60 leading exponents of the first-class game.[39]

In the major winter game of association football the 1914/15 season had started when the war broke out and instead of abandoning play, as happened in other sports, the football authorities let it continue, causing unfavourable press comment and leading to a loss of reputation which lasted for a full 20 years. Amongst other results of this was the action of many schools in dropping football as the main sporting activity to be replaced by rugby union.[40] However, by the end of hostilities *The Times* at least had come around to an acknowledgement 'that the round ball did more than anything else to revive tired limbs and weary minds. Everyone knows that association football is the game soldiers and sailors love best'.[41] The business of the game naturally also suffered through declining gates and there was a formal proposal for a reduction in players' wages in order to 'assist the financially weaker clubs, since workers in all trades and professions were having to sacrifice in a similar manner'.[42] An indication of the loss of business can be found in the annual report and accounts of the Tottenham Hotspur Football and Athletic Company for 1915 which state that 'since the war receipts are 65% lower than normal but the loss this year has been kept to £3,968. 19. 4d.'[43] Play continued in a restricted form with 'friendlies' and charity matches and the club played its part by raising £1,000 towards various war charities. The temptation to carry on paying the players at the full rate, with bonuses to keep a winning team, was considerable, and at least one First Division club was caught deriving a competitive advantage by doing so throughout the war. Leeds City FC was banned from all competition in 1919 and re-surfaced as Leeds United in 1920. At the amateur level play continued in an ad hoc fashion with juniors and veterens making up the weekly village and neighbourhood fixtures. The Kinson FC in Dorset, like many others, established a junior club to see it through the hostilities and planned practice nights for Mondays, Wednesdays and Fridays, no doubt as much to maintain morale as improve techniques. Perhaps not surprisingly the Professional Footballers' Union itself suffered more than many clubs and went defunct during the war due to unremitted subscriptions, leaving liabilities of over £700. But during 1919 the level of new subscriptions was the highest ever and left the Union in a much stronger position in relation to the Football League and Association. Negotiations with club chairmen brought about a small rise in players' wages, a share in transfer fees and a winning bonus scheme, whilst the union officers had managed to organise financial aid for relatives of members injured or killed and comprehensive legal advice for subscribers, with the result that 'there was no reason why the Union should not be ten times as strong and the officers meant to have it so'.[44]

In the years immediately prior to the war the bowling fraternity had been exercised mainly by a succession of wet winters followed by exceedingly dry springs which played havoc with the greens. Nevertheless the sunny summers helped to boost membership figures for many clubs, the Moseley Bowling Club being no exception and its annual report for 1913 goes as far as to conclude that 'the very first concern of a bowling club is the weather which has been exceedingly good resulting in a large increase in membership and a record income from the championships'.[45] Whilst the onset of war caused cancellation of inter-club matches, most clubs continued to function at a basic level since their middle-aged membership remained untouched by conscription until 1917 when practically all able-bodied men were needed for the 'final push'. Little mention of the war can be found in the minutes of clubs except for the odd allusion to 'the circumstances of the times' which were cited to justify some relaxation of normal procedures, often, as in the Headingley Club's case, 'that subscriptions be allowed to lapse'.[46] In March 1917 the Westbourne Recreation Club committee felt that 'the nation had a greater claim on the groundsman's services than the club', whilst in August of the same year the Headingley Club was mourning the loss of its groundsman who died from gas poisoning in France and was 'our first loss in this great war'. The records of clubs show no substantial fluctuations in fortune throughout the war years, although some like the Crosthwaite Bowling Club simply leave a gap from 1915 to 1920, but after the war they usually record a Peace Day Championship in the summer of 1919, to which, like that at Bebington Bowling Club on the Wirral, there was always 'a splendid muster which turned up to compete'.[47] After the war everything was done to return to normality as quickly as possible: fixture lists were soon re-established, subscriptions levied at pre-war prices[48] and membership numbers soon returned to and exceeded the 1914 levels, due to a general retention of middle-aged and elderly members supplemented by juniors. However, unlike several other sports, post-war club bowling remained a female-free zone.

The war actually seemed to encourage the participation of women in swimming. In Bolton in 1916 there were 87 men, 116 boys, 89 women and 50 girls enrolled as members of the local swimming club.[49] There continued to be so many male members because the club had decided to admit all soldiers and sailors to free membership so that they could enjoy the baths while on leave, but even so by 1917/18 women comprised 40 per cent of total club membership. In Warrington, by way of contrast, the local swimming club practically folded during the war save for issuing a few reduced season tickets for schoolboys. Much other sporting activity in the town came to a halt, no doubt due, as the minutes of the Warrington Anglers' Association explained, to 'the large number of members who responded to the call to arms and the suffering of those in want of employment consequent to the war'.[50] Other sports throughout the country followed the national trend for curtailment of activity either from necessity or a desire to show solidarity with the forces overseas. Hammersmith Sailing Club, for instance, closed in March 1915 'until further notice'; the committee of the Darlington Cycling Club thought in October 1914 'that in the present state of affairs it would not be advisable to do anything'; Dunmow Park Tennis Club closed completely from 1915 to 1920; and Sunningdale Ladies Golf Club involved itself only in competitions held on behalf of the Queen's 'Work for Women Fund' with its members making bandages for the Red Cross Emergency Aid Committee and cotton bags for the Ministry of Munitions.

If a discontinuation of sporting activity typified reaction to the First World War then a dogged determination to carry on regardless was the general response to the Second. Despite initial panic, during which the Football Association cancelled players' contracts, cut wages to 30s and limited crowds to 8,000, the game nationally was soon reorganised into a system of district competitions which, unlike those in the First World War, were given both popular and official approval. The suppression of bonus money and championship points actually resulted in high scoring matches and excellent football. A Football Association circular of April 1939 expressed the hope that the game would provide a patriotic example to the youth of the country, and so it did with Brentford FC players joining the Reserve Police and both West Ham and Bolton Wanderers Football Clubs encouraging entire staffs to enlist. On this one issue at least the Football Association and the Players' Union were agreed, for the Union were to declare that 'the professional footballer is determined to carry on this great game of ours for the benefit of the community in spite of the threats made by evil minded dictators to weaken the morale of the people'.[51] Early Mass Observation reports during the first months of the war declared that the outbreak of hostilities had 'shattered many sports organisa-tions due to an absence of a policy of transformation to a war time situation' and a contemporary survey showed that 70 per cent of people no longer took part in sport due to lack of time and money, together with the impossibility or inconvenience of travel.[52] During the 'phoney war' there were restrictions placed on crowd sizes at sports venues throughout the country, but by the middle of 1940 football clubs were allowed to fill their grounds to half capacity and just before Easter the ban on the use of Birmingham City Football Club's ground was lifted partly due to the campaign led by the *Birmingham Post* which declared that 'the Germans are foul and dirty fighters but even they could hardly be expected to choose Saturday afternoon as the time and St Andrews as the locale for their first manifestation of frightfulness'.[53] As the hostilities wore on, public support for the continuation of football was maintained, whilst it became obvious that 'there was a strong feeling that horse-racing should be stopped mainly due to the feeling that it is a minority sport for the rich'.[54] That horse-racing was saved despite a considerable groundswell of opinion from all quarters against it[55] was due to the advocacy of Lord Derby who represented what he called the 'horse racing industry' and its enormous vested interests at the highest governmental level. Despite its survival, attendances at meetings were very poor with consequently low levels of gambling, winnings and purses, and there were also poor attendances at other sporting events, with a survey of Worcester during October 1940 reporting small crowds of 2,000 at football and cricket matches. Although the normal County Championship matches had been can-celled, the MCC improvised a programme of 19 games during the 1940 season and thus gave a practical lead to counties who were wavering on the subject of wartime play. At club level we can see that many organisations 'carried on as usual with the help of locally billeted members of H.M. forces',[56] and club finances often improved during the war, for not only was there less expense incurred from inter-club matches but also a steady income from continuing social attendances.[57]

There were, however, disadvantages and Bolton Cricket Club's purely recreational bowling green made the supreme sacrifice when it was dug for use as a vegetable garden. Many clubs were obliged to alter constitutional arrangements in order to deal with the new circumstances. The Warrington Public Parks Bowling League introduced War Emergency Rules which laid down procedures for dealing with games disrupted by air-raids and set levels of subscriptions for those serving in the forces; the Corinthian Sailing Club in Hammersmith changed the level of quoracy from eighteen to three; the Tyldesley Swimming Club managed to rub along with junior members only; and the Walsall Cycling Club committee decided that several co-options were needed to compensate for members called up for military service and that 'all future club transactions be strictly cash since so many members are likely to be conscripted'.[58] The Mass Observation Report on Oxford clubs in June 1941 featuring sports clubs concluded that all had been hit hard and most activities had been cut down owing to petrol rationing, with all away matches being abandoned. A notable exception to this was the local Cyclists' Touring Club which was able to maintain its normal level of activity without difficulty, and the Cheltenham Cycling Club reported 'a good position considering the troublesome year that we have had'.[59] Rugby also managed to carry on despite early talk of an official shut down of all activities; the *Daily Mail* reported that 'it will surprise clubs and players to know that the watchful eye of the Rugby Union is still upon them and that it is still very much alive, indeed even Rugby 13 in the North is carrying on determined to keep the fans cheerful'.[60]

One major effect of Britain's involvement in wars abroad was an increasing awareness that the country's international importance was dwindling and its strategic role was being usurped by the United States of America. As we have seen there was a public school tendency to equate military conflict with sporting competition and to judge the nation's virility by its sporting success, with the result that defeats by foreigners at cricket and rowing, together with evidence of poor physical standards amongst the population at large, prompted some to identify a creeping moral decline in English society. The London Olympic Games of 1908 had left many English sportsmen feeling decidedly ambivalent about international competition and the failure of the British Empire team to beat the medal tally of the United States at the Stockholm Olympics in 1912 allowed critics to conclude that 'its performance has prejudiced our position in the eyes of other people and has given an excuse for not a little patronising talk of England's decadence'.[61] Shortly following the First World War and the first intimation of Britain's industrial and military decline, a withdrawal from all international sporting conflict was contemplated in some quarters, particularly in that bastion of amateurism the Amateur Rowing Association, which in 1923 concluded that 'organised international athletic activity is contrary to the true spirit of amateur sport and endangers friendly relations'.[62] The following year *The Times* endorsed this approach by stating bluntly that 'the Olympic Games is a cause of ill will, nothing has been generated in Paris but international ill will', and that in the interests of international relations there should be 'No more Olympic Games'.[63] However, in this as in so much else, the sporting establishment and governing bodies were out of tune with sportsmen themselves who relished the prospect of stronger competition and argued persuasively to be given a chance to emulate the foreign levels of performance. Four years later the establishment attitude began to change and *The Times* endorsed the Olympics of 1928 as 'being more satisfactory than any which have preceded them' because 'the success of our athletes in the track events should dispose once and for all of the undignified inferiority complex suffered when Britons are beaten'.[64] Finally in 1939 even the rowing establishment, in the form of the stewards of Henley Royal Regatta, was embracing internationalism in offering to defray the expenses of visiting crews 'since foreign competition is of such great value to English rowing'.[65] In this respect the English attitude to international sport mirrored the domestic scene, with the former insularity complementing the reduction in sporting activity during the First World War and a broadening of horizons reflecting the continuation of organised games during the Second World War.

To this burgeoning internationalism in post-war English sport and society must be added the elements of democratisation and commercialism, the importance of which had been underlined by six years of hardship and sacrifice. It is to these and several other minor themes that we shall turn in a survey of post-war developments in the following chapter.

NOTES

1. P. Mantoux, *The Industrial Revolution in the Eighteenth Century* (Methuen, 1964), p. 350.
2. *Manchester Guardian*, editorial (24 June 1872).
3. For example in Birmingham where construction of new factories encouraged the middle class to move into the new 'smaller homes adapted to the means of the family man of limited income who likes to live just outside the artisan belt encircling the city' (*Birmingham Daily Mail*, 26 Nov. 1903, 4a). This movement resulted in the establishment of several tennis clubs in these areas.

4. See a protracted debate on such use in the *Daily Telegraph* letters, page 8, 21 Jan. 1869. Some correspondents thought that such idleness was socially damaging whilst others thought indulgence in competitive sport was character building.
5. *Staffordshire Bowmen* minutes (29 April 1871).
6. *Tyldesley Swimming Club* minutes (1 Aug. 1879).
7. *Appleby Golf Club* minutes (5 Nov. 1903), 'it is desirable that the club members give their support to a new club at Brackenber to be called the Appleby Brackenber Golf Club'.
8. *Lancaster Golf Club* Annual Report for 1912.
9. *Bolton Rugby Union Football Club* AGM (6 May 1910).
10. *Warrington Anglers' Association* Annual Report for 1931.
11. N. Wigglesworth, *The Social History of English Rowing* (Cass, 1992), pp. 38–40.
12. A. Trollope, *Autobiography* (Virtue and Spalding, 1883).
13. For example, *The Racing Calendar* for Tuesday 28 April 1840 cited 36 meetings from the Scottish borders and Wales to the south coast, 33 of which were newly accessible by train.
14. *Whitfield Cricket Club* minutes (16 April 1898).
15. *Netherfield Swimming Club* minutes (14 May 1934).
16. *North Staffordshire Hounds* minutes (8 Nov. 1926). Their records show that 67 foxes were killed in 1876–77 and 86 were killed in 1926–27.
17. *The Tyldesley Cricket Club* minutes (25 Aug. 1884) cite the detail of tenders for this work ultimately carried out by its part-time groundsman Mr Smith who was also instructed 'to prevent any persons from removing the manure deposited by the sheep from the field'.
18. *Appleby Golf Club* minutes (18 Oct. 1900).
19. Climate could have devastating effects. The Kendal Skating Club established in the 1860s dissolved permanently in 1907 because for several seasons there had been no ice to skate on.
20. *Instruction to Architects* for the Construction of New Baths for the Borough of Stockport 1893. These new baths were to replace the old baths which had been built soon after the 1850 Baths Act and which had consisted of 'one swimming bath, eight private baths, one family bath and one washing bath'.
21. Not surprisingly the 'league' areas were the industrial areas and the 'union' were the relatively rural areas. Where the two combined it was possible to find both traditions flourishing side by side, e.g., Wigan RLFC and Orrel RUFC, Leeds RLFC and Headingley RUFC. The geographical theme also features in the phrase 'going north' which denotes a change of codes from Union to League football.
22. For example, between 1919 and 1926 40 rugby union internationals 'went north', mostly from Wales.
23. The original 12 significantly all represented towns of 80,000 population or more: Preston North End, Blackburn Rovers, Bolton Wanderers, Accrington Stanley, Everton, Burnley, Wolverhampton Wanderers, West Bromwich Albion, Stoke City, Derby County, Nottingham County and Aston Villa.
24. Tottenham certainly were not the only club to invest heavily in the future; the league system of competition encouraged spectator support to such an extent that between 1889 and 1910 no fewer than 58 football clubs moved into new grounds with substantial capacities. By 1910 one million people a year paid to watch First Division football alone.
25. *Kinson Football Club* minutes (14 Sept. 1899).
26. *Kendal Ladies Hockey Club* minutes (25 April 1900).
27. W. Hickey, *Memoirs* (Hurst and Blackett, 1923), Vol. 1, p. 297. Much of the decline of interest in rowing at various times in the past has been put down to the difficulties of the sport and the existence of less arduous, more fashionable activities. Let *Poole Rowing Club* minutes of 18 April 1932 speak for all such explanations, 'Today the boys fight shy of really hard work. Perhaps it is because of motor cycles.'
28. For example the *Kinson Football Club* in Dorset in the minutes of 12 Sept. 1900 which

lament the 'prospect of getting together a team especially for playing matches away'.

29. In Leeds, for example, the numerous golf clubs enforced a covert policy of Jewish exclusion with the result that the Jewish community established its own club, the Moor Allerton Golf Club, in 1932, which nevertheless welcomed gentile members.

30. *The Times* (20 May 1882), 7a.

31. Archery was a particularly social sport and in Lancaster, for example, as elsewhere, its periodic revivals, specifically those in 1869 and 1901, can be traced to a few leading local families who resuscitated the local club for purely social and cultural reasons, the main result being the re-establishment of the Bowmen's Ball as a major social attraction.

32. Thames watermen had been 'pressed' since the earliest times, e.g. John Taylor 1580–1654, known as the Watermen's Poet and apprenticed to a Westminster waterman, was pressed into the navy on no fewer than seven occasions. More fortunate than most he ended his life as a publican in Oxford.

33. *The Nineteenth Century Journal* (May 1903).

34. Quoted in A. White, *Efficiency and Empire* (Longman, 1901). It is worth pointing out here that healthy conscripts were those who regularly indulged in sporting activity of one form or another and so a disproportionately high percentage of successful candidates were members of sports clubs. Confirmation of this can be found in members lists and casualty figures not only for the Boer War periods but also for subsequent wars. It was said and was demonstrably true that sports clubs were 'breeders of patriotism'.

35. *Casterton Rifle Club* minutes (29 June 1910).

36. *The Times* (4 May 1914), 8b.

37. *The Sportsman* (27 Aug. 1914).

38. *Huyton Cricket Club* minutes (16 Jan. 1919).

39. If one looks at all the clubs in the present survey the mortality rate during the First World War approaches 1 in 5. This really only tells half the story since there were hundreds of thousands of returning combatants who were to remain incapable of taking part in sport again, mainly due to gas poisoning. The majority of all sports clubs thus became youth orientated of necessity. In cycling, swimming, tennis and golf the female element was often predominant during the 1920s.

40. In contrast the *Northern Rugby League Football Union* taking note of these unfavourable comments pronounced that 'excepting for schoolboys and juniors under 18 all competitive football under Northern Union rules be suspended for the duration of the war' (minutes, 8 June 1915).

41. *The Times* (25 Sept. 1919), 7a. It is worth finishing this particular quotation: 'The authorities should devote particular attention to the training of officers of the future in the game that their men will play.' As we have seen many public schools gave the game up in disgust and turned to rugby, nevertheless the underlying lesson was learned by the authorities who were more disposed to encourage sporting activities during the Second World War.

42. *Professional Footballers' Union* minutes (9 Oct. 1914).

43. This is almost precisely the sum spent on 'trainers and players wages and bonuses' being £3,940 3s 6d.

44. *Professional Footballers' Union* (25 Aug. 1919). There was of course no insurance cover for those members killed or injured in the war. Eighty leading players were killed in the conflict.

45. *Moseley United Quoits and Bowling Club* minutes (11 Oct. 1913).

46. *Headingley Bowling Club* minutes (15 Oct. 1916).

47. *Bebington Bowling Club* minutes (19 July 1919).

48. This was most unusual, post-war prices generally were way above pre-war levels as the *Headingley Bowling Club* minutes confirm when recording the renewal of 1914 level subscriptions 'about the only thing at 12 shillings, that hasn't gone up as far as I know' (14 March 1919).

49. *Bolton Swimming Club* minutes (9 Feb. 1916). The same minute mentions 102 members in the forces of whom at this relatively early point 17 had been killed.

50. *Warrington Anglers' Association* Annual Report for 1914.

51. *Football Players' Union* minutes (26 Aug. 1940).
52. *Mass Observation Archive* Weekly Intelligence Service (3 April 1940) (University of Sussex).
53. *Birmingham Post* (26 March 1940).
54. *Report on attitudes to the continuation of sport in wartime* (April 1942) (Mass Observation Archive, University of Sussex).
55. See correspondence in *The Times* throughout October 1940 both decrying (mostly) and supporting the activity.
56. *Irthing Vale Cricket Club* minutes (13 March 1942).
57. *Bolton Cricket Club* exemplifies this, indeed during 1940 for the very first time modern beer pumps were installed in the bar to meet the increased demand, minutes (28 May 1940). Other beneficiaries of this improvement were the various charities for which many domestic 'friendlies' were played. Between 1939 and 1943 the amounts raised by each activity was as follows: Whist, Bridge and Dancing (£365,478); Billiards and Snooker (£79,919); Darts and Bowls (£72,186); Soccer (£70,236); Golf (£67,000); Greyhound Racing (£50,561); Boxing (£25,183); Cricket (£22,996); Rugby (£10,580); Athletics (£9,319); Cycling (£6,365); Swimming (£1,758); Hockey (£480). Figures taken from A. McCarthy, *War Games: The Story of Sport in World War Two* (Queen Anne Press, 1989).
58. *Walsall Cycling Club* AGM (1 Dec. 1939).
59. *Cheltenham Cycling Club* AGM (27 Feb. 1940).
60. *Daily Mail* (23 Oct. 1939).
61. *The Times* (18 July 1912), 12f.
62. *The British Rowing Almanack* for 1923 under 'Proceedings for 1922'.
63. *The Times* (22 July 1924), Leading Article 12a.
64. *The Times* (7 Aug. 1928), Leading Article 12a.
65. *Henley Royal Regatta* minutes (20 March 1939).

8

Post-war developments

An early opportunity should be taken to apply
for admittance to the association of unions
associated with entertainment, broadcasting
and television.

(*Minutes of the Professional Footballers' Association*,
23 October 1955)

Professional cycling is a sport but mostly it's
just a huge business.

(Stephen Roche, *Guardian*, 1 July 1994)

Immediately following the Second World War in October 1945 Britain successfully applied to host the first Olympic Games to be held for twelve years. Despite their makeshift character and the exclusion of teams from Germany and Japan the London games attracted 6,000 participants from 59 countries whose exploits were regularly watched by capacity crowds of 80,000 at Wembley Stadium and for the first time by over half a million television viewers. The British team came away with three gold medals in the gentlemanly sports of rowing and yachting, helped no doubt by the 'charm and domesticity of Henley where the family atmosphere was absorbed by the crews from abroad',[1] which together with the unusual distance and nature of the course may have given the host team a distinct home advantage. The lack of success on the track was once again put down to the British disinclination to indulge in the intense preparation and specialisation increasingly required to compete at international level, and the secretary of the Amateur Athletic Association promised that a much better showing would be forthcoming at the 1952 event.[2] The war, national service and rationing all had a part to play in explaining Britain's continuing lack of international sporting success and the Labour government certainly had different priorities, notably welfareism, housing and education, with sport only being officially considered as an educational issue. Another legacy of the war was the general recognition that sport was as likely to provide a boost for morale in the peacetime struggle for national prosperity as in the wartime battle for national survival. Both in war and peace the communal pleasures of sport complemented communal work in factories, and football particularly exemplified the growth of sporting spectatorism as a manifestation of social solidarity. It should be no surprise that attendances at football matches peaked in the late 1940s when the Attlee government embodied the collective strength of the working classes but has been on the downward trend ever since as increasing prosperity has eroded social and cultural affiliations.

Another example of such solidarity during this period was provided by greyhound-racing which eventually became the second biggest spectator sport after football. Having officially begun as recently as the General Strike summer of 1926 at Belle Vue in Manchester, it grew quickly to the point where crowds of 25,000 at venues like Hackney Stadium were not uncommon, with other big meetings being held at the White City, Haringey, Owlerton in Sheffield and of course Belle Vue. Apart from these large meetings and following in a long historical tradition, there were also scores of small rural meetings around the country.[3] At the lower socio-economic levels such solidarity was also evident in rugby league which maintained and strengthened its hold on the public imagination in Yorkshire and Lancashire, whilst at the upper levels cricket, horse-racing, rowing, golf and rugby union entered a period of slow but steady democratisation. Whilst staunch fashionable and genteel support continued for events like the Eton and Harrow cricket match, which was re-established in 1946 on such austere lines that the Etonians lacked their top hats and the Harrovians their straw boaters, there began a gradual breakdown of social hierarchy in the sport which culminated in 1963 when the distinction between gentlemen and players was finally abolished.[4] Economic and financial imperatives required that horse-racing was made available to a wider cross-section of the public and determined attempts were made after the war to shed race meetings, particularly those at Newmarket, of their old-fashioned exclusiveness, and gradually admission to the members' enclosures was made more accessible. Despite a loss of public confidence in the administration of the sport, brought about by a series of doping scandals in the 1950s, its future as a popular attraction was assured by the injection of further capital through the application of the Betting Levy Bill in 1960 which empowered the new Levy Board to collect contributions from bookmakers and the Tote.

In rowing the seeds of social change had been sown in 1890 when the National Amateur Rowing Association was established for working men as an alternative to the gentlemen's Amateur Rowing Association. Following the Second World War this governing body became increasingly aware that in most boat classes, particularly the blue riband Eights, the foreign competition had not only caught but easily surpassed the English crews formed entirely of Oxbridge gentlemen. It thus became necessary to widen the recruitment of oarsmen for national selection and with this end in view the two organisations amalgamated in 1956. Two sports which proved less receptive to the post-war democratisation were golf and rugby union, of which the former continued to discriminate against potential recruits on grounds of sex, class, religion and occupation, whilst the latter restricted itself at least ostensibly to considerations of social class and occupation, stipulating ironically that only 'professionals' were acceptable.[5] During the 1980s particularly, the social constitution of golf clubs changed considerably, many being affected not only by the commercial necessity of a wider membership but also by the activities of the Equal Opportunities Commission. The Northwood Golf Club in Middlesex exemplifies this national trend in its recent acceptance of all those capable of paying its subscriptions as members, although there continue to exist several classes of membership.[6] From the 1950s onwards the game of rugby union has struggled with the problems of paying expenses to ostensibly amateur players and with a strained relationship with the Rugby League.[7] Cultural divisions can be discerned within the club structure, particularly when clubs like Bath and Harlequins play each other since such games reveal an intriguing subtext of regional and class rivalries: London versus the provinces, futures markets versus farming, and old school tie versus new school titans. Peter Yarranton, Vice-President of Wasps RUFC laments the passing of the 'golden days' when the top clubs played each other in a network of contests stretching back through schools and universities, but realises that, ironically, 'the sport has got to become as professional as possible so that the game remains amateur'.[8] In 1986 the International Rugby Board endorsed a 'Free Gangway' agreement which allowed for players to be members of both the Amateur Rugby League and Union and in January 1995 the first meeting in 100 years took place between the presidents of the two codes in order to agree a *modus vivendi* for the future.

The position of women in sport improved gradually and grudgingly during the post-war period and is only now approaching anything like parity with men. As we have seen, women in golf are often treated as second-class citizens and further examples of this are available in the constitutions of most golf clubs which state that 'lady members shall not be eligible to take part in any management of the club or to act as officers' even though they often represent a significant proportion of the membership.[9] Despite the sexual equality of the war years much sporting culture reverted to traditional pre-war custom, so that even in those clubs where it was possible for women to gain access it was unlikely that they would be treated civilly.[10] Most of the older sports were considered to be male territory and most women were content for them to remain so, but the more recent recreational activities of archery, cycling, tennis and swimming became equally accessible to both sexes and club membership in these sports often shows a predominance of women. There are, of course, clubs like The Leander Club and the Marylebone Cricket Club which continue to exclude women even as social members, but they represent the prosperous few which can manage without the extra income brought in by a wider membership. Few smaller clubs in any sport now operate a ban on women, due almost entirely to the economic necessities of an increasingly commercial world and the advent of the Sports Council in 1965 which offered grant aid only to those clubs operating an open-door policy. It is significant that discrimination against women, as enshrined not only in club constitutions but in habitual behaviour, diminished sharply in the latter half of the 1960s as the take-up of grant aid became a major part of club development programmes.[11] Even a dyed in the wool club like the Manchester Wheelers Club established in 1890, which specialised in competition cycling, was constrained to admit females in 1969 despite grave misgivings on the part of the older members; and many rowing clubs only became feminised at this time.[12]

Unlike hunting, horse-racing remained male-dominated until the mid 1960s when Florence Nagel became the first woman ever granted a training licence, followed in 1975 by the first woman professional jockey ('jokette' in contemporary parlance), and in 1977 the first female member of the Jockey Club. In more recent times women have begun to encroach upon the remaining male bastions of rugby and football, having already established themselves in most other sports either in association with the original governing bodies or as separate organisations.[13] The Rugby Football Union and the Football Association finally recognised the growth of female participation in their sports in 1994 by granting associate status to the women's governing bodies. Despite their acceptance into the majority of contact sports, women continue to be officially denied access to boxing by the Amateur Boxing Association, but, again in 1994, some enthusiasts established a Women's Professional Boxing Association and women's bouts are attracting considerable spectator interest in the London area. Women's take-up of sport generally in the post-war period continued to give cause for concern to the Sports Council, whose research department showed how serious the problem was.[14] Several initiatives designed to improve the situation were subsequently implemented with moderate success and a further strategy to encourage their participation was published in 1993.[15]

Along with the process of democratisation came an understanding that in order to survive the economic difficulties of the immediate post-war period it was necessary for those involved in sport to treat their activities with greater seriousness than before. In professional football this was exemplified in a strike called in November 1945 for better wages and conditions, and although club chairmen cited the entertainment tax of 40 per cent as evidence of their inability to pay more, they finally agreed to a maximum wage of £9 a week, bonus schemes and an injury compensation settlement. On the amateur side, all sports clubs were forced to re-assess their positions in the light of greatly changed circumstances. In cycling, for instance, the Catford Cycling Club managed its post-war debt by reviewing its affiliations to governing bodies and by forming a subsidiary company for the management of the Herne Hill track in conjunction with the National Cycling Union. Poorly attended Saturday afternoon meetings were abandoned and the club joined forces with other local clubs to establish the London Cyclists' Defence Association for the purpose of protecting cyclists against any further restrictions of their liberties.[16] A similar tightening up of administration was commonplace in the sport and the Bristol Cyclists' Touring Club drastically reduced the size of its committee, delegating much of its business to the governing body; whilst the Cestreham Club initiated a 'black book' scheme in 1950 to deter inappropriate behaviour amongst members with a further threat of suspension from all competitive events.[17] Renewal of club activities sometimes after a prolonged lay-off placed strains on administration and some clubs like the Portsmouth Corinthian Yacht Club were compelled to employ professional secretaries for the first time in 1946 and to seek mergers with similar organisations (as Portsmouth did with the Royal Anglian Yacht Club) with a view to effecting economies. New wage rates affected many clubs as groundsmen at cricket, tennis and bowling clubs and instructors at athletic and swimmming clubs expected to receive improved post-war terms,[18] and the cost of petrol proved a further burden to those clubs with away fixtures.[19] New, higher insurance rates made life very difficult for the smaller club, like the Huyton Cricket Club which was constrained to rent out its field to the Sefton Hockey Club in order to meet the increased premiums on its pavilion.[20] Inevitably many clubs found the transition to a more businesslike post-war climate impossible to sustain. Archery suffered a substantial decline in support at individual and club level, only halted during the 1950s by the establishment of Country Archery Associations,[21] whilst many of the smaller local events like Holme Athletic Sports found it difficult to continue and succumbed to the inevitable during this time. Many small clubs decided that closer co-operation with a neighbour was the only viable option for them and this happened often throughout the post-war era. A good example was that between the Blackheath Hockey Club and the Forest Hill Cricket Club following the realisation that 'we rely on each other and have a lot in common'.[22]

During the 1960s similar financial imperatives allied to fiercer competition, brought about in most sports by the spread of local and regional leagues, encouraged the growth of a commercial attitude towards sporting activity even at the amateur and recreational levels. Club committees were required to consider, often for the first time, the availability of social facilities for players and spectators alike and the sponsorship potential of their core activity. It was during this period that breweries particularly invested millions of pounds in club bars up and down the country, with the Tetley and Whitbread Companies chief amongst them, and the ubiquitous fruit machine first made its appearance as an important source of income for beleaguered club treasurers. New licensing restrictions, including the introduction of Club Registration Certificates for nominally non-profit making organisations, required many club constitutions to be amended to include reference to the provision of 'recreational and other social facilities including the supply of alcoholic refreshment to members.'[23] Awareness that sponsorship, even at the level of equipment purchase, required some public profile for the club's activities prompted the encouragement of more supporters on the touchline and in the bar after the game. Spectator appeal became almost as important for amateur sport as it had always been for the professionals.[24] Not everyone welcomed the new commercial initiatives and the amateur dilemma in microcosm was illustrated by the 1962 Cyclists versus Harriers event held by the Walsall Cycling and Running Club. A meeting was convened to hear a proposal from the secretary of the National Cyclo Cross Association who suggested that a new venue for the event would attract more spectators and pave the way for a British application to host the 1963 World Championships. The club committee rejected the proposal out of hand feeling that 'if we fell in with the secretary's views it would change the whole character of the event'.[25] It was for the preservation of just this 'character' that most amateur clubs continued to strive in the face of growing commercialism and a professionalism born of higher competitive standards.[26] There were, however, clubs which employed some commercialism simply in order to survive. For example, the huge growth in sponsored rowing events during the 1970s and 1980s owes more to the instinct of self-preservation in a sport where clubs are financially dependent on the success of one or two annual regattas than on any planned development policy.[27] In those sports involved in league-style competition the pressure for success has led to levels of business activity unheard of before. In 1980, for instance, the Durham Cricket Club, recognising that 'the accounts showed the need for a great deal of hard work' and 'seeking to maintain its position as one of the foremost clubs in the country' amended its constitution to appoint a chairman who could revitalise the club by securing commercial sponsorship and an experienced professional.[28] Similar activity was being repeated throughout the premier leagues. Whilst leagues in cricket were already 100 years old in the 1980s, it was at this time that the Rugby Union first introduced them with a view to encouraging much needed spectator, commercial and media interest during a period when the Rugby League itself was reaping the commercial benefits of substantial television coverage. The traditional competition network of rugby union clubs was largely destroyed by the new league system and has led inevitably to a professionalisation of the sport throughout the country as the larger clubs establish trust funds to recruit and retain the best players. One worrying result of fiercer competition has been an increase in on-field violence, the growth of which has been explained by the pressures exerted by media scrutiny, the obsession with winning brought about by the greater availability of large prizes, and the failure of the governing body to develop an adequate framework of regulation and control.[29] Rugby union is becoming a professional sport but as yet lacks the framework of control that has helped to keep rugby league in check, a gap which has been partly filled latterly by an arbitration panel established by the Central Council for Physical Recreation in 1993 designed to deal with contentious issues in any sport.[30]

Commercial activity in professional sport continued to grow inexorably during the post-war period, so that by the 1980s it had attained the status of big business in England and a huge industry worldwide. Responsibility for this lies with the seductive financial appeal of television which first made itself felt at the Wimbledon Lawn Tennis Championships of 1937 when a few hundred Londoners viewed 25 minutes of a men's single match. By the early 1970s fees from television coverage provided 20 per cent of total income, by 1987 at £9 million they represented 60 per cent, whilst today (1995) they bring in over 70 per cent thanks to the hard work of the television marketing executive and his team.[31] Well aware of the power of media exposure the Professional Footballers' Association established a sub-committee in 1955 to explore its potential with the remit to 'take a firm stand on the question of Broadcasting and Television or be guilty of dereliction of duty to our members'. The sub-committee knew only too well that clubs would make as much money as possible from the media and that little or none of it would be shared with the players who provided the entertainment, whilst perversely many club chairmen feared the growth of media coverage as likely to reduce match attendances.[32] The chairman of the PFA during the early 1970s, Derek Dougan, was largely responsible for extending the game's commercial profile with a view to maximising his members' income in the belief that football was 'an art and craft combining commercial exploitation and having a product to sell we should sell it the best way we can'.[33] The full commercial potential of the game has only recently become obvious with the coming of satellite television, which has opened up a global market for those clubs big enough to exploit it. As in other eras football continues to hold up a mirror to English society in exemplifying the Thatcherite revolution in which locally based club chairmen were replaced by thrusting entrepreneurs who knew how to market the game to consumers. The free market perspective has meant that top clubs are creaming off most of the television revenue, whilst those in the lower divisions are finding it more and more difficult to make ends meet despite promises that prosperity would eventually 'trickle down' to them.[34] The failure of this to happen, at least in the first years of the Premier League, would suggest that the new market system needs adapting since the domination of a few successful clubs is 'likely to neuter the appeal of professional sport which thrives on the uncertainty of result'.[35]

Such uncertainty has always been the lure for gamblers on horse-racing and explains the severity of offical reaction which generally follows any discovery of cheating in the sport. Following several stringent inquiries by the Jockey Club in the 1950s and the establishment of the Levy Board in 1960, the domestic scene was at last deemed to be in a satisfactory state, but due to the increasing commercial interest particularly shown by the companies of Independent Television, the Jockey Club and the National Hunt Committee amalgamated in 1968 in order to facilitate contract negotiations. Although greyhound-racing at national level suffered a reduction in popular support during

10. The medium has finally become the message.

the 1960s following a resurgence in the fortunes of horse-racing, it began to revive somewhat during the next decade when some re-furbishment of stadiums took place. Businessmen began to take interest in their own local tracks during the 1980s simply as land and property investments without realising their full entertainment potential as relatively cheap and convenient alternatives to football and horse-racing. The British Greyhound Racing Club was not slow to point this out with the result that much modernisation took place throughout the country, and the Hackney stadium, for example, which hosted some of the first meetings in the country has recently undergone a multi-million pound face-lift, including the installation of a restaurant and hospitality boxes which would not disgrace a Premier League football club. Apart from the commercial returns from such facilities, the sport nationwide is currently followed by 4 million supporters and generates some £2 billion pounds in gambling turnover per annum.[36] The long-term financial success of the sport may well have been secured in April 1994 when Sky Television began broad-casting selected meetings. Early regional television coverage of rugby league matches encouraged the Rugby Football League to solicit commercial sponsorship during the 1970s, which had such a beneficial effect on individual clubs that by the 1980s it had become the most important determinant of the state of the game. Almost unnoticed, television became essential to the game as sponsors took advantage of associating themselves with a sport so much in the public eye. The reduction of the First Division into a super league of 14 clubs in 1987 was a manoeuvre calculated to encourage greater commercial support and it bore fruit in 1989 when the governing body announced that its three main competitions alone would yield £2.5 million in sponsorship, a figure since doubled. Similar television coverage of the one day 'knock-out' competitions in cricket introduced the idea of brand marketing, advertising and sponsorship to a game which had become almost moribund by the 1960s. The Test and County Cricket Board was responsible, along with the newly established Cricket Council, for encouraging further television coverage of county games, for example the 'Roses' match, and of Test cricket, the income from which is used to promote the game nationally. Individual county clubs have begun to use their facilities for overtly commercial purposes wherever possible, often constructing pavilion extensions to cater for the conference market, whilst sponsors for teams and players, many of which are breweries, are avidly sought for each and every competition.[37]

The availability of financial support for sport exemplified by the growth of sponsorship in the professional sector over the last few decades has undoubtedly affected perceptions about the acceptability of commercialism in the amateur sector. Even as early as the 1950s Horst Dassler was handing out free pairs of running shoes to athletes at the Melbourne Olympic Games, a practice that enabled Adidas to dominate the industry for the next 25 years. Sponsorship from English firms like Prudential Assurance and Trustee Savings Bank, together with televison contracts negotiated by consultancies such as Alan Pascoe Associates, has promoted athletics even at club level into a lucrative business for the successful athlete who soon has access to a substantial trust fund built up from prize winnings and commercial endorsements. In order to increase the potential for television coverage and sponsorship of athletics, a sport which continues to be nominally amateur and governed nationally and internationally by amateur associations, a four-yearly World Championship event was introduced in 1983, the commercial success of which encouraged the organisers to establish a biennial event in 1993. International commercial inducements have led to the establishment of a World Cup competition in rugby union, and the introduction of leagues into the domestic scene has resulted in television coverage of club matches and sponsorship worth £7 million from Courage Brewers.[38] Most golf clubs of any size now rely heavily upon proceeds from the professional's shop, catering and bar profits, and income from gaming machines,[39] whilst even cycling clubs have derived commercial benefits from greater television coverage of the sport during the 1980s and 1990s.[40] In rowing, that most Corinthian of all sports, commercialism entered in 1985 with television broadcasts of the 'Leyland Daf Challenge Sprints', and those two bastions of the amateur ethic, the Oxford and Cambridge University Boat Clubs, have fully professional staffs paid for out of the considerable income derived from television contracts and sponsorship from Beefeater Gin.[41]

This inexorable commercialisation has thus professionalised much formerly amateur activity and at the same time redefined professional sport as a business. Those sports which first became professionalised as a means of providing much needed supplemetary incomes have now become so specialised as to exclude all but the most talented who will have emerged only after years of grooming, training and sponsorship by some form of institutionalised management. The sport of boxing, for example, only attained official, formal status with the establishment of the British Boxing Board of Control in 1929 at a time when the economic depression encouraged the unemployed to try their fists at prize-fighting. For centuries before this time and for half a century afterwards, men had dabbled in a semi-professional way with the sport at a variety of venues, one of which was the fairground boxing booth. In the immediate post-war period there were 1,000 fighters registered with the board of control, many of whom would have found seasonal employment in the hundred or so fairground booths travelling around the country. One such was the Excelsior Pavilion run by Ron Taylor which had been in the family since its inauguration by his grandfather in 1843 and like many others was valued for providing as much ring experience in one month as a gymnasium might provide in three. As the number of registered boxers diminished throughout the 1950s and 1960s, the booths gradually went out of business and the Excelsior was reckoned to be the last when it too closed for business in 1994, the very year that saw the formation of the Professional Boxing Association established to set new professional standards for its 350 members. Its President Barry McGuigan commented at the Association's first Annual General Meeting that the sport had 'for too long far too many seedy connotations with the boxers being the least consideration of all'. Once again television has created a commercial business from a sporting activity, with the result that the journeyman professional has been largely replaced by expertly managed super athletes whose success depends almost as much upon their media profile and personality as their boxing skills.[42]

The immediate post-war situation in football reflected that in boxing since there was a record number of members affiliated to the Players' Union, which in 1958 was renamed the Professional Footballers' Association when for the first time it gained representation on the Council of the Football Association.[43] Following protracted discussions with both the Football League and Association, the PFA finally brought about the abolition of the maximum wage and the introduction of a minimum wage for the First Division of £15 per week which was close to the average earnings of the time. The owners of football clubs through the administration of the League itself continued to operate the original 'retain and transfer' system of players' employment which denied a player any independence, and reaction to this came to a head with the celebrated case of George Eastham in 1963. Eastham wished to move from Newcastle United FC to Arsenal FC but was prevented from doing so by the Newcastle board, a decision successfully contested by the player in the courts with the backing of the Players' Association.[44] From that time onwards, at first slowly but with increasing rapidity after the introduction of television cameras, the importance of individual players grew to the point where they have become, along with their agents, the dominant factor in the football industry.[45] Agent representation of professional sportsmen was already big business in golf and what was to become Mark McCormack's International Management Group began with the development of Arnold Palmer's career which included his promotion of the Open Championship from 1960 onwards. For the largest part of the previous century the domestic game had been overwhelmingly amateur and middle-class in character, but the wealthier clubs had long employed golf 'professors' as coaches and trainers who augmented their wages with prizes from professional tournaments often sponsored by the popular newspapers of the day. Television coverage of selected events began during the 1950s, and in the years following the Centenary Open Championship in 1960 and the influx of foreign players there grew up a class of tournament professional whose income derived exclusively from prize monies and endorsements. As more players joined the tournament 'circus' attracted by ever greater financial inducements, it was found that the existing number of traditional events was no longer adequate and so in 1976 the Professional Golfers' Association established the European Tour which provided players and sponsors alike with greater commercial potential. By this time the best English professionals were travelling the globe seeking the most lucrative events, so that once again commercial pressures have resulted in an elite standard of play which can only be attained by a relative few who monopolise the major championships and prize funds. Similar commercial pressures were responsible for the inclusion of professional players for the first time in Wimbledon Championships of 1968, which led directly to the abolition of the distinction between amateur and professional by the International Tennis Federation. The rise of commercialism in lawn tennis has resulted in huge prize funds, a proliferation of tournaments and the emergence of a few 'star' players who play far too often for their own good in order to meet contractual obligations to their sponsors.[46]

The coming of 'open' competition has necessarily blurred the distinction between amateur and professional to the point where it has become irrelevant.[47] Even in the most Corinthian of sports the concept of payment in some form or another for participation is generally acknowledged as acceptable, and the International Olympic Committee dropped the word 'amateur' from its charter as far back as 1972.[48] The professionalisation of the English attitude towards the Olympic Games may be gauged by the employment of a Competitors' Employment Officer by the British Olympic Association to secure jobs for sportsmen and women 'whose careers are affected by the heavy demands of their training schedules', with further financial support for them coming from the Sports Aid Foundation.[49] The poor showing of the British athletic team in the first post-war Olympic Games in London encouraged the Amateur Athletic Association for the first time to employ professional coaches to establish a coaching infrastructure throughout the country. Even so Chris Brasher's gold medal in the steeple-chase in 1956 was Britain's first individual gold medal in track athletics since 1932. Only relatively recently has substantial commercial sponsorship of both teams and individuals enabled athletes to attain and maintain the degree of fitness necessary to compete successfully at the highest level. British success in the newly commercialised post-war world of international sport has taken many years to come since the domestic governing bodies persevered in an attitude of 'British is Best' long after it had become untenable. Not until well after the war did they fully realise the implications for their members of specialisation funded by commercialism in the West and state subsidy in the East, and once they had done so the transition from well-meaning amateurism to businesslike professionalism took a generation to achieve results.[50]

It would seem that the post-war developments in the domestic sporting scene reflect the capacity of sport to respond to a variety of societal forces exhibiting, as they do a commercialism and professionalism ideally suited to the business ethic of a new entrepreneurial age. It is to this very responsiveness over the centuries that we shall turn in the next and final chapter with a view to placing the present situation in an appropriate historical context and sketching a scenario for the future.

NOTES

1. *The Times* (18 Aug. 1948), 5f.
2. *The Times* (20 Aug. 1948), 5e.
3. Greyhound racing is currently promoted as a family experience. One of the results of the 1994 amendment to the Sunday Observance Act of 1780 has been the development of 'Family Afternoons' on Sundays at the tracks at Hove, Canterbury, Wembley and Peterborough.
4. Arguably a more significant milestone in the democratisation of the game for both participant and spectator was the introduction in 1968 of foreign players into county cricket.
5. Ludovic Kennedy in his autobiography (*On My Way to the Club*, Harper Collins, 1990) recalls being blackballed by his golf club due he thinks to his criticisms of the judicial system. Other discriminations were also present in the game and anti-jewish feelings amongst club members generally led to the establishment of the Association of Jewish Golf Clubs and Societies. Quotas were in force until recently, e.g. allegations against the Moor Park Golf Club in Hertfordshire during the 1960s. *The Professional Golfers' Association* records that there are currently 3,400 professionals and retired members in the UK, of whom two are black: Jim Howard at Pontypool CC and Roland West at Altrincham Municipal CC
6. Speaking in 1994 the secretary of *Northwood Golf Club* lamented this open door policy as 'a change for the worse' putting it down to financial necessity and the subsequent influx of prosperous traders from the East End of London ('The Club', Cutting Edge, Channel 4 TV, 11 Jan. 1994). As with many other golf clubs, Northwood neither allows its 110 female members to vote or sit on committees and restricts their playing time to benefit the male members. Proposals to rectify this situation were heavily voted down in 1987 and 1992.
7. After decades of censure of the League's policy of 'broken time' payments, the Rugby Football Union sanctioned what it described as 'legitimate expenses' for those Union players who were 'in the early stages of a profession' (see O.L. Owens, *The History of the Rugby Football Union*, Playfair, 1955, p. 55).
8. *Guardian* (18 March 1989), Weekend section.
9. The Equal Opportunities Commission was set up in 1975 as a result of the Sex Discrimination Act of that year. The position of women in sports clubs is however outside its legal remit even though a past chair has said that 'Discriminatory rules within mixed sports clubs are a source of constant complaint to the Commission' (Joanna Foster, *Guardian*, 21 Dec. 1988). At this point it is worth mentioning that there are Ladies' clubs whose male members are not accorded votes, e.g. The Wirral Ladies Golf Club, estd. 1894.
10. For example, *The Darlington Billiard Club* had a rule which forbade members from even buying a drink for a lady (minutes, 10 Feb. 1947).
11. In the present survey 65 per cent of the clubs have received grant aid from the Sports Council since 1965.
12. Perhaps the older cyclists knew something – witness an item in *The Graphic* of 13 July 1895 (around the time when many cycling clubs were established): 'The Newest Woman – Forward but not Fast. A certain lady cyclist in the suburb of Finchley riding on the wrong side of the road ran into another lady and using 'language' knocked her down,

pulled her hair and dragged her across the road. The wearing of rational dress does not apparently make the wearer rational'.

13. Cricket and Hockey have separate governing bodies for women since the men's governing bodies at the time felt unable to 'officially recognize the existence of the new organisation' (*Ladies Hockey Association minutes*, 23 Nov. 1895). The following sports are administratively 'unisex': Archery, Basketball, Bowling, Cycling, Rowing, Rugby League, Swimmming, Lawn Tennis.

14. M. Talbot, *Women in Leisure* (Sports Council, 1979).

15. *Women and Sport* (Sports Council Policy Document, 1993). Evidence of the greater involvement of women in sporting activity comes in a 1994 report by Headland Research (1, Henry Smith Terrace, Headland, Cleveland), entitled *Local Authority Sport*, which identifies the greatest growth in leisure activity as swimming and aerobics both of which attract a disproportionately large percentage of women. The proportion of adults taking part in sport or physical recreation regularly has thus risen from 35 per cent in 1975 to 50 per cent in 1994 due to women's participation.

16. *Catford Cycling Club* minutes AGM (24 Jan. 1946).

17. *Cestreham Cycling Club* minutes (6 Dec. 1950).

18. For example, pre-war swimming instruction was generally £10 per season and post-war around £16 per season; groundsmen charged £4 per season pre-war and £10 post-war.

19. *Tyldesley Swimming Club* for example spent £90.5s.0d. on away fixtures for the 1953 season.

20. *Huyton Cricket Club* minutes (28 April 1947).

21. The dearth of archery clubs was highlighted in a leading article in *The Times* (26 July 1948). For example there were just six archery clubs in the north west of England in 1945 and in 1990 there were 71 due largely to the endeavours of the Lancashire and Cheshire Archery Association established in 1951.

22. *Blackheath Hockey Club* minutes, 19 May 1954.

23. *Warrington Golf Club* Rules and Constitution for 1968.

24. After 1965 higher levels of fund raising were experienced in the amateur sector in order to maximise the 50 per cent grant aid from the newly established Sports Council (see note 11 above). Around this time many clubs were suffering for the first time from what some minutes called a 'plague of vandalism' and funds were needed to repair premises.

25. *Walsall Cycling and Running Club* minutes (4 June 1962).

26. The trend away from 'amateur' behaviour was causing worries elsewhere – witness a remark made at a conference concerning physical education and its future in boarding schools held at Marlborough College, 15–17 April 1970: 'As school teachers one of our greatest enemies may be the increasing expertise of win at all costs professionalism'.

27. Some regattas have reverted to an eighteenth-century level of commercialism employing fairground attractions to subsidise the rowing events, e.g. Burton on Trent, Whitby, Putney Town.

28. *Durham Cricket Club* minutes AGM (14 Jan. 1980).

29. E. Grayson, *Sport and the Law* (Butterworth 1994). The overall thesis of the book links the apparent decline in sporting standards with a collapse of values in society.

30. Two particular examples of sporting violence precipitated the panel's establishment: the severe head injury suffered by Gary Mabbutt, the Captain of Tottenham Hotspurs FC, and the death of Seamus Lavelle, the Hendon RFC player whose manslaughter by fellow player William Hardy resulted in a six-month prison sentence. Nigel Hook of the CCPR told the inquiry that 'the rules of sport should primarily govern the behaviour of the players not the law of the land. In an ideal world there is no place for sport in the courts since it is essentially an affair between two consenting adults.'

31. In 1992 the *All England Lawn Tennis and Croquet Club* advertised for a Television Marketing Executive on the grounds that 'Television coverage of the Championships has increased dramatically in recent years and a senior executive is sought to market and manage these contracts worldwide'.

32. Over the long term this would seem to have happened. Average First Division attendances dropped from 28,704 in the 1970s to 18,766 in the 1980s to 18,273 in the

1990s which gave ammunition to those who promoted and established a Premier Division in order to consolidate attendances and maximise television income. This has come about for those clubs involved but has arguably disadvantaged those clubs in the lower divisions.

33. *Guardian* (12 Oct. 1973). The game in England was not quite ready for Dougan's commercial vision and he went to America to help with the growth of the game there.

34. Each Premier League club is guaranteed £1.5 miilion per year for five years under the £340 million deal with BSkyB Television signed in 1993. In paying for exclusive coverage the company forced those unwilling or unable to pay their subscription charges to do without, along with some Test cricket and many other minor sports broadcast on its Sports Channel.

35. *Soccer – A Game without Vision* (IPPR, Southampton, 1993). In 1995 there was talk of readjusting the football market by establishing a Premier Second Division as a link between the most successful clubs and the rest. Further evidence of the influence of television on the game is the serious suggestion that televised matches could be played in four quarters to allow for more advertising.

36. In correspondence with the author, Geoffrey Thomas of the *British Greyhound Racing Club* maintained that the success of the sport in the modern era relies almost exclusively on the ability of the new stadiums to 'win the leisure pound and not just the gambling pound'.

37. For example, Tetley Breweries (since 1994 Carlsberg/Tetley) sponsor cricket at county level (Yorkshire CCC) and international level (England) and in the process invest several million pounds annually. They are a little coy about saying exactly how much.

So great has the business element in sport become that in 1988 a coalition of companies involved in owning and operating sports facilities launched 'Business in Sport', an initiative aimed primarily at commercialising leisure centres under local authority control. The association included the Metropolitan Group, the Brent Walker Group (since bankrupt), the First Leisure Corporation, Whitbread Retail Division and All Weather Sports Activities. According to its spokesman the group is 'part of a fast growing but very fragmented industry that has not until now sought to speak with one voice' and seeks to 'encourage greater commitment from the private sector in the development of first class sporting facilities on a national level'.

38. Bath RUFC, the most successful club in England over the last decade, proposes to set up a trust fund for players (1995), since it believes that it has a responsibility to reward players who have put service to the club before their careers.

39. This has certainly been true since the 1970s when rateable values, insurance premiums and maintenance costs were badly affected by inflation and subscriptions no longer covered clubs' basic expenditure, e.g. *Warrington Golf Club* accounts for 1978 show subscriptions supplemented by sponsorship from Greenhall's Brewery (£5,000), Bar Income (£23,000), and Gaming Machines (£7,000). The overall deficit still came to £2,300.

40. A good example of this commercial 'fall-out' on the domestic club scene is provided by the Manchester Wheelers' Club which suffered a significant post-war decline but was rescued by sponsorship from Trumann's Steel. This enabled the club to recruit some of the leading riders of the day who have added to the club's long record of achievement. Some of these riders went on to become successful professionals: Steve Joughlin, Malcolm Elliott and Daryl Webster.

41. In 1995 a new three-year contract was signed with Beefeater Gin which gave each club £225,000 per annum, and television income brings that to £300,000 p.a.

42. In the pre-television age there was only one recognised world champion for each weight classification but the last 15 years have seen the formation of three new governing bodies and several new weight categories, all designed to maximise the sport's commercial potential.

43. The minutes of the *Football Players' Union* for 14 Nov. 1949 show an all-time record membership of 2,714 and a comment that 'it is almost unbelievable that any professional player would refuse to join the Union at the same time as receiving the extra

benefits obtained through it'.

44. The summing up by Lord Justice Wilberforce as recorded in the minutes of the Professional Footballers' Association for 4 July 1963 found that 'the old retain and transfer system was an employers' system set up in an industry where the employers have established a monolithic front where they are more strongly organised than the employees and represents an unjustifiable restraint of trade'.

45. This has led to many compromising situations with regard to transfer fees. At the time of writing the latest of these is the allegation that George Graham, the Manager of Arsenal FC, received £285,000 from an agent as an inducement to employ his client. Graham was dismissed on 21 Feb. 1995.

46. The three times Wimbledon champion Boris Becker made the point in 1992 that the top ten players of that year 'were all badly injured or having a nervous breakdown' (*Guardian*, 28 July 1992). During the 1980s both Andrea Jaegar and Tracy Austin were forced out of the game with permanent injuries whilst still teenagers.

47. The top ten money earners in sport for 1995 comprised four boxers, three football players, two golfers and one athlete (nominally amateur).

48. As Christopher Chataway has noted, international sport has become 'War without Weapons' not without encouragement from the Olympic movement itself, whose oath speaks of 'honour of country and the glory of sport', not the other way around. Add to this the commercial pressure exerted by global sponsorship and there exists a potent mix of vested interests.

49. The most successful Olympian of recent times, Steve Redgrave, three times gold medallist in rowing, has been a full-time athlete with an income ranging from £20–50,000 per annum for the last ten years.

50. This is exemplified in the sports featured in the present survey, eight of which have now produced European or World champions at individual or team level, following a lack of competitiveness first shown up against those countries shown in parenthesis: Athletics (USSR), Cycling (France), Football (Hungary), Golf (USA), Hockey (Pakistan), Rowing (Germany), Rugby (New Zealand), Swimming (Australia). Whilst Boxing and Bowling have maintained traditional success, Cricket and Tennis have evidently not embraced the new competitive ethic with sufficient enthusiasm.

9

Conclusions

So long as sport is true to itself its only
purpose is the enjoyment of the players and if
the interest of the spectators predominate then
corruption has set in and the essence of the
game is lost.

(H.A. Harris, *Greek Athletes and Athletics*, 1964)

We don't live in a fair society
so why should sport be fair.

(Dennis Brailsford, *British Sport: A Social History*, 1992)

If one fact above all others is evident from the foregoing review of English sport over four centuries it is that no sport can be insulated from the wider society in which it is played, and yet we have also seen that it has been common from the earliest times for gentlemen to use their recreations as badges of social and physical superiority over the lower order. 'What's a Gentleman but his pleasure?' rings as true in 1995 as it did in 1595,[1] but if we accept the conclusion of William FitzStephen in the twelfth century that all sport derives from a basic human inclination to playfulness then we must ask why the evolution of English sport has largely maintained the social and cultural differentials of so long ago.

A major shift in emphasis in the evolutionary process occurred when any activity indulged in for the 'sport' or fun of it was first seen as socially disruptive and injurious to the patriotic practice of archery. From that time onwards all such indulgences were likely to be judged not only un-English but unmanly and unchristian due to the unruly nature of such sports commonly played on Sundays. The discipline imposed upon society by a web of manorial rights and obligations was extended to include the recreational activities of ordinary people in an attempt to adapt and limit their playfulness to a style more consistent with genteel behaviour and conducive to civil obedience. A gentle-man's recreations at this time consisted mainly of field sports, dancing and games of chance which all reflected a ritual and regulation inherited from courtly etiquette, the acquisition of which identified the player as socially superior to those who participated in similar activities from baser motives. The hired man's field sports born of necessity were thus condemned as poaching whilst his 'gambolling' and 'betting' were dismissed as licentious and cited as evidence of his inherent unreliability. As activities such as bowling and football became socially disruptive, the authorities sought to limit their extent by curtailing people's free time and by outright prohibition, whilst at the same time making provision for regulated participation with the construction of football crofts and bowling alleys. There is evidence of genteel appropriation of bucolic sport in the introduction of football as a therapeutic exercise into some school curricula and in the laying of bowling greens, and these activities supplemented the existing recreations for gentlemen which now included real tennis in emulation of royalty. A withdrawal from field archery was occasioned by the introduction of the musket which joined the horse as another badge of superiority and separateness, the use of which was legitimised by the gentlemen's 'game privilege' preserved and endorsed by Charles II. By this time royalty had led the way in promoting horse-racing but its national popularity became so great that gentlemen sought to regulate it by means of the Jockey Club established in 1750, whose strictures encouraged some to forsake the turf and take up cricket as a less expensive but no less noble alternative form of gambling. To do this it was necessary to appropriate an already well-developed rural pursuit, a process which began with gentrification and continued with regulation and enclosure following the establishment of the Marylebone Cricket Club in 1787, a metropolitan body of self-appointed gentlemen which took upon itself to legislate for the game nationally.

The growth of mercantilism throughout the eighteenth century not only encouraged gentlemen to seek further sporting opportunities for gambling, but also made the commercialisation of leisure activities a profitable concern. The promotion of race meetings became a much needed source of revenue for town councils up and down the country, whilst genteel sponsorship of sport extended from cricket and horse-racing to rowing, boxing and running with the result that more sporting activity than ever before took place in enclosures adapted to facilitate payment and exclude undesirables. Even the first Thames Regatta in 1775 took place out of public view between huge barges full of fee-paying aristocratic spectators. One result of this sponsorship of sport was the rise of the sporting journeyman who supplemented his trade income with prize-winnings and profits from gambling, the pursuit of which frequently involved levels of fixing and fouling which were to become quite unaccceptable to the first generation of gentlemen educated in muscular Christianity by the newly revived public schools. This descent into what became known later as quasi-amateurism or pseudo-professionalism was accompanied by the first intimations that sport was becoming a business, with the organisation of cricket tours, boxing promotions and athletics meetings providing managers and agents with lucrative contracts. The 'prodigious conflux'[2] of people into urban centres, which was the most obvious result of the commercialisation and subsequent industrialisation of the country, provided both the demand for and supply of sporting entertainment, the style of which changed from a free-ranging, rural activity for participants to an enclosed, urban display for spectators.

This change of style embodied the second major shift in the evolution of sport which became for some an activity providing financial reward for competitive success. The new generation of classically educated gentlemen condemned such activity on the grounds that it encouraged unsporting behaviour and was therefore likely by example to be injurious to society. They endeavoured to thwart the trend towards 'the accursed greed for gold' by the traditional means of licensing and prohibition or appropriations and withdrawal, so that the Victorian period saw an enormous growth in the number of sporting clubs whose membership was strictly limited to 'gentlemen amateurs'. Withdrawal into such clubs, which for social, cultural, financial and geographical reasons were unavailable to the working man, was the predictable response of a middle class seeking to distance itself from the crowd. In earlier centuries the landed gentry maintained such a distance with the help of feudal precedents and legal safeguards, but at a time of growing democratisation the sporting club offered a haven of separate development. In emulation of the gentry of the seventeenth century the nouveau riche equivalent of the nineteenth century strove 'to have some knowledge of all the arts but not to seek excellence in any',[3] concluding that any who did had ceased, in Trollope's phrase, 'to be a gentleman in the best sense'.[4] Thus sportsmen who strove for excellence in order to win money became social pariahs and 'to keep them out was a thing desirable on every account'[5] since they represented for the gentlemen amateurs as great a threat to the established order of society as the licentiousness of earlier times. Although the sporting establishment was successful at maintaining the amateur ethic in middle-class culture, it failed to do so in those sports where spectator demand justified substantial payments to players, so that football and rugby league became predominantly professional activities.[6]

The story of twentieth-century English sport, particularly after the Second World War, has been the widespread erosion of amateurism even in the most traditional areas of support. This has been caused through the influences of internationalism which offers the governing bodies the prospect of enhanced prestige for their sports, and television broadcasting which provides huge financial incentives for them, their constituent clubs and the players. The desire for international sporting success placed the amateur governing bodies in a severe dilemma since it became obvious that in order to compete successfully at international level it was necessary to professionalise much of their activities. Naturally this cost large amounts of money and explains why they all levy such exorbitant registration fees upon their constituent clubs and apply for equally substantial grants from the Sports Council, the justification for both being that 'sport must become more professional in order to remain amateur'.[7] The prospect of television fees and consequent commercial sponsorship designed to further excellence of performance in elite groups has persuaded the amateur bodies governing sports like athletics, rowing and rugby union to allow deferred payments to players, thus undermining their amateur credentials in that very 'accursed greed for gold', the condemnation of which brought about their own establishment over a century earlier. The most recent broadcasting innovation of satellite television has brought the elements of international prestige and financial gain to bear upon sport simultaneously by offering staggering fees for participation in worldwide competitions. Such inducements have lowered the amateur resolve of all those sports which have any spectator appeal. Even those activities like cricket, golf and tennis which were appropriated as safe havens for gentlemen during the nineteenth century have succumbed to the blandishments of the Packers, McCormacks and Hunts of the twentieth century.[8] This movement into a business culture based upon the competitive success of elite sporting groups in international leagues, represents the third major shift in the evolution of domestic sport, the latest example of which is the appropriation by Rupert Murdoch of the English Rugby League as part of Sky television's plans for global coverage of the sport.[9] At the same time, those activities once thought of as embodying the genteel purity of English leisures – the centuries-old field sports of hunting, shooting and fishing – have evolved into so much cultural heritage with a market value realised through sales to Japanese, American and Arab businessmen.

In telling the above story it is difficult to avoid the conclusion that although the players may have changed, the tactics have remained remarkably similar. Time and again we find evidence of this as situations present themselves which, though shaped by contemporary circumstances, are nevertheless entirely recognisable as products of a timeless energy. The very essence of sport itself, being the recreation of the human spirit through the sheer joy of play, has imbued all those activities looked at in the present survey and the ritualistic aspects of such behaviour can be seen today as clearly as ever. What was described in the fifteenth century as the licentiousness of footballers destroying property in and around the villages which formed the field of play has evolved into the hooliganism of supporters who destroy property in and around stadiums. The efforts made by the authorities in the fifteenth century to contain such aberrant behaviour are mirrored almost exactly by those made today and exemplified in the terms of the Football Spectators Act passed in 1989. The ritual of early genteel recreations which derived from even earlier courtly etiquettes gave rise to the formalisation of games organised by the gentlemen of the nineteenth century who wished to emulate the aristocratic customs in order to consolidate their social position. We can see, therefore, a *noblesse oblige* attitude in the implementation of concepts of fair play, together with a patronage of those lower down the social scale, and more mundanely an emphasis on codes of discipline and dress all of which were utilised to exhibit and maintain their peculiar privilege.[10] The inter-village tribalism engendered by early sporting activity manifested itself later in the cleavage between town/country and London/ provinces and is particularly evident today in the fanatical support of football teams from different towns. Even today much antipathy is born of the cultural divide between the north and south of the country, a recent example being the disagreement within the National Cricket Association concerning semi-professionals in its one-day competition, the involvement in which was supported by northern clubs but condemned by those in the south.

The element of gambling that was so prevalent in both the bucolic and genteel cultures of earlier centuries was formalised and legitimised by the stock-jobbers of the eighteenth century whose money helped to commercialise and urbanise much of English sport. An exactly similar effect today is produced by the 'spread betting' of city analysts on every aspect of sporting activity from the number and frequency of goals scored in football matches to the likelihood of a sinking in the Boat Race.[11] The recognition by the genteel classes of earlier centuries of the therapeutic aspects of sport, particularly with reference to swimming and football, which was introduced at St Paul's School in the sixteenth century, has continued to inform much educational thought.

The poor physical health of army recruits encouraged the government to introduce physical training into state schools in the early years of this century, but as recently as 1993 the army once again claimed that its recruits were unable to tackle the prescribed fitness programmes. Whereas football was seen at one time as a disruptive influence, the reintroduction of this and other team games into schools is now seen by government as productive of much needed discipline and morale.[12] These attributes can be seen as the natural products of activities deemed from the earliest times to be essentially unintellectual, a judgement underlined by the Rugby School Book of 1856 which comments that 'we are not students in England, our nature is abhorrent of the study'. This goes some way to explain the English mistrust of the pursuit of excellence, whilst also identifying sport as one of the very few avenues of advancement for the less academically inclined.[13]

The medieval concept of authority based upon the support for an established social order presided over by God, represented on earth by the monarch and exercised through an unchanging hierarchy of the great and good, remains largely intact today. The power of the landowner over the daily activities of his tenants, including their recreation, has been modified over the centuries through Acts of Parliament, Game Privileges and Laws of Trespass, and was institutionalised during the eighteenth century in the form of bodies such as the MCC and Jockey Club, both of which enclosed land in order to restrict and control sporting activity. In emulation of these aristocratic clubs many of the governing bodies of the nineteenth century were similarly constituted and it is only since 1945 that they have, often grudgingly, made any effort to represent their constituent members democratically.[14] The social structure of England, despite all the innovations of recent history, remains essentially that which was produced by the public school graduates of the late eighteenth and early nineteenth centuries. The working-class element is better educated today and has a higher representation in Parliament, but the real levers of power remain in the hands of Oxbridge-educated men, half of whom continue to come from the independent sector of education. These people still form the majority of Conservative governments and at all times control the financial aspects of society while continuing to own the lion's share of land and property.[15] The gentlemen of the Star and Garter tavern who codified the laws of cricket in 1784 and those of the Star and Arrow coffee house who established Leander Club in 1819 were the very same 'substantial men' who appointed everyone in their own counties from members of parliament to clergymen. Their contemporary equivalents as the great and good can be found on governing bodies, sports councils, development corporations and quangos of every description, placed there by governments or ministers to implement established policies.

The idea of using enclosures first to control and later to exclude trouble-makers has developed to such an extent over the centuries that the Taylor Report of 1990 will require £1 billion to be spent modifying the grounds of those activities likely to attract crowds of any size. This concept of physical exclusion has had obvious repercussions on sports such as football, cricket, racing and rugby, but also significance with regard to enclosures at regattas which sought to maintain during the nineteenth and twentieth centuries the social exclusivity enjoyed during the seventeenth and eighteenth centuries by artistocrats at their private boating lakes. It is interesting to make a direct comparison between these early artificial lakes and the modern artificial international rowing courses, since the former managed to exclude undesirables on social and cultural criteria whilst the latter continue to do so on those of finance and athletic ability. Similar restriction of public access was rigorously maintained in the countryside for many centuries as landowners used large areas for the preservation of game and hunting and prosecuted trespassers with extreme force. Although the penalties for trespass have been reduced over the centuries, there remains the age-old tension between the landed and the landless which resulted in the Kinder Trespass of 1932 and, following the privatisation of much Water Board land, a further organised trespass of the same area in 1995.[16]

The decline of amateurism can be traced as far back as the classical era, but in the English context began in earnest during the eighteenth century when the commercialisation of sport introduced payment for sporting entertainment and competitive success. As society itself fragmented to accommodate different socio-economic classifications, so sporting activities and players were themselves placed into categories ranging from pure Corinthian amateur to salaried professional, and this process carries on today with as much terminological prevarication as ever. In rugby union particularly, the sport into which the gentlemen amateurs withdrew to avoid the professional contamination of football, the definitions of former times no longer apply now that all the best players receive some form of payment. Whilst the Rugby Football Union 'wants the game to remain a recreational sport' it admits that 'pure amateurism went out of the window some time ago' and concludes, due to the professional ethos of the 1990s, 'that perhaps we need a new word to define the present players'.[17]

The amateur ideal in sport, which is the sheer joy of playing, has been eroded in direct proportion to the rise of commercialism in society at large, and in so far as commercial activity is driven by demand for a given product we must recognise that the professionalisation of games playing is the result of spectatorism. By extension of this argument we should realise that the more spectators there are, the further from that ideal we shall surely travel, and that the growth of a global television audience will take us so far from it that the very nature of those games involved will change irrevocably.[18] The enduring popularity of football, not only in England but in all those countries to which it has been exported, has made it the biggest business in sport and it is confirmed in this position by television magnates such as Murdoch and Berlosconi. Although many clubs in England began as purely recreational organisations, the commercial prospects offered by the growing number of spectators encouraged local entrepreneurs to develop them as business ventures. Share option schemes like that promoted by Tottenham Hotspur FC in 1899 became an accepted way of raising the large sums of money needed to build the bigger capacity stadiums. Like many other clubs, Tottenham suffered fluctuating fortunes and was bought after the Second World War by the Richardson family who, unwilling to invest the necessary capital, sold out to a business consortium in 1983 which immediately sought a stock market listing – the first for any football club in England. 'Spurs' plc was a paradigm of the late 1980s when involvement in leisure was seen as a licence to print money, but the recession of 1990 caused falling attendances and the debt on the east stand became impossible to service. The establishment of the Premier League and Murdoch's huge investment in it brought financial security to the club, as it did to many others, and together with income from club shops the better supported Premier Division clubs now make substantial profits each year.[19] Much of the money that football clubs spend goes on wages for very highly paid professional players who can supplement their incomes through product endorsements and other commercial ventures, and this is now common for many of the players in televised sports. As we have seen, the sporting hero over the centuries has usually been well-recompensed materially for his efforts but today the earning potential for sporting 'stars' is unprecedented.[20]

A final historical parallel worth drawing concerns the place of English sport in the international arena. The Victorian gentlemen's denigration of foreign sporting etiquette led directly to English exclusion from many of the world governing bodies, a situation only rectified many years later when it was finally realised that international co-operation was necessary for domestic development.

Foreign leadership of international sport continues and some distance still remains between the often blatantly professional foreign approach to the promotion of sport and the more measured but now quasi-amateur English approach. Recent illustrations of this ongoing problem concern complaints over the less than favourable treatment of some foreign competitors at the athletics World Cup held in London in 1994 (interestingly echoing those made at the London Olympic Games of 1908) and the behaviour of the Princess Royal in missing both the opening and closing ceremonies of the Barcelona Olympic Games in 1992, the only member of the IOC to do so. During the 1980s and 1990s the trend towards a thoroughgoing professionalisation of sport has been supported by the godfathers of international sport: Samaranch, Havelange, Nebiolo, Parker, Murdoch, Tapie, Ecclestone, McCormack, King, Berlosconi, Un Yom Kin, the most powerful eleven in the game having between them taken sport from the nineteenth century to the twenty-first century and all but extinguished its Corinthian spirit in the process.

The evolution of English sport, and by extension much of English society, has been a story full of petty snobberies, class selfishness, hypocrisy, religious bigotry, racism and sexism, the constant theme of which has been the exclusion of all those groups identified as socially undesirable by the contemporary customs of succeeding generations. It would seem that the sporting gentlemen, establishment and governing bodies of today have very largely elected to connive at the appropriation of sport by television companies in the pursuit of profit and prestige, a process which by accident or design has again excluded many people not only from direct participation but also from active support as spectators. As in the past those with most money will purchase privileged access, whilst those with least will have no choice but to accept whatever they are offered and be left with a participation which also has its price, since competitive sport is increasingly concentrated in clubs whose spiralling costs force them to levy ever higher subscriptions.[21] It is not surprising then that the growth areas in sporting activity are those in non-club, non-competitive pursuits such as jogging, aerobics, swimming, rambling, cycling and fishing, where few of the traditional exclusions apply.[22]

The message of the past which continues to be repeated loud and clear today is that exclusion can breed resentment and disaffection with unfortunate results for the whole of society. With that in mind, those in positions of influence must realise that the long-term future for both sport and society involves working together for the benefit of the whole community rather than divisively in the interests of a few.

CONCLUSIONS

NOTES

1. J. Lando and H. Runt, *Banks Bay Horse in Trance* (London, 1595).
2. D. Defoe, *A Tour through the whole island of Great Britain* (London, 1726).
3. A. Peacham, *English Recreations* (London, 1641).
4. A. Trollope, *British Sports and Pastimes* (Virtue and Spalding, 1868).
5. *The Times* (26 April 1880), 6a.
6. See Appendix.
7. Peter Yarranton of the Sports Council and Wasps RUFC, *Guardian* (18 March 1989).
8. Television sponsorship of sport can be summarised as follows (1995):

   BBC Bowling (World Indoor Championships), Cricket (domestic Test Matches), Football (FA Cup), Golf (Open Championship and four domestic events), Racing (Grand National and selected provincial meetings), Rowing (Boat Race), Rugby League (Championship Trophy and Challenge Cup), Rugby Union (Five Nations Championship).

   ITV Athletics (seven international events), Football (selected League matches and the League Cup), Rugby Union (World Cup matches).

   C4 Racing (Gold Cup and The Derby and selected meetings).

   Sky Boxing (all Frank Warren promotions), Cricket (overseas Test Matches and one day matches), Football (England internationals, Premier Division and FA Cup), Golf (Ryder Cup and nine tour events), Rugby League (League Championship and World Super League), Rugby Union (League and Cup competitions).

   Sky TV now (April 1995) accounts for 75 per cent of all televised sport in Britain.

   Commercial sponsors involved: Beefeater Gin, Martell Brandy, Endsleigh Insurance, Coca-Cola, Ever Ready, Courage Brewers, Pilkington Glass, Tetley Brewers, Scottish and Newcastle Brewers, Cadbury Schweppes, Commercial Union, Barclays Bank, Gallagher Ltd.

   The two sides of the argument concerning the televising of sport can be summarised: BBC spokesman: 'Our aim is to ensure that the key national events can still be seen by the whole nation.' Sky TV spokesman: 'Viewers know there is no such thing as a free lunch.' (Both taken from *Guardian*, 7 April 1995.)
9. £77 million has been paid for the television rights of the whole English Rugby League. The international competition as envisaged will require the amalgamation of traditionally fiercely independent clubs representing almost tribal loyalties and has been opposed by many supporters. Nevertheless 25 out of the 32 clubs are technically on the verge of bankruptcy because of insufficient support on the terraces. Maurice Lindsay of the League hails the arrangement with Sky 'as a glorious opportunity of taking the game to the world' and the club chairmen welcome the money as 'a godsend' whilst sounding a note of alarm in recognising that Sky's investment is 'aimed purely at an armchair audience' (*Guardian*, 8 April 1995).

   A point made time and again concerning the appropriation of sport by subscription broadcasting is summed up in *Guardian* (8 April 1995): 'Something important has been torn from the heart of Britain when big sporting events are high jacked from the public domain for minority gain', a sentiment expressed more poignantly by a supporter contemplating the amalgamation of his beloved team with a rival in order to qualify for the Super League, an action 'which would make a hole in my life that could never be filled' (*Guardian*, letters, 15 April 1995).
10. The 'tradition' of wearing whites in cricket for example only dates back to the 1880s and is an emblem of purity representative of some mythical Corinthian past which was sacralised as a bastion against uncivilised behaviour.
11. Investment firms involved in betting on sporting events:

City Index with	5,500 clients and £180 m turnover
Sporting Index with	4,500 clients and £150 m turnover
I.G. with	9,000 clients and £400 m turnover
12. It is significant that the promotion of sport at school continues to be a priority in the independent sector where it can represent up to 20 per cent of the curriculum, whereas

the state sector allows only six per cent to be available. Between 1983 and 1993 the introduction of the national curriculum has encouraged 70 per cent of state schools to reduce the amount of PE whilst only 14 per cent of fee paying schools have followed suit.

13. Examples of this exist as far back as records go: Greek athletic champions were kept by the state in some splendour; medieval English champions were made members of the Lord's household and often given official positions as 'stewards'; eighteenth-century champions of various sports were given sinecures in the households of their patrons; nineteenth-century champions often finished their careers as landlords of public houses or retired on the proceeds of substantial testimonials; the twentieth century equivalents include the advancement of socially deprived ethnic minorities through sports such as boxing, football and athletics and the opening up of careers particularly in the media for past champions.

14. Most sports bodies are self-perpetuating oligarchies including the British Olympic Committee (and of course the International Olympic Committee). None of the major sporting organisations has, for example, any senior female administrators or any from the ethnic minorities and there are few from any source under 50 years of age. The Amateur Rowing Association continues to allow Leander Club, OUBC and CUBC each to appoint a representative to the governing council, a privilege not accorded to any other club. In cricket the era of aristocratic ownership of teams is recalled in the rule that no player is allowed to comment about anything publicly without consulting their county and the MCC. The Jockey Club maintains its exclusivity and independence by regenerating from within. It effectively took over the National Hunt Committee in 1968 and in 1993 established the British Horse Racing Board whose first chairman was Lord Huntingdon, the ex-senior steward of the Jockey Club. He was followed as senior steward by Thomas Henry Milbourne-Swinnerton-Pilkington. Football, according to Kate Hoey, MP, 'is a multi-million pound business and yet it is run like a seedy private club' (*Independent*, 16 March 1995).

15. H. Perkin, *The Structured Crowd* (Harvester, 1981), a study of 4,500 elite positions in English society.
    It would appear that the other end of the socio-economic scale also remains much the same as before. For example, comparing the figures for infant mortality produced by the Registrar General in 1931 and those in *Social Trends* for 1991, we find the discrepancy between the 'Independent Class/Labouring Class' (1931) and 'Class 1/Class 5' (1991) almost exactly similar. The unchanging nature of the gap between the 'haves' and 'have nots' is graphically illustrated by two comments made 128 years apart: the first, at a testimonial dinner of 1866 in Newcastle for a local professional sculler, made by a speaker denigrating those who talked of working class improvidence by citing the common local family situation of ten members living on 18 shillings a week, commenting that this was 'as improvident in one week as many men would spend on one meal' (*Newcastle Chronicle*, 10 Jan. 1866, 7d.); the second, as before denigrating criticism of the less well off, by commenting that 'Many householders on council estates eat for a week on the price of a Fleet Street lunch' (*Guardian*, 24 Jan. 1994, 5c).

16. An interesting example of such exclusions stretching back over the centuries is afforded by Gerald Grosvenor, Duke of Westminster, on his Abbeystead estate in Lancashire where preservation of grouse takes precedence over public access to open moorland. His forebear, who came to England with William in 1066 and was named after his prediliction for hunting (Le Gros Veneur), had a similar attitude to trespassers on his estates north of the Thames with admittedly more terrifying results.

17. Dudley Wood, secretary RFU, *Observer*, 12 Feb. 1955. In other sports the new word is 'fundholder', indicating a nominally amateur athlete who uses a trust fund to subsidise his activities, the balance of which can be accessed on his retirement. Athletics has operated this scheme for over ten years and rowing endorsed it for the first time in 1994: 'The competitor shall be entitled on his retirement to receive the balance of any cash prize held on his behalf by the national association' (*The Rowing Almanack*, 1995, Amateur Status Regulations).

CONCLUSIONS

Some other sports maintain a purely amateur stance, e.g. the Hockey Association defines an amateur as 'a person who plays hockey as a diversion or for physical or moral wellbeing and does not directly or indirectly derive any profit therefrom'.

The level of commercial interest in a sport is largely responsible for its playing status and this in turn is largely dependent upon television coverage. Therefore hockey with little coverage can remain comfortably amateur. Athletics, rowing and other sports must quasi-professionalise, whilst rugby union will soon join football, cricket and others as fully professional, thanks to global television contracts.

18. The trend away from active participation to passive viewing has continued despite official efforts to reverse it. The latest available breakdown of sporting income published by the Sports Council in 1993 shows that £5 billion was spent on spectating (admissions, books, videos, newspaper, television licence/subscription, football pools, betting and fashion) and £4.7 billion on participation (sports goods, bicycles, boats, footwear, travel and club subscriptions).

19. *Preliminary Report on Research on the Premier League* (Centre for Football Research, Leicester University, 1995). The average expenditure at club shops is £92.33 per season and the average home game expenditure is £24.42. Together with television income and commercial sponsorship, the turnover for one of the larger clubs is around £20 million, with profits of around £4 m.

20. It is instructive to compare contemporary earning capacity with that of a century and more ago (see note 42, chapter 4).

    Endorsements for a sports wear company by a well-known sporting personality are valued at £50,000–£80,000, similarly a single television advertising fee would be £10,000–£30,000; personal appearances come in at £1,000–£3,000; and a weekly newspaper column £200–£500.

    Although the remuneration available has increased immeasurably over this period, the identification with individual champions, at least in England, has, one suspects, been weakened by their media induced proliferation: would Newcastle close for the day to pay respects to Paul Gascoigne as it did in 1871 when 100,000 turned out onto the streets to mourn James Renforth? Perhaps.

21. Price rises in subscription rates and entrance fees from 1985 to 1995: athletics 211 per cent, cricket 208 per cent, football 146 per cent, golf 185 per cent, racing 142 per cent, rugby 200 per cent, tennis 371 per cent (*Social Trends*, HMSO, 1995).

    As further evidence of exclusion it is worth noting here the decrease in television viewing following the introduction of subscription TV into a sport: the Premier League drew nine million viewers when as Division I it was on BBC, but only 800,000 after BSkyB took over the franchise.

22. Participation increases from 1985 to 1995 as follows: hiking nine to 27 per cent, swimming 28 to 56 per cent, cycling 15 to 28 per cent, fishing 35 to 63 per cent (*Social Trends*, HMSO, 1995).

APPENDIX
SYNOPSIS OF SPORTING EVOLUTION

(based on E. and S. Yeo's four means of repression of popular activities put forward in *Popular Culture and Class Conflict*: (i) Joining and taking them over – appropriation; (ii) Organising rival activities – withdrawal; (iii) Licensing and pricing them – exclusion; and (iv) Outright banning – prohibition)

Archery   Appropriated and priced largely out of reach in club structures

Athletics   As pedestrianism was often banned, but as athletics was later appropriated as an Olympic sport

Bowling   Banned as socially disruptive but appropriated by the leisured class and largely abandoned when popularly available

Boxing   As pugilism was often banned, but as boxing was appropriated as the 'noble art'; later abandoned owing to fixing

Cricket   Appropriated and priced largely out of reach in club culture

Cycling   Initially appropriated, subsequently licensed but soon abandoned owing to popularity withdrawal to motor sports

Fishing   Banned and/or licensed; growth of popularity forced withdrawal from coarse fishing into game fishing which was priced out of reach

Football   Banned and appropriated, subsequently abandoned at the onset of professionalism in favour of rugby union

Golf   Appropriated and priced out of reach in club culture

Hockey   Appropriated and developed in a club culture

Hunting   Banned and/or licensed and priced out of reach

Racing   The 'sport of kings', always of privileged access, continues to be run in the interests of the owners

Rowing   Appropriated and gentrified and priced out of reach in clubs

Rugby   Established as an amateur alternative to football into which gentlemen withdrew; priced out of reach in club culture

Shooting   Banned and/or licensed and priced out of reach

Swimming   Initially appropriated as therapeutic but abandoned following mass popularity and availability

Tennis   Appropriated and priced out of popular reach in club culture

Note: The above helps to explain why those sports that either have maintained open access or were not susceptible to regulation are now the most popular participation sports: athletics (all forms of running), bowling, cycling, fishing, swimming.

Bibliography

INDIVIDUAL SPORTS

Altham, R. and Swanton, J. *A History of Cricket* (Allen & Unwin, 1962)
Ascham, R. *Toxophilus* (1545) (Scolar Press, 1971)
Batchelor, D. *British Boxing* (Faber, 1940)
Bellamy, R. *The Story of Squash* (Cassell, 1976)
Bird, D. *Our Skating Heritage* (N.S.A., 1979)
Brailsford, D. *A Social History of Prize Fighting* (Lutterworth, 1988)
Brookes, C. *English Cricket* (Weidenfeld & Nicolson, 1978)
Browning, R. *A History of Golf* (Allen Lane, 1956)
Burke, E. *The History of Archery* (Fawcett Muller, 1958)
Cardus, N. and Arlott, J. *The Noblest Game* (Longmans, 1969)
De Beaumont, R. *Fencing, Ancient Art and Modern Sport* (Kaye Ward, 1970)
Downer, A.R. *Running Recollections* (Blairgowrie Books, 1982)
Fleischer, N. *A History of Heavyweight Boxing, 1719 to the Present* (Putnam, 1949)
Gate, R. *Rugby League* (Arthur Barker, 1989)
Grimsley, W. *Tennis, Its History, People and Events* (Prentice, 1971)
Harding, J. *For the Good of the Game* (Robson Books, 1991)
Harris, H.A. *Greek Athletes and Athletics* (Hutchinson, 1964)
Hawkes, J. *The Meynellian Science* (Leicester U.P., 1932)
Heath, E.G. *A History of Target Archery* (David & Charles, 1973)
Hill, C. *Horse Power, the Politics of the Turf* (Manchester U.P., 1988)
Itzkovitz, D. *Peculiar Privilege, A Social History of English Fox-Hunting* (Hassocks, 1977)
Lake, A. and Wright, D. *Bibliography of Archery* (Manchester U.P., 1988)
Lemon, D. *The Crisis of Captaincy* (Christopher Helm, 1988)
Longrigg, R. *A History of Horse Racing* (Macmillan, 1972)
Lord Aberdare. *The Book of Tennis and Raquets* (Stanley Paul, 1980)
Lunn, A. *A Century of Mountaineering* (Allen & Unwin, 1957)
Lunn, A. *The Story of Skiing* (Eyre & Spottiswoode, 1952)
Lyttleton, B. and Padwick, E. *A Bibliography of Cricket* (Clarke, 1977)
Macklin, K. *The History of Rugby League* (Stanley Paul, 1974)
Malherbe, W. *A Chronological Bibliography of Hockey* (Hockey Ass., 1965)
Marshall, M. *Gentlemen and Players* (Grafton, 1987)
Mason, A. *Association Football and English Society 1863–1915* (Harvester Press, 1980)
McNab, T. *A History of Professional Athletics* (Athletics Ass., 1972)
Moorhouse, G. *Lords* (Hodder & Stoughton, 1983)
Mortimer, R. *A History of the Derby Stakes* (Joseph, 1962)
Mortimer, R. *The Jockey Club* (Cassell, 1958)
Owen, O.L. *The History of the Rugby Football Union* (Playfair, 1955)
Philips-Birt, D. *The Cumberland Fleet* (David & Charles, 1975)

Robertson, M. *Wimbledon, 1877–1977* (Arthur Barker, 1977)
Rowley, P. *The Book of Hockey* (Batsford, 1963)
Scott, J. *The Athletic Revolution* (Free Press, 1971)
Seth-Smith, M. *A History of Steeple-Chasing* (Joseph, 1966)
Shearman, M. *Athletics* (Longman Green, 1889)
Sissons, R. *The Player, A Social History of the Professional Cricketer* (Kingswood Press, 1988)
Smith, R. *A Social History of the Bicycle* (American Heritage, 1972)
Smyth, J. *Lawn Tennis* (Batsford, 1966)
Solomon, J.W. *Croquet* (Batsford, 1966)
Tabner, B. *Through the Turnstiles* (Yore Publications, 1993)
Thomas, P. *The Northern Cross Country Association, Centenary History* (N.C.C.A., 1982)
Thompson, L. *The Dogs, A Personal History of Greyhound Racing* (Chatto and Windus, 1994)
Walvin, J. *The People's Game, A Social History of British Football* (Arrow Books, 1975)
Watman, M. *A History of British Athletics* (Hale, 1968)
Whyte, J.C. *A History of the British Turf* (Longmans, 1840)
Wigglesworth, N. *A Social History of English Rowing* (Cass, 1992)

COLLECTIVE SPORTS

Arlott, J. *The Oxford Companion to Sports and Games* (Paladin, 1977)
Bale, J. *Sport & Place – A Geography of Sport* (Hurst & Co, 1982)
Briggs, A. *Essays in the History of Publishing* (Longman, 1974)
Burke, P. *Popular Culture in Early Modern Europe* (Temple Smith, 1978)
Burrows, H. and Wood, L. *Sports & Pastimes in English Literature* (Nelson, 1925)
Cone, C. (ed.). *Sundry Sports of Merry England* (Kentucky U.P., 1981)
Cox, R. *Sport – A Guide to Historical Sources in the U.K.* (Sports Council Information Series No.9, 1983)
Ford, J. *This Sporting Land* (New English Library, 1977)
Goodman, P. *Sporting Life – An Anthology of British Sporting Prints* (British Museum, 1983)
Harris, H.A. *Sport in Britain* (Stanley Paul, 1975)
Lady Greville. *The Gentlewomen's Book of Sports* (Spalding, 1880)
Lennox, W. *Pictures of Sporting Life and Character* (Hurst, 1860)
Longrigg, R. *The English Squire and his Sport* (Joseph, 1977)
Maclaren, A. *Training in Theory and Practice* (Macmillan, 1866)
McCrone, K. 'Sport at the Oxbridge Women's Colleges to 1914' (*British Journal of Sports History*, Sept. 1986)
Nickalls, G.O. *With the Skin of Their Teeth* (Country Life, 1951)
Peek, H. *The Poetry of Sport* (Longmans & Co, 1896)
Reekie, H.M. 'A History of Sport and Recreation for Women in G.B. 1770–1850' (Ohio State University, Ph.D., 1982)
Rodgers, H.B. *Pilot National Recreation Survey* (Keele University, 1966)
Trollope, A. *British Sports and Pastimes* (Virtue, 1868)
Vale, M. *The Gentlemen's Recreations 1580–1630* (Brewer, 1977)
Walsh, J.H. *A Manual of British Rural Sports* (Routledge, 1856)
Whitney, C. *A Sporting Pilgrimage to Oxford, Cambridge and the Shires* (Osgood McIlvaine, 1894)

BIBLIOGRAPHY

SOCIAL COMMENTARY

Allison, L. *The Politics of Sport* (Manchester U.P., 1986)

Arnold, J. 'The Influence of Pilkington Brothers on Sport and Community in St. Helens' (M.Ed., Liverpool University, 1977)

Aspin, D. 'The Nature and Purpose of Sporting Activity' (*Physical Education Review*, Spring 1986)

Bailey, P. *Leisure and Class in Victorian England* (Routledge, 1978)

Ball, D. and Loy, J. *Sport and Social Order* (Addison Wesley, 1975)

Berryman, J.W. 'Sport as Social History' (*Quest*, Summer, 1973)

Bert, E. *An Approved Treatise on Hawking* (London, 1619)

Blanchard, E. and Cheska, P. *The Anthropology of Sport* (Bergin Garvey, 1985)

Brailsford, D. *Some Factors in the Evolution of Sport* (Lutterworth, 1993)

Brooke-Smith, M. 'The Growth and Development of Popular Entertainment in the Lancashire Cotton Towns 1830–1870' (M.Litt., Lancaster University, 1971)

Cardus, N. *Cardus on Cricket* (Souvenir Press, 1977)

Carter, J. *Sports and Pastimes of the Middle Ages* (U.P. of America, 1988)

Cashman, E. and McKernan, R. *Sport in History* (Queensland U.P., 1979)

Chataway, C. and Goodhart, G. *War Without Weapons* (Allen, 1968)

Clarke, J. *The Devil Makes Work: Leisure in Capitalist Britain* (Illinois U.P., 1985)

Cross, G. *A Social History of Leisure Since 1600* (Venture, 1990)

Cunningham, H. *Leisure in the Industrial Revolution* (Croom, 1980)

Dando, J. and Runt, H. *Banks Bay Horse in Trance* (London, 1595)

Dobbs, B. *Edwardians at Play* (Pelham, 1973)

Donajgrodski, J. *Social Control in Nineteenth-Century England* (Croom, 1980)

Dunning, Maguire and Pearson. *The Sports Process: A Comparative and Developmental Approach* (Routledge, 1993)

Dunning, E. and Sheard, K. *Barbarians, Gentlemen and Players* (Robertson, 1979)

Ensor, E. 'The Football Madness' (*Contemporary Review*, lxxiv, 1898)

Ford, J. *This Sporting Land* (New English Library, 1977)

Golby, J. and Purdue, A. *The Civilisation of the Crowd – Popular Culture in England 1750–1900* (Batsford, 1984)

Haley, B. *The Healthy Body and Victorian Culture* (Harvard U.P., 1978)

Haley B. 'Sports and the Victorian World' (*Western Humanities Review*, 22, 1968)

Hammond, L. and B. *The Age of the Chartists 1832–1854* (Anchor, 1962)

Hargreaves, J. *Sport, Power and Culture* (Polity Press, 1986)

Hawkins, B. and Lowerson, J. *Trends in Leisure* (Sussex U.P., 1979)

Holt, R. *Sport and the British* (O.U.P., 1989)

Holt, R. *Sport and the Working Class in Modern Britain* (Manchester U.P., 1992)

Ingham, R. and Loy, J. *Sport in Social Development* (Hutchinson, 1993)

James, C.L.R. *Beyond a Boundary* (Hutchinson, 1963)

Krawczyk, B. *Social Origin and Ambivalent Character of Ideology of Amateur Sport* (International Review of Sport Sociology, 1977)

Lowerson, J. *Sport and the English Middle Classes* (Manchester U.P., 1993)

Lowerson, J. and Myerscough, G. *Time to Spare in Victorian England* (Harvester Press, 1977)

Lucas, J. *The Future of the Olympic Games* (Routledge, 1992)

Malcolmson, R. *Popular Recreations in English Society 1700–1850* (C.U.P., 1973)

Mangan, J. *Athleticism in the Victorian and Edwardian Public School* (C.U.P., 1981)

Mangan, J. *The Cultural Bond: Sport, Empire & Society* (Frank Cass, 1992)

165

Mangan, J. and Park, B. *From Fair Sex to Feminism* (Frank Cass, 1992)

Mangan, J. and Park, B. *Pleasure, Profit and Proselytism* (Frank Cass, 1988)

Marx, K. *Capital* (Lawrence & Wishart, 1970)

Mason, A. *Sport in Britain* (Faber & Faber, 1988)

McCrone, K. *Sport and the Physical Emancipation of English Women* (Lutterworth Press, 1988)

McIntosh, P. *Fair Play – Ethics in Sport and Education* (Heinemann, 1979)

McIntosh, P. 'Historical View of Sport and Social Control' (*International Review of Sport Sociology*, Vol.6, 1973)

McIntosh, P. *Sport in Society* (Watts, 1963)

Mellor, H. *Leisure and the Changing City 1870–1914* (Routledge, 1976)

Metcalfe, A. 'Sport in Nineteenth-Century England' (Wisconsin U., Ph.D., 1968)

Midwinter, E. *Fair Game* (Allen and Unwin, 1986)

Natan, A. *Sport and Society* (Bowes and Bowes, 1958)

Pimlott, J. *An Englishman's Holiday* (Harvester Press, 1976)

Pimlott, J. *Recreations* (Studio Vista, 1968)

Plumb, J. *The Growth of Leisure 1630–1830* (O.U.P., 1972)

Plumb, J. *The Commercialisation of Leisure in the Eighteenth Century* (Reading U.P., 1974)

Rees, R. 'The Development of Physical Recreation in Liverpool in the Nineteenth Century' (M.A., Liverpool U., 1968)

Roberts, J. *The Commercial Sector in Leisure* (Sports Council, 1979)

Roberts, J. *The Economic Impact of Sport in the U.K.* (Henley Centre for Economic Forecasting, 1992)

Simson, A. *The Lords of the Rings* (Simon and Schuster, 1992)

Smith, S. 'Remarks on the System of Education in Public Schools' (*Edinburgh Review*, August 1810, Vol.XVI)

Strutt, J. *Sports and Pastimes of the People of England* (White, 1801)

Talbot, M. *Women and Leisure* (Sports Council, 1979)

Tomlinson, A. and M. *Insights into Leisure and Culture* (Sports Council, 1984)

Trollope, A. *British Sports and Pastimes* (Virtue and Spalding, 1868)

Trollope, A. *The New Zealander* (Clarendon Press, 1972)

Walton, J. *The English Seaside Resort, 1750–1914* (Leicester U.P., 1983)

Walton, J. and Walvin J. *Leisure in Britain* (Manchester U.P., 1983)

Walvin, J. *Beside the Sea* (Allen Lane, 1978)

Walvin, J. *Football and the Decline of Britain* (Macmillan, 1986)

Walvin, J. *Leisure and Society* (Longman, 1978)

Waszack, P. 'The Development of Leisure and Cultural Facilities in Peterborough 1850–1900' (B.A., Huddersfield Polytechnic, 1972)

Whitney, C., *A Sporting Pilgrimage to Oxford, Cambridge and the Shires* (Osgood McIlvaine, 1894)

Wood, A. *Memoirs of the Holles Family* (Camden 3rd series, 1937)

Wood, H. and Burrows, H. *Sports and Pastimes in English Literature* (Nelson, 1925)

Worsley, T. *Barbarians and Philistines* (Robert Hale, 1940)

Worsley, T. *The End of the Old School Tie* (Secker & Warburg, 1941)

Yeo, E. and S. *Popular Culture and Class Conflict* (Harvester, 1981)

CULTURAL BACKGROUND

Adams, R. *Paradoxical Harvest: Energy and Explanation in British History 1870–1914* (Cambridge U.P., 1982)

BIBLIOGRAPHY

Baumann, Z. *Memories of Class* (Routledge and Kegan Paul, 1982)

Beeton, Mrs. *The Book of Household Management* (1888) (rep. Cape, 1968)

Benson, J. *The Working Class in England 1875–1914* (Croom Helm, 1985)

Briggs, A. *Victorian Cities* (Odhams, 1963)

Campbell, R. *The London Tradesman* (1747) (rep. Kelly, NY, 1969)

Cannadine, D. *Patricians, Power and Politics in Nineteenth-Century Towns* (Leicester U.P., 1982)

Cannon, J. *Aristocratic Century, The Peerage of 18th-Century England* (Cambridge U.P., 1984)

Chandos, J. *Boys Together, English Public Schools 1800–1864* (Hutchinson, 1984)

Checkland, S. 'English Provincial Cities' (*Economic History Review*, Jan. 1954)

Christie, I. *Stress and Stability in Late Eighteenth-Century Britain* (Oxford U.P., 1985)

Cole, J. and Postgate, R. *The Common People* (Methuen, 1961)

Crouch, C. *The Scope for Socialism* (Fabian Society, 1985)

Daverson, J. and Lindsay, K. *Voices from the Middle Class* (Hutchinson, 1975)

Davidoff, L. *The Best Circles* (Croom Helm, 1973)

Davidoff, L. and Hall, C. *Family Fortunes: Men and Women of the English Middle Class 1780–1850* (Hutchinson, 1985)

Davis, I. *The Harlot and the Statesman* (Kensal Press, 1987)

Dore, L. and Jerrold, M. *In London – A Pilgrimage* (Grant, 1872)

d'Ormesson, J. *Grand Hotel* (Dent, 1984)

Dunkereley, D. *Occupations and Society* (Routledge & Kegan Paul, 1975)

Dyson, A. and Lovelock, J. *Education and Democracy* (Routledge & Kegan Paul, 1975)

Escott, T. *Social Transformations of the Victorian Age* (Seeley & Co., 1897)

Evans, E. *Social Policy 1830–1914* (Routledge & Kegan Paul, 1978)

Fried, G. and Elman, P. *Charles Booth's London* (Hutchinson, 1969)

Fulford, R. *The Greville Memoirs* (Batsford, 1963)

Gash, N. *Aristocracy and People* (Arnold, 1985)

Gay, J. *Trivia et al.* (rep. Fyfield Books, 1979)

Grego, J. *Rowlandson, the Caricaturist* (Chatto, 1880)

Hampden, J. *An Eighteenth-Century Journal 1774–1776* (Macmillan, 1940)

Harrison, B. *Drink and the Victorians* (Faber, 1971)

Harrison, B. *Peaceable Kingdom* (Clarendon Press, 1982)

Hawker, James *The Journal of a Victorian Preacher* (Oxford U.P., 1961)

Hayes, J. *Rowlandson – Watercolours and Drawings* (Phaidon, 1972)

Heald, T. *Networks* (Hodder & Stoughton, 1983)

Hecht, J. *The Domestic Servant Class in Eighteenth-Century England* (Routledge & Kegan Paul, 1956)

Henisch, B. *Cakes and Characters* (Prospect Books, 1984)

Heward, C. *Making a Man of Him – Parents and Their Sons' Education at an English Public School 1929–1950* (Routledge, 1988)

Hibbert, C. *The English – A Social History* (Grafton, 1986)

Himmlefarb, G. *The Idea of Poverty* (Faber, 1984)

Hopkins, H. *The Long Affray* (Secker & Warburg, 1979)

Jeffries, S. *The Spinster and her Enemies 1880–1930* (Pandora, 1985)

Jenkins, P. *The Making of a Ruling Class 1640–1790* (Cambridge U.P., 1983)

Lady Bell. *At the Works – A Study of a Manufacturing Town* (Arnold, 1907)

Lansdell, A. 'Costume for Oarswomen 1919–1979' (*Costume*, No.13, 1979)

Lauwerys, J. 'The Philosophical Approach to Comparative Education' (*International Review of Education*, Vol.5, 1959)

Lorimer, D. *Colour, Class and the Victorians* (Leicester U.P., 1978)
Mann, M. *Socialism Can Survive* (Fabian Society, 1985)
Mantoux, P. *The Industrial Revolution in the Eighteenth Century* (Methuen, 1964)
Marsh, D. *The Changing Structure of England and Wales* (Routledge, 1965)
Mingay, C. *The Transformation of Britain* (Routledge & Kegan Paul, 1986)
Munsche, P. *Gentlemen and Poachers 1671–1831* (Cambridge U.P., 1981)
Neale, R. *Class and Ideology in the Nineteenth Century* (Routledge, 1972)
Newby, H. *Country Life: A Social History of Rural England* (Weidenfeld, 1987)
Owen, C. *Social Stratification* (Routledge & Kegan Paul, 1968)
Paulson, R. *Hogarth, His Life and Times* (Yale U.P., 1971)
Payne, P. *British Entrepreneurship in the 19th Century* (Routledge, 1974)
Pearson, G. *Hooligan – A History of Respectable Fears* (Macmillan, 1983)
Penn, R. *Skilled Workers in the Class Struggle* (Cambridge U.P., 1984)
Pepys, S. *Diary* (Bell & Hyman, 1973)
Perkin, H. *Professionalism, Property and English Society since 1880* (Reading U.P., 1981)
Perkin, H. *The Social Tone of Victorian Seaside Resorts in North West England* (University of Lancaster, 1976)
Perkin, H. *The Structured Crowd* (Harvester Press, 1981)
Perkin, H. 'The Origins of the Popular Press' (*History Today*, Vol.7, 1957)
Perkin, H. *The Origins of Modern English Society 1780–1880* (Routledge, 1969)
Philips, K. *Language and Class in Victorian England* (Blackwell, 1984)
Pick, J. *The West End – Mismanagement and Snobbery* (Offord, 1984)
Plumb, J. *The Birth of a Consumer Society: The Commercialisation of 18th-Century England* (Hutchinson, 1983
Read, D. *The English Provinces 1760–1960* (Arnold, 1964)
Reed, M. *The Georgian Triumph 1700–1830* (Routledge & Kegan Paul, 1983)
Richards, J. and Mackenzie, J. *A Social History of the Railway Station* (Oxford U.P. 1986)
Roberts, E. *A Woman's Place 1890–1940* (Blackwell, 1984)
Robinson, J. *The Latest Country Houses 1945–1983* (Bodley Head, 1985)
Robson, B. *Where is the North?* (City of Manchester, 1985)
Sanderson, M. *The Universities in the 19th Century* (Routledge & Kegan Paul, 1975)
Scott, A. *The Early Hanoverian Age 1714–1760* (Croom Helm, 1980)
Sharpe, J. *Crime in Early Modern England 1550–1750* (Longman, 1984)
Stanley, L. *The Diaries of Hannah Cullwick* (Virago, 1984)
Stevenson, J. *English Urban History 1500–1780* (Open U.P., 1982)
Stone, L. and J. *An Open Elite* (Oxford U.P., 1986)
Walker, S. *Sporting Art 1740–1900* (Studio Vista, 1972)
Wigley, J. *The Rise and Fall of the Victorian Sunday* (Manchester U.P., 1980)
Wingfield, R. *Victorian Sunset* (Murray, 1932)
Wright, T. *Some Habits and Customs of the Working Class* (rep. Kelly, NY, 1967)

CLUB MINUTE BOOKS

Alcester Cricket Club, Warwick County Records Office, Warwick CV34 4JS (Ref. CR114A/743)
Alnmouth Golf Club, Northumberland Record Officer, Newcastle NE3 5QX (Ref. NRO 530.20/438)

Anson Hunt Races, William Salt Library, Stafford ST16 2LZ

Appleby Golf Club, Cumbria Record Officer, Kendal LA9 4RQ (Ref. WDSO/40)

Astley Bowling Club, Tameside Local Studies Dept., Stalybridge SK15 2BN (Ref. DD 37)

Bebington Bowling Club, Birkenhead Reference Library, L41 2XB (Ref. YBB)

Beccles Golf Club, Suffolk Records Officer, Ipswich IP4 2JS (Ref. HD49 405/122)

Bedale Bowling Club, North Yorkshire County Record Officer, Northallerton DL7 8AD

Bellingham Bowling & Lawn Tennis Club, Lewisham Archives, Lewisham SE13 5SY

Blackheath Hockey Club, Lewisham Archives, Lewisham SE13 5SY

Bolton Cricket Club, Bolton Metropolitan Borough Archives, BL1 1SA (Ref. 22/193)

Bolton Municipal Officers Rifle Club, Bolton Metropolitan Archives, BL1 1SA (Ref. FZ/1)

Bolton Playing Fields Society, Bolton Metropolitan Borough Archives, BL1 1SA (Ref. S3/17)

Bolton Rugby Football Club, Bolton Metropolitan Borough Archives, BL1 1SA (Ref. 22/243

Bolton Swimming Club, Bolton Metropolitan Borough Archives, BL1 1SA (Ref. FZ/8)

Bowmen of Edgbaston, Birmingham Reference Library, B3 3HQ

Bristol Cyclists Touring Club, Bristol Records Officer, BS1 5TR (Ref. 31415(7))

Bristol Long Range Club, Bristol Record Officer, BS1 5TR

Bullingdon Club, Wiltshire Records Officer, Trowbridge BA14 8OG (Ref. WRO 947)

Bungay Steeple Chase, Suffolk Records Office, Ipswich IP4 2JS (Ref. HD49 405/118)

Casterton Rifle Club, Cumbria Record Office (WDSO/87)

Catford Cycling Club, Lewisham Archives, Lewisham SE13 5SY

Caxton Cricket Club, Cambridge Record Office, CB2 0AP (P37/24/1)

Cestreham Cycling Club, Buckinghamshire Record Office, Aylesbury HP20 1HA (D/x 566)

Cheltenham Cycling Club, Gloucestershire Record Office, Gloucester GL1 3DW

Corinthian Sailing Club, Hammersmith Archives, London W12 8LJ

Crosthwaite Bowling Club, Cumbria Record Office, Kendal LA9 4RQ (WDSO/7)

Cumberland & Westmorland Wrestling Society, Cumbria Record Office (D/SO/48)

Darlington Archers, Darlington Public Library, DL1 1ND (D/X/D30)

Darlington Billiard Club, Darlington Public Library (D/X/22)

Darlington Cycling Club, Darlington Public Library (D/HP/109–110)

Didsbury Archers, Manchester City Archives, M2 5PD (M62/1/2)

Didsbury Archers & Hunters, Manchester City Archives (M62/1/2)

Didsbury Bowling Green, Manchester City Archives (M62/1/2)

Dresden Boat Club, Nottinghamshire Record Office, NG1 1HR (DDBB 119)

Dunmow Tennis Club, Essex Record Office, CM5 1LX (D/DW 23)

Dunmow Park Tennis Club, Essex Record Office (D/DW 23)

Durham City Cricket Club, Durham County Records, DH1 5UL (D/DCC)

Durham Cyclists Touring Club, Durham County Records (D/DCT)

Durham National Playing Fields Association, Durham County Records (D/HH 10/13/1/1–6)

Fambridge Yacht Club, Essex Record Office, BM1 1LX (D/226)

Finsbury Park Cycling Club, Haringey Museum, N17 8NU

Fleetwood Gala, Lancaster City Archives, LA1 4AW

Fulwood Race Course, Lancashire Records Office, PR1 8ND (DDX/03/4)

Gateshead Fox Hounds, Northumberland Records, NE3 5QX (ZSI.316)

Hambledon Cricket Club, Hampshire Record Office, SO23 9EF (F/239)

Headingley Bowling Club, Leeds Archives, LS7 3AP (1978)

Hexham Steeple Chase, Northumberland Records, NE3 5QX (ZMD 2/15)
Hinton St George Cricket Club, Somerset Records, TA2 7PU (DD/HW/Z)
Holme Athletic Sports, Cumbria Records, LA9 4RQ (WDSO/37)
Hull Athletic Ground Company, Kingston on Hull Record Office, 79 Longate (DBHT/9/390)
Hutton in the Forest Cricket Club, Cumbria Records, Carlisle CA3 8UR (Vane Family Collection)
Huyton Cricket Club, Knowsley Central Library, Liverpool L36 9DJ
Irthing Vale Wanderers Cricket Club, Cumbria Records, Carlisle CA3 8UR (D/SO/9)
John O'Gaunt Bowmen, Lancaster City Archives LA1 4AW
Jolly Anglers Society, Central Library, Warrington WA1 1JB
Kempsford Cricket Club, Gloucestershire Records, GL1 3DW
Kendal Amateur Swimming Club, Cumbria Records, LA9 4RQ (WDSO/71)
Kendal Ladies Hockey Club, Cumbria Records (WDSO/10)
Kendal Rugby Union Football Club, Cumbria Records (WDSO/80)
Kendal Skating Club, Cumbria Records (WD/RG)
Kindon Football Club, Dorset Records Office, DT1 1XJ (P362/PCCI)
Lake Hatherton Fishery, William Salt Library, Stafford ST16 2LZ
Lambton Tally Ho Club, Durham County Records, DH1 5UL (D/lo/F 1013)
Lancaster Football Club, Lancashire Records, Preston PR1 8ND (DDX 411/35)
Lancaster Golf Club, Lancashire Records (DDX 411/36)
Lancaster Races, Lancashire Records (DDX 441/32)
Lancaster Regatta, Lancashire City Archives, LA1 4AW
Lichfield Races, William Salt Library, Stafford ST16 2LZ
Linton Sports, Cambridgeshire Records, CB2 0AP (L95/15A)
Maldon Bicycle Club, Essex Records, Chelmsford CM5 1LX (T/A475)
Mersey Archery Society, Manchester City Archives, M2 5PD (M5645/1–3)
Minnesingens Yacht Club, Portsmouth City Records, PO1 2LE
Morpeth Olympic Games, Northumberland Records, NE3 5QX (NRO 1565)
Moseley United Bowling Club, Birmingham Reference Library, B3 3HQ
National Fitness Campaign, Tyne & Wear Archives, NE1 4JA (1407)
Netherfield Amateur Swimming Club, Cumbria Records, LA9 4RQ (WDSO/71)
Newton Racecourse, Records held at the racecourse, Haydock
North Staffordshire Hunt, Staffordshire Record Office, ST16 2LZ (Colonel Dobson Collection)
Northumberland Cockfighting, Northumberland Records, NE3 5QX (ZALA 19)
Oken Bicycle Club, Warwick County Records, CV34 4JS (CRI 844)
Old Raby Hunt, Durham County Records, DH1 5UL (D/St/V 1633)
Park Swimming Club, Haringey Museum, N17 8NU
Porlock Golf Club, Somerset Records, Taunton TA2 7PU (DDBR/6n33)
Preston Mutual Improvement Society, Lancashire Records, PR1 8ND (DDX 411/37)
Quayside Sports (Lancaster), Lancaster City Archives, Lancaster LA1 4AW
Ross Men's Hockey Club, Hereford Records Office, Hereford HR1 2QX
Royal Portsmouth Yacht Club, Portsmouth Records Office, PO1 2LE
Rugeley Bowling Green, Staffordshire Record Office, ST16 2LZ (Dobson collection)
Society of Staffordshire Bowmen, Staffordshire Records, ST16 2LZ (Farley Hill Papers)
South Durham Steeple Chase, Durham County Records, DH1 5UL (D/X/480/1)
South Saxon Archers, East Sussex Records, Lewes BN7 1UN (SHR 3703-5)
Stafford Races, William Salt Library, Stafford ST16 2LZ
Stansted Park Cricket Club, Essex Records, Chelmsford CM1 1LX (T/P68/55/6)

Stayley Hunt, Manchester City Archives, M2 5PD (DD 96/2)

Stockport Races, Stockport Central Library, SK1 3RS

Sunningdale Ladies Golf Club, Berkshire Records, Reading RG2 9XD (D/EX 531/2)

Sutton Sports, Cambridgeshire Records, CB2 0AP (R79/95)

Tees Salmon Fisheries, Durham Records, DH1 5UL (D/St/Box 144)

Tottenham Hotspur Football Club, Haringey Museum, Arts Dept. N17 8NU

Tring Village Football Association, Hertfordshire Records, SG1 8DE (AR 138/79. D/X 675)

Trowbridge Recreation Club, Wiltshire Records, Trowbridge BA14 8JG (WRO.583)

Tyldesley Cricket Club, Wigan Record Office, Leigh WN7 2DY (D/DS 16)

Tyldesley Swimming Club, Wigan Record Office, Leigh WN7 2DY (D/DS 16)

Vale of Derwentwater Angling Ass., Cumbria Records, Carlisle CA3 8UB (D/SO/67)

Walsall Cricket Club, William Salt Library, Stafford ST16 2LZ

Walsall Cycling & Running Club, Walsall Central Archives, SW1 1TR (3103)

Walthamstow Bicycle Club, Waltham Forest Library, E17 9NH (W37.3875. WBC.2)

Walthamstow Ferry Fishery Society, Waltham Forest Library, E17 9NH

Walthamstow Tennis & Bowling Club, Waltham Forest Library, E17 9NH

Warrington Golf Club, Central Library, Warrington WA1 1JB

Warrington Parks Bowling League, Central Library, Warrington WA1 1JB

Warrington Sailing Club, Central Library, Warrington WA1 1JB

Warrington Swimming Club, Central Library, Warrington WA1 1JB

Warwick Angling Society, Warwick County Records, CV34 4JS (W37.223. W1)

Warwick Races 1754, Warwick County Records, CV34 4JS (CR229/Box 2/2)

West Kent Wanderers Cricket Club, Lewisham Archives, SE13 5SY

Whitfield Cricket Club, Northumberland Record Office, NE3 5QX

Wood Green Cricket Club, Haringey Museum, N17 8NU

Worcester Tricycle Club, Hereford & Worcester Records, Worcester WR1 1TN

Worksop Cricket Club, Nottinghamshire Records, NG1 1HR (DD4P 62/ 108/4)

Other original sources

Accounts of a Dancing Master, Nottinghamshire Records, NG1 1HR (DD 5P.7)

Bearbaiting in Cambridge, Cambridgeshire Records CB2 0AP (PB vol.31)

Charles Shaw's Shooting Diary, Northamptonshire Records, NN4 9AW

Death of Lord Shaftsbury's Son, Northumberland Record Office, NE3 5QX (ZMI/ 576.50)

Edward Harbottle Grimston's Diary, Hertfordshire Records, SG1 8DE (D/EV/ F154)

Game Duty Certificates 1802, 1824, Buckinghamshire Museum, Aylesbury HP20 2QP

Horse Racing on Skircoate Moor, Calderdale Archives, Halifax HX1 5LA (Misc. 3–4)

Prize Fighting in Cambridge, Cambridgeshire Records, CB2 0AP (R58/5/5)

Index